K

Making Sense of Illness

DATE DUE

Making Sense of Illness

The Social Psychology of Health and Disease

Alan Radley

SAGE Publications

London • Thousand Oaks • New Delhi

SAGE Publications Ltd
6 Bonhill Street
London EC2A 4PU

SAGE Publications Inc
2455 Teller Road
Thousand Oaks, California 91320

SAGE Publications India Pvt Ltd
32, M-Block Market
Greater Kailash - I
New Delhi 110 048

British Library Cataloguing in Publication data

A catalogue record for this book is available from the British Library.

ISBN 0 8039 8908 3
ISBN 0 8039 8909 1 (pbk)

Library of Congress catalog card number 94-068553

Typeset by Type Study, Scarborough
Printed in Great Britain at the University Press,
Cambridge

Contents

Acknowledgements

I have been fortunate to have had the advice of several colleagues at various stages of this book's preparation. Wendy Stainton Rogers and Doug Carroll were encouraging about the original book proposal, for which I thank them. Particular thanks go to those who took time to read draft chapters, correcting errors in the manuscript and advising upon changes of emphasis – Ellen Annandale, Paul Bennett, Mildred Blaxter, Mike Bury, Robert Dingwall, Mark Levine and Kristian Pollock. Any remaining shortcomings in the text are, of course, my sole responsibility.

I am also grateful to the following publishers for permission to reproduce figures and tables that appear in the text: to the Office of Population Censuses and Surveys for extracts from tables in the *General Household Survey 1992*; to the World Health Organization for material from *Demographic Trends in the European Region*, 1984; to Macmillan Ltd and to St Martin's Press Incorporated for a figure from Kane, 1991, *Women's Health*; to the British Medical Journal Publishing Group for material from Moser et al., *BMJ*, 1988; to Elsevier Science Ltd for a table from Nathanson, which appeared in *Social Science and Medicine*, 1980, and for allowing me to reproduce the 'Social Readjustment Rating Scale' from an article by Holmes and Rahe in the *Journal of Psychosomatic Research*, 1967.

Preface

This book is an introduction to the topic of 'health and illness', as viewed from both a social and a psychological perspective. It reviews some of the more important research that has been carried out in recent years, mainly by medical sociologists, health psychologists and medical anthropologists. The reasons for drawing upon a wide range of work is, quite simply, that the efforts of these different disciplines often overlap. This overlap occurs because questions of how people fall ill, and how they stay well, have a human significance that no discipline can overlook. Of course, this significance is not restricted to the inquiries of academics. Most people are interested in illness and its treatment – first, perhaps, from a distance, and then later in a personal way.

What often grasps our interest is not the disease itself, not the germs or the symptoms, but the way that becoming ill faces people with all kinds of personal choices and moral dilemmas. Once we begin to look into it, this is a topic that seems to touch all other aspects of life. Perhaps that, too, is what makes it interesting to so many people. When we try to make sense of illness we find that we are, often unintentionally, also making sense of these other aspects of life, and perhaps of ourselves as well.

For social scientists of whatever hue, these questions make 'health and illness' more than just another topic to be investigated. It promises something more in the way of telling us about ourselves, about our society and the way that we live within it. One other reason for this interest is that it concerns something which social scientists find difficult to analyse, but (eventually) impossible to ignore – the body. Health and illness are not just abstract states, but also physical ones. Our bodies matter to us, and how they matter is surely something for any sociologist, psychologist or anthropologist to want to explain.

If the book has any single approach, it is to look at illness in this way – as something that we have to 'make sensible', if our own lives are to 'make sense'. This is a task not just for individual sufferers, but for others around them, for medical staff, and for society as a whole. It invites questions about how people think about health; how they conduct themselves when ill; the part played by family, friends and strangers; relationships with doctors and nurses; and the place of the sick in the social world. In my terms, this makes for a 'social psychological' approach to these questions, and this is the perspective that I have adopted in the text.

In the pages to follow I have tried, wherever possible, to relate the argument to everyday life. Therefore, the book follows a path that leads from health – when illness appears a distant prospect – through diagnosis and treatment, to the experience of having a chronic, and perhaps serious, disease. Although it is not essential that readers start with Chapter 1 and proceed onwards, many of the later arguments build upon ideas presented earlier on in the text.

There are, inevitably, several omissions in a book of this length. There is no discussion of mental illness, even though many points raised in the text are relevant to this question. Also, the reader will find little here about the hospital experience, and nothing concerning terminal care, dying or specialist services such as dentistry. Instead, much of the coverage concerns what might be called 'everyday illness', and how this is managed by medical staff and by laypeople in their turn. For that reason, I hope the reader will bring to bear on the text his or her own experience, thus not only making sense of it, but making sense with it as well.

1
Explaining Health and Illness: An Introduction

A metaphor and an introduction

Health and illness, Susan Sontag (1991) wrote, are like two different countries. If we are lucky, we spend most of our time dwelling in the first, though nearly all of us are, at some time or other, passport holders of both domains. It might be this universal aspect of illness which makes it compelling as a subject for study, together with the fact that it is linked to matters of life and death. Studying in the 1990s it is almost impossible to be unaware of the problem of AIDS, and of sickness among the destitute and disadvantaged. Also, one is constantly being urged, from all quarters it seems, of the need to adopt a healthy lifestyle. Alongside these high-profile issues there remains, for many people, the day to day experiences of minor ailments and of visits to the doctor. These visits are punctuated by the knowledge that what began as something minor, could turn out to be more serious. In truth, many of us who can claim to be firmly domiciled in the world of health have spent sufficient time at the border to have spied the outcrops of the terrain on the other side. Others, less fortunate, must make regular visits across the divide.

To extend this metaphor a little further, this book is about the beliefs that people hold about what it is to be a citizen of each country. It is also about the ways and means of making crossings between them, and about what people do to ensure that they remain in the kingdom of the healthy rather than in that of the sick. Putting the matter more directly, this is an introduction to the study (a) of health and illness as experienced by people, and (b) of the actions taken by them to avoid illness or to regain their health.

Two guidelines to the book's focus are identifiable in the ideas of illness *experience*, and of *action* to determine good health. First, the question of experience points to individuals not only having beliefs about these matters, but also *feeling* well or *feeling* ill. This means that, while we may share ideas about what it means to be healthy or ill, the location of one's affliction is one's own *body*. Any study in this area is bound to be concerned with social or cultural issues, as well as with questions of being (as well as having) a body.

Second, the mention of action relates to the fact that staying well and getting better involves other people. In special circumstances, this means seeking help from doctors and nurses, who are experts in what has been referred to as 'health work' (Stacey, 1988). Health work includes what, in

Western societies, are commonly recognized as treatment and curing. It also includes other health practices, such as care by dependants, and the control of matters to do with birth, mating and death. It should be emphasized that much of this other health work involves ordinary people in society (especially women), not just paid medical employees. Therefore, the relationships in which we live, and the groups to which we belong, have a distinct bearing upon both the maintenance of good health and the care of the sick.

Because our discussion will involve a study of experience in the context of social life, it will traverse ground that has, by tradition at least, been thought of as the overlap of sociology and social psychology. This does not mean that researchers in other disciplines have not investigated this topic as well; the work of anthropologists and epidemiologists will also appear in the pages to follow. However, the book's aim is not to present an account of what any one social science discipline has found out about health and illness. Instead, it will draw upon the work of various disciplines to illustrate different approaches to the field. At this point we need to take a closer look at some of these approaches, so that we shall be in a better position to set out the perspective and the boundaries of the chapters to follow.

Disease, illness and sickness – some initial distinctions

Just what does it mean if we say that someone is ill? This depends upon who is making this interpretation and the basis for their doing so. Doctors make diagnoses of disease based upon their readings of patients' symptoms, while ill people are likely to make such decisions (at least partly) on the basis of their own bodily feelings. The family and friends of these individuals might notice that they 'don't look well' but then again they might have to rely on their verbal reports of feeling unwell. This suggests that being ill is a state that results from interpretations of changes in bodily states and in personal capabilities. While doctors make specialized interpretations of this kind, each of us does something similar in the course of assessing our own state of health and that of others with whom we are involved. What is the basis upon which we make the judgement that someone is 'ill' rather than 'well'?

The reader is invited to consider the following descriptions and decide, in each case, whether the person is sick and what action should be taken.

[A] Here's a man who developed a sore throat and a running nose the day before yesterday. He feels feverish and aches and has a tight feeling in his chest. He doesn't feel like doing anything.

[B] Here's a man who has been feeling very tired a lot of the time for the past six months. He gets tired soon after he gets up in the morning. Sometimes he feels dizzy for a few minutes. He doesn't feel like doing as much as he usually does. (Apple, 1960: 220)

These descriptions are taken from a study by Apple (1960), who asked people to judge illness from vignettes such as these. The vignettes varied according to the degree to which they showed the condition to be (a) interfering with usual activities, (b) of recent onset and (c) ambiguous in its symptomatology. (In the above descriptions, [A] is of recent onset, interferes with life and is unambiguous; [B] is chronic and stable, interferes with usual activities and is ambiguous.) Apple found that people judged illness to be present when the individuals were described as having an ailment of recent origin that interfered with their usual activities.

This study is cited here more for illustration than for its specific findings. It shows that people detect illness on the basis of information about bodily conditions, and about expectations of how social activities should be undertaken. While laypeople might have little medical knowledge, they are able to distinguish between conditions they regard as sufficient, and those they see as insufficient to label someone as sick. This is not surprising, given that everyone is used to some degree of discomfort or pain in everyday life, and therefore in having to decide how to cope with it. Apple's study does, however, raise other questions. For example, do laypeople and medical practitioners differ in their ways of thinking about illness? Do doctors and patients concentrate to different degrees upon bodily symptoms and the disruption to the patient's everyday life?

At this point it is useful to make some distinction between the terms 'disease', 'illness' and 'sickness'. The reason for doing this is not to give definitive answers to the questions posed above, but to show how we can begin to understand some of the assumptions upon which they are based. Effectively, *disease* is something that physicians diagnose and treat. Examples include influenza, cancer and tuberculosis. For comparative purposes, it can be said that disease refers to pathological changes in *the body*, so that a main symptom of each of the diseases just mentioned might include fever, a growth, and extreme coughing. *Illness* can be taken to mean the experience of disease, including the feelings relating to changes in bodily states and the consequences of having to bear that ailment; illness, therefore, relates to a way of being for *the individual* concerned. *Sickness* can be defined as a social condition that applies to people who are deemed by others to be ill or diseased. It refers to a particular status or role *in society* and is justified by reference either to the presence of disease or to the experience of illness (Eisenberg, 1977).

Distinguishing between these three terms provides a useful way of approaching the question of how people are deemed to be 'ill'. By linking them to the concepts of body, individual and society it becomes possible to appreciate (a) how confusions can arise through using the terms interchangeably; and (b) how different linkages point to interesting questions about how people come to be labelled 'healthy' or 'ill'.

Consider, first, the two terms 'disease' and 'illness'. The mixing of these in everyday speech arises from the assumption that 'normally' the two occur together. Someone is 'ill' because he or she 'has a disease'. However, it is possible for a disease to be diagnosed on the basis of bodily signs that the person concerned has not perceived. For example, as part of a routine medical examination, a person might be found to be HIV positive, or to have high blood pressure. Up until this point, the individual might not have felt unwell at all. Here the diagnosis of disease precedes the experience of illness. The latter might appear immediately afterwards if the doctor informs the patient of the result of the examination. (That is, knowing that one is diagnosed as having a disease, or that it is likely to develop, might well incline the individual to feel unwell.)

In other cases the experience of illness precedes diagnosis, so that the person concerned must presume (or at least question) the presence of disease. However, people may suffer symptoms for some time before seeking medical advice, perhaps trying to treat themselves or simply putting up with feeling unwell. However, if on seeing the doctor they are told that no disease can be determined, this does not necessarily banish their claim to be 'feeling ill'. Clearly, then, the designation of pathology (disease) and the consciousness of suffering or debility are not the same, and should not be confused in our explanations.

Before examining this distinction further we need to say something about sickness. People speak of feeling sick and of feeling ill. In the terms used here, an individual's consciousness of being unwell should not be confused with the social status accorded to people diagnosed as having a disease. Again, this perhaps occurs because we have in mind examples where, as with influenza, to feel ill means to retire to bed and to take medicine. This removal of ourselves from the demands of the everyday world constitutes the adoption of what Parsons (1951a, 1951b) called the *sick role*. 'Sickness', therefore, is the term we should reserve for what we began by calling the 'world of the ill'.

It is possible, however, to feel ill and yet not be termed 'sick'. For example, following our protestations of 'feeling dreadful', the doctor might not agree that we have a disease, but only be suffering from 'the cold he had last week and he got over it'. Alternatively, people might feel ill but for various reasons refuse to take time off work and insist that they 'only have a headache and are not really sick'.

Why should people refuse to occupy the status 'sick', and what does this tell us about this category in relation to the others? If we return to the example of the person who is told that s/he is HIV positive, the question arises as to whether that individual informs others of this fact. It is likely that s/he will choose not to do so, given that there are strong prejudices about AIDS patients in society. That is to say, to occupy this social role, whether or not one suffers from the symptoms of disease, is to be subject to social categorizations that have their origin in society. We need to look beyond the experience of the individual patient to understand how the term 'sickness' relates to the public awareness and designation of disease.

One source of ideas about sickness is the medical survey itself, where screening programmes provide information about the extent and the patterning of diseases in society. Independent of individual complaints of illness, such surveys bring disease directly into social consciousness, via the media, as beliefs about sickness (Frankenberg, 1980). It is in this way that most of the population 'knows about' AIDS, which groups suffer from it, how it is contracted and what could or should be done to minimize its spread.

So far we have separated disease, illness and sickness and related each to its conceptual focus – the body, individual experience and society. The focus upon disease, upon its classification and its treatment, is the concern of biomedicine. By comparison, the experience of illness is the concern of individuals who suffer from ailments. In the past this distinction has been used to justify the different interests of social science as compared with medicine. Medicine is concerned with classification in order to produce knowledge which will be effective in the course of healing (Kleinman, 1973); social science is concerned with the meanings and behaviours that organize the experience of illness for the individuals involved (Idler, 1979). The point of making this distinction is to show that disease, illness and sickness do not stand in some kind of practical or theoretical vacuum. Instead, they have their independent meaning because they can be spoken about within different theoretical perspectives.

At this stage of our discussion it is possible to see that, whatever the diagnostic and therapeutic power of medical knowledge, it cannot answer questions about illness and sickness, as we have been using these terms so far. This does not mean, of course, that medical knowledge and practice has no place in our account of health and illness. What it does mean is that the concepts of biomedicine cannot define the field of interest for a social science approach to the topic. Having said that, we shall see that what health professionals believe, and what they do, remain key to our understanding of illness experience and the social context of sickness.

The relationship of health to illness

It might be thought that health and illness are simply polar opposites, so that a person is either at one or other end of this dimension. In fact, this is not the case, as a brief analysis will demonstrate. Health refers to a state of being that is largely taken for granted. By this, I mean that being able to live one's life untroubled by pain or disease forms a background to everyday existence. Arguably, it is only when symptoms appear, or where a diagnosis of disease is made, that one's health is brought into question. Then it is the disease, the illness experience, the condition of being a sick person that we are aware of. And it is the shadow that this figure of illness casts upon the backcloth of health that gives the latter some shape in our consciousness. Only then do we know, at some remove as it were, what we have lost or what is at risk.

Later on in the book I shall provide some evidence for these claims. For the moment, they can be understood by noting that the relationship of health to illness in experience is consistent with its form in linguistic usage. A simple question shows what is meant here: 'How healthy would you say you are?' has a quite different meaning to 'How ill would you say you are?' The former leaves open the whole spectrum of 'healthiness', while the latter assumes illness and then asks about its degree. The point is that 'health' defines the whole dimension, while 'illness' is restricted to being the subordinate opposite of 'health'. This inequality between opposites is common in language structure, where the defining label (health) has been called the 'unmarked pole' and its opposite (illness) the 'marked pole' (Greenberg, 1966). The relevance of this distinction is that it alerts us to the unequal attention given to health and to illness in many studies. It also raises the question of what this difference means for the way that people think about these issues in everyday life.

In the main, the consciousness of illness, and the attention given to disease by medicine, have ensured that it is this marked pole (rather than health) that has received most attention from researchers. There is a far greater range of terms to do with disease, its causes and its cures than there is to do with being well. In the next chapter we shall explore some of the historical factors that created this difference. For the moment, it is enough to note that in recent years there has been a definite shift in this balance. Now, more researchers are concerned to study the conditions that promote and maintain good health. Partly, this is to do with a greater concern with the experience and behaviour of ill people. This has led to the identification of behaviours seen as contributing either to the prevention or to the continuation of disease (Diekstra, 1990). Having identified what they see as illness-producing behaviours, medical experts have attempted to turn around these definitions in order to say how people should avoid them and thus stay healthy. A major initiative has been taken by the World Health Organization (1987), which has argued that modifying lifestyles will lead to better health for all. However, there is a problem with this recom-mendation. It fails to recognize that simply inverting findings about illness will not produce complementary results concerning health. To mention one issue only, the methods that have been used to study the illness of individuals might not be appropriate to study the healthiness of the community as a whole (Brown, 1981).

Raising this question in the introduction to this book alerts us to the need to treat the relationship between health and illness with some caution. If what we have outlined in this section is true, then the metaphor with which we began already requires some modification. The two kingdoms are not equal, and inasmuch as our consciousness of membership of each territory is important, then it will affect our citizenship in each case. I said before that in casting a shadow against the backcloth of health illness gave it some form. This point can be made for social scientists trying to understand health, just as it can for individuals suffering from disease. In a paradoxical way, the form that the shadow of illness casts on health also throws some light on what it means to be healthy. This should not be seen as a perverse summary of affairs, but as the potential for this topic to tell us about other aspects of everyday life. In this book we shall not only be reviewing explanations in terms of established theory, but also be asking about the kinds of explanation required to account for the findings of our investigations.

Explaining health and illness: three perspectives and their associated disciplines

In order to introduce the book's perspective, it is necessary to say something about existing approaches to the study of disease and illness experience. The reasons for this include the fact that some disciplines have a long tradition of work in this field. They have focused upon problems and used methods of study that are either 'social psychological' or 'micro-sociological'. They have also made explicit some of the difficulties associated with investigating what people believe to be essentially 'medical questions'. Indeed, one of the initial stumbling blocks to a social scientific understanding of health and illness is that, as members of Western societies, we experience our ailments (and our body in general) in medical terms. This can have the effect of making it difficult to see how matters to do with viruses, heart attacks, head injury or vaccination are anything but 'really medical', in the sense of being biological events. On the other hand, the fact that we experience our illnesses (if not our health) using medical terminology means that these terms carry significance and meaning for us. This is as true for social scientists as it is for anyone else, and means that their explanations must, in one way or another, all come to terms with 'the reality of medicine'.

There are three perspectives, apart from biomedicine, that have been used in the study of illness and its treatment. These can be called the *behavioural*, the *societal* and the *cultural*. Because they are perspectives – 'ways of taking a view upon' – they are not to be confused with the disciplines with which they are normally identified. The behavioural perspective is typically adopted by psychologists, the societal by sociologists, and the cultural by anthropologists. The key word here is 'typically' – the theoretical outlook characterizes the discipline, it does not by itself define it. Therefore, in describing these perspectives I am not claiming that, for example, all sociologists take a societal view, or that all psychologists adopt a behavioural one. The fact is that investigators from the different disciplines have, at various times, utilized all three. This, however, has served to show that these perspectives remain distinct, not that they are interchangeable.

Let us examine each perspective in turn, with a view to saying what our approach will be to questions concerning health and illness. To help us do this, a schematic representation of the relationship of each perspective to biomedicine is shown in Figure 1.1.

(a) The behavioural perspective – behavioural medicine and health psychology

Behavioural medicine has been defined as the field of work in which behavioural science knowledge is applied to problems in the prevention, diagnosis and treatment of physical illness (Gentry, 1982). Its definitions of health and illness are, therefore, derived from biomedicine, which circumscribes its efforts (see Figure 1.1). This approach sprang from the application of behaviourism to specific problems such as chronic pain,

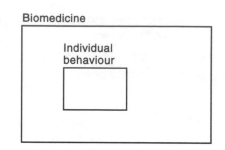

(a) **Behavioural**

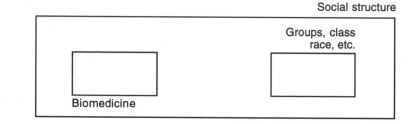

(b) **Societal**

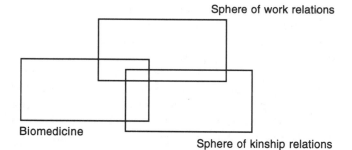

(c) **Cultural**

Figure 1.1   *A schematic representation of the three perspectives on illness in relation to biomedicine*

alcoholism and the non-compliance of patients with medical treatment. Although it has been described as an interdisciplinary field, its basic assumptions stress individual responsibility for illness prevention and health care. This stated emphasis upon changing behaviour means that it draws heavily upon individualistic psychology and its methods. For example, techniques such as self-monitoring or relaxation training might be used to help control chronic pain, high blood pressure or spasms associated with cerebral palsy.

The growth in the application of psychological concepts and techniques, beyond those that are clearly behavioural, has led to the emergence of a field that claims to stand on its own – *health psychology*. This has been described as the aggregate of psychology's contribution to the promotion of health and the prevention of illness (Matarazzo, 1982). More recently, it has been defined as 'the disciplinary area of psychology which is concerned with human behaviour in the context of health and illness' (Weinman, 1990: 9).

The difference between behavioural medicine and health psychology would appear to be a shift in standpoint: away from medically defined problems tackled by any 'behavioural science', towards questions of health and illness conceptualized within the terms of 'psychological science'. The reason for making this point is that it suggests something about the close relationship of the behavioural perspective to medicine. This relationship, in turn, tells us much about the practical orientation of the behavioural perspective, and its continuing influence upon the work of psychologists researching this field (Johnston, 1994).

Medicine, too, has a perspective, which is termed *biomedicine*. It applies the concepts of physiology, anatomy and biochemistry to questions of the origins and treatment of disease. The methods of biomedicine are those of natural science, and its assumptions about the onset and treatment of disease are recognizably those concerning cause and effect relationships. It rests, therefore, upon a dualism of mind and body, privileging the latter through reducing all problems to its pathologies, which are understood as disease. In a critique of this perspective, Engel (1977) suggested that disease might not be due to physico-biological causes alone, but that people's vulnerability to disease and their reactions to it are also affected by psychological and social factors. This argument is an extension of the biomedical model, in the sense that it accepts as potential causes of illness those matters that are to do with the individual's personal and social context. Equally important, it allows for the possibility that interactions between body, mind and society might be crucial in the onset of disease, or in the propensity to fall ill (Taylor, 1990; Temoshok, 1990).

The medical perspective – often termed 'the medical model' – has two features that it shares with the behavioural perspective. One concerns the assumptions of natural science in its methods of research; the other concerns its aim to cure disease and to relieve suffering. Both of these features continue to influence health psychology in ways that need to be outlined here if we are to see how it differs from the perspective to be adopted in this book.

The first aspect has been signalled in the claim that the medical perspective has been extended to embrace the personal and social context (see Figure 1.1). In practice, this allows measures to be made of person and situation alongside established diagnostic categories and measures of physiological change. For example, one group of researchers studied the risk factors that might lead to the development of heart disease (Lehr et al., 1973). They selected 12 'biological variables' and 12 'social variables', correlating these with a measure of Type A Behaviour Pattern, believed to be a risk-factor for heart disease. What they found was that certain variables, including systolic blood pressure, parental religious beliefs, age, serum cholesterol level and father's occupation, were key predictors of likelihood of having this predisposing behaviour pattern.

The question remains, however, in what direction, and in what way exactly do these variables influence each other? While there is a sense in which all of these are 'variables', there is an important sense in which they are not. Parental religious belief and father's occupational status are *social phenomena* that do not 'connect' with serum cholesterol in any meaningful way. This connection could only be provided by a theory that acknowledged the qualitative differences between these distinct phenomena. This is actually obscured by turning them all into variables and continuing to cross-relate them, hoping that statistical associations will, by themselves, explain their relationships to each other (Radley, 1982). The use of an experimental design involving statistical manipulation of the data gives the illusion that these variables are all the same kind of thing, when palpably they are not. In a changing social world, religious beliefs and labour markets could not be expected to retain their meaning over time, so that any correlational finding would not be a natural association. This goes for all of what we would regard as matters concerning our personal and social involvements. The conclusion must be that, while the extension of the medical model makes psychology and sociology relevant to its questions, it does this at a price; it transforms their data into its own kind of 'stuff' – factors that cause disease.

The second feature relating the behavioural perspective to the medical model concerns the development of psychology as a profession allied to medicine. While the behavioural perspective is not exclusively taken up by psychologists, their adherence to the experimental approach, and their focus upon the individual rather than the social group, mean that they have developed techniques for changing behaviour. The isolation of what have been regarded as 'behavioural risk factors' has meant that psychologists have seen how, for example, they might influence individuals to refrain from smoking and drinking alcohol, reduce their salt or dietary cholesterol intake, exercise regularly or use dental floss (Matarazzo, 1982). Recently, this list has been extended to changes involving personal outlook and social relationships, such as teaching people how to reduce their stress levels or modify behaviours believed to be deleterious to health (Taylor, 1990; Weinman, 1990). These recommendations can be advanced more readily where psychologists are employed in clinical settings, in which the relationship of doctor to patient assumes that medical knowledge will result in some form of treatment. The existence of clinical psychology as an established profession allied to medicine provides the basis for the development of health psychology in Western societies (though not in the Third World; see Holtzman et al., 1987). What this means, however, is that it has provided yet another reason for health psychology to adopt the medical model (Marteau and Johnston, 1987). The diagnostic categories and treatment needs arising from medical practice can all too often become the unquestioned basis for psychological inquiry and intervention.

In summary, the behavioural perspective rests upon a natural scientific view of disease that it shares with biomedicine. It also assumes the importance of changing the behaviour of individuals in ways defined as desirable. This is in order to reduce the likelihood of disease occurrence, and to alleviate pain and suffering. In terms of the distinctions made earlier in this chapter, this perspective focuses upon disease rather than illness and sickness, the different forms of which it only vaguely discerns. While psychology has contributed much to the behavioural outlook (and continues to do so), there has been an expansion of health psychology into contexts outside the clinic. This has led to the application of theories other than behavioural ones, and to the recognition that health psychology lacks the framework of understanding that has been built up by medical sociology (Marteau and Johnston, 1987).

To what degree we can make use of the behavioural perspective in this book will be a matter for discussion after we have examined the remaining approaches. The reason for giving it detailed attention, at this stage, is because we might have wanted to adopt the perspective of health psychology at the outset; or else, have tried to extend the behavioural perspective still further. From what has been said already, the reader is probably aware that this will not be the case. Instead, we shall look closely at alternative approaches, particularly those adopted by sociologists and anthropologists wishing to study health, illness and disease.

(b) The societal perspective – medical sociology

The societal perspective is identifiable with the emergence of medical sociology. However, it is important not to identify all of medical sociology with this perspective, because this sub-discipline is now diverse both in its theory and in its methods (Gerhardt, 1989). Indeed, we shall see that some sociologists of health and illness are pointedly critical of the societal perspective as it will be outlined here.

The work of Parsons (1951a) is most important in putting forward the idea that illness and health are social dimensions. This idea is significant because it sets questions about this topic outside of the biomedical model. Interpretations of the Parsonian view stress that falling ill involves the individual in taking up what is called the 'sick role'. This follows from the person's inability to carry out satisfactorily his or her normal roles, so that a period of relief from everyday duties is allowed. This relief is provided so long as the individual makes efforts to seek professional help and to get well as soon as possible. Parsons described the doctor as aiding the patient to recover, not just 'biological health', but his or her ability and willingness to resume normal social life. Therefore, the work of the doctor, and of medical practice in general, is a form of re-socialization in that it works as a mechanism of social control. The sick role is an adaptive device within society, ensuring that deviations from social norms are countered by restoring the ill to the world of health. What matters is the functioning of the social order, which is maintained in part by medicine and the role that it plays in society.

The point to be made here is that Parsons brings medicine – the practices of the doctor – into consideration alongside the activities of the patient. Medicine is part of society, and its relationship to laypeople can be considered within that wider context (see Figure 1.1). This means that instead of working, as behavioural medicine does, within an extended biomedical model, sociologists have been able to frame their questions outside of that perspective. On the one hand there are doctors, and on the other individuals who become patients. This means that the actions of doctors – how they classify disease, how they treat patients, how they admit individuals to the sick role – also become subjects for sociological study. Medical knowledge can be treated as something that does not merely reflect states of the body; it is also a means for doctors to exercise authority over their clients (Freidson, 1970). If doctors admit patients to the sick role, on what basis do they do so? What rules do they employ? Which groups of sufferers do they view as being more (or less) deserving of treatment?

These and other questions are reflections of the view that illness is not caused by biological agents, but is a condition *ascribed* by societal interpretation. Thus, the diagnosis of diseases, like colds and heart attacks, can be discussed in the context of everyday responses to minor or major infringements of the law, such as parking violations and murder (Freidson, 1970). During the 1960s this view was given impetus by critics of psychiatry, who argued that personal problems are fabricated as a mental illness; it is a label made up by doctors (Gerhardt, 1989).

By calling into question the right of medical knowledge to its dominant position, the ground was prepared for attention to be focused upon the knowledge held by laypeople. This view was justified by criticisms of Parsons' theory as being functionalist, meaning that it assumed that medicine worked for the good of society as a whole. Instead, it has been argued that society is made up of competing groups with different interests, having unequal opportunities to share in its rewards (Morgan et al., 1985). Studying the differences between social groups has become one of the main branches of empirical research in medical sociology. Indeed, it is the comparative treatment of two or more groups within a common frame of reference that exemplifies the societal perspective.

Examples of this approach include studies of the varying amount of illness reported by different sections of the population. By defining social class in terms of occupation it is possible to compare the frequency of illness with the relative use of health services (Brotherston, 1976; Townsend and Davidson, 1982). The finding that the prevalence of illness is lower in the top social groups, while their use of medical services in relation to need is greater than that of lower groups, provokes questions about the social context in which illness arises. Are these features to do with material deprivation, which can then be determined as a cause of disease? Do these class differences stem, in part, from different attitudes that people have towards their health and how they should look after it?

The interesting feature of these questions is that they suggest a collective source of disease, at a distance, so to speak, from biomedicine. The idea that disease might originate in this way means that it is *the conditions of people taken collectively* that deserve study. Therefore, the societal perspective highlights general issues such as the effects of economic booms and recessions (Eyer, 1977), as well as more specific factors such as the conditions of people in the workplace (Doyal, 1979). Even though illness will be suffered by individuals, the origin of their diseases, and how these are dealt with by medical authorities, will be defined by forces within society itself. To take this particular line is to make the 'social causes' of illness primary, and their biomedical explanation and treatment secondary.

The idea that individuals are more or less susceptible to disease, as a result of their social position, allows for another relationship of the social to the biological. This, the approach of *epidemiology*, demonstrates differences between social groupings in the prevalence of specified diseases. For example, Marmot and Syme (1976) investigated the presence of coronary heart disease among groups of Japanese men who had migrated to California. They found that those immigrant men retaining traditional Japanese culture had levels of disease consistent with the relatively low levels found in Japan. Those who had taken on an American way of life had levels three to five times greater, and similar to those found amongst men in the USA. Marmot and Syme made a point of showing, statistically, that these differences could not be accounted for by the 'traditional risk-factors' of smoking, diet or high blood pressure levels.

The explanation underlying this type of finding is presumed to lie in the common experiences or way of life of the groups concerned. In this particular variant of the societal perspective, such reasons are often difficult to find within the statistical comparisons carried out. What is common to a group or culture often requires a different sort of analysis, in which the experiences of the individuals concerned, and the meanings that they place on these, are given greater weight. We shall, in a moment, turn to an approach that does just this.

Before doing so, it is worth emphasizing that where the behavioural perspective has worked within biomedicine, the societal perspective has done quite the reverse. It asserts that because being sick and being treated are both part of the workings of society, it is as important to consider the views of laypeople as it is to study the behaviour of medical practitioners. That is, by stepping quite outside biomedicine, and framing its questions in sociological terms, this approach gains a perspective on medicine itself.

(c) The cultural perspective – medical anthropology

The concept of culture has provided the basis for a third perspective on health and illness, associated with the work of medical anthropologists. The idea of a cultural view derives from this discipline, which, in the past, was identified with the study of non-literate or pre-industrial countries. The term 'culture' directs attention to the complex of practices, rules and values that are shared by a particular people or significant group in society. The broad contribution of culture studies has been to alert other social scientists to the relativity of their ideas about the individual, and about people's relationships to society. What are taken-for-granted realities in Europe or the USA, for example, are not so in many non-Western countries, and this applies to matters of disease as much as to anything else.

As with the previous two perspectives, we need to see how this one relates to biomedicine, and what biomedicine looks like from its point of view. For the anthropologist, biomedicine is the Western way of understanding and treating disease. This does not mean that it is just knowledge exercised by doctors. It is also the way that health and illness 'make sense' in the light of the layperson's cultural traditions and assumptions about reality (Fabrega, 1975; Scheper-Hughes and Lock, 1987).

An example of a cross-cultural difference in medical belief systems has been offered by Young (1976), based on his study of the Amhara people who live in Ethiopia. Young argues that, where Western culture explains disease in terms of the *internal* workings of the body, the Amhara focus upon *external* matters to account for sickness. They believe that disease can occur for a variety of reasons: people eat the wrong foods (upsetting worms that live in the stomach), ingest food contaminated by contact with creeping animals or demons, are poisoned, or are attacked by the spirit aspects of an enemy. These beliefs are supported by a range of cures, many based upon herbal remedies. The way that these remedies work is not explained in terms of any unified theory involving bodily organs. Instead, the Amhara find their healing system meaningful (and therefore helpful) because it restores balance to the individual within the moral order of society.

In terms of the structure and workings of beliefs, this appears to be very different from the experience of being ill in Western society. In this culture, the development of a unified body of specialized knowledge (biomedicine) has produced an *internalized* belief system involving detailed descriptions of the inner workings of the body (Young, 1976). And yet Western medicine, taken as a belief system, does more than classify diseases and offer remedies. It, too, also structures that experience and creates the terms in which people can become sick and make a proper recovery (Kleinman, 1973). Therefore, the cultural perspective poses biomedicine, not at a distance from lay beliefs, but as itself a set of ideas that connect events in the social world with mental and bodily feelings (see Figure 1.1). As well as using medical knowledge to organize their own experience of illness, individuals grasp the social significance of medicine through sharing in its cultural meanings. If we think of the various areas of life as providing the individual with different domains of experience, then Western medical knowledge is important in organizing aspects of those experiences into one realm that we term 'sickness' (see Figure 1.1).

In focusing upon beliefs about sickness in cultural settings, the cultural perspective brings biomedicine and everyday beliefs together. This can be envisaged in two ways. Either one sees medical knowledge and cultural beliefs as overlapping systems 'within' the individual; or else medical knowledge and lay beliefs are seen as different, and hence potentially conflicting ideological positions 'within' the one culture. On the one hand, this gives rise to a study of how medical knowledge enables individuals to make illness adaptations (i.e. to make discomfort or injury meaningful). On the other, it offers a view of medical knowledge as privileged, in its power to decide how particular signs of disease are given socially recognizable meanings, thus designating the course of sickness that particular groups can follow (Young, 1982).

The cultural perspective is different from both the behavioural and the societal viewpoints in its refusal to take the assumptions of either Western medicine (e.g. diagnostic categories of disease) or Western society (e.g. terms like middle class, stress, lifestyle) as absolute. By studying the medical system as one domain of cultural knowledge amongst others, the rigid frames of (a) disease categories and (b) social groupings are dissolved. Considered at this stage of an introductory text, this is rather an elusive point to grasp. For that reason, it is sufficient to take the following point from this discussion: the cultural perspective opens up questions about how disease is 'made social' in the overlap of medical and lay beliefs about health and illness (Frankenberg, 1980).

This book's approach to the study of health and illness

The previous section pointed out that there is no one-to-one relationship between each perspective and its associated discipline. Therefore, we shall not rely upon only one perspective when discussing social and psychological issues of health and illness. Certainly, the research carried out in this field does not, as yet, exemplify one distinct approach.

The behavioural perspective is lacking for our purposes because it ignores both the experiential and the social aspects of illness and health. This is true even in social psychology, where researchers have adopted an experimental approach to medically defined problems. The objection to this is that the focus upon individuals – their predisposition to disease and recovery from illness – simply ignores the social settings in which becoming sick and regaining health take place. For that reason, this book does not review work that some might consider central to social psychology (e.g. 'locus of control'). The application of existing social psychology theory to health problems is not, in itself, sufficient to tell us what is special about this topic.

Nor are we primarily interested in questions of health outside of individual experience, at the level of social class or institution. This means that the societal and cultural perspectives, inasmuch as they address issues about the delivery of health care in the population, or about illness in other cultures, will remain at the fringes of our concern. This does not mean that these perspectives will be missing from our discussions in the chapters to follow. Many of the studies that we shall consider have been carried out by sociologists or by anthropologists. Questions of individual experience and social conduct still require that we adopt one, or both, of these perspectives at various times.

To say what the approach of this book will be, it is necessary to address some of the questions raised earlier on in this chapter. What do people believe about staying healthy, and what do they do to recover from illness? How do they decide when they are ill, and what part do others play in the decision to seek medical aid? What is the role of the doctor and other health professionals in deciding when someone is sick and how they should be treated? What happens when individuals live with a long lasting condition, or must undergo treatment over a period of time? And finally, how do the prevailing cultural beliefs about how to stay well affect people in their everyday lives?

These questions will form the basis for the discussion in the pages to follow. Notice that they bear directly upon two aspects of social life – (a) how people experience health and illness, and (b) how the passage from one of these domains to the other involves relationships between individuals and between groups. These two aspects give the book its focus, and provide the theoretical orientation for answering the questions raised above. In particular, we shall be concerned with the way that people interpret illness, so that questions of meaning will often be central to our review. This is not limited to the study of individual ways of thinking. How people think about health and illness, and what they do about these things, are matters of joint concern. As we shall see, illness matters because it 'means' something to others as well as to the person directly affected. And what it 'means' extends to other areas of life shared by people in a particular group and culture.

There is one other aspect to the book's approach that should be mentioned here. Health and illness are not abstract affairs: they concern the body – or more precisely *my* body or *your* body. Again, we must be wary of thinking that this means it is necessary to look towards physiology, or somehow inside the body considered as an object. Our physical existence is intimately tied up with social life, with its rules and meanings. When, later on, we consider what it means to fall ill, or to be diagnosed as having a serious disease, it will quickly become apparent that these are questions that demand we take the lived body into consideration. Individuals do not just *have* diseases, they *bear* illnesses. The way that they do this is with, or through, their bodily conduct.

In summary, the approach of this book will be to examine health and illness with an eye to seeing how these matters 'make sense' to people. This means how people collectively make sense of disease; how individuals make sense of their own illness experience; and how being sick can make someone's world 'make sense' in new and different ways.

The chapters are organized to show the experience of individuals as they move between the realms of health and illness, and the role of other people who influence, and sometimes share, this passage. For readers new to this topic, there is good reason to follow a line that traces the everyday experience of becoming ill and receiving medical treatment. For that reason, Chapter 3 examines the everyday beliefs that people hold about why they become ill and how to stay healthy. In Chapter 4 we discuss the way that bodily changes come to be perceived as symptoms, and the transition that people make from feeling unwell to being sick, which may involve seeking medical aid. The relationships of patient and doctor is the focus of Chapter 5, which examines the practices of diagnosis and treatment in the application of medical knowledge. Chapter 6 takes up the question of gender in relation to illness, paying particular attention to the health of women. The problems of those with a chronic illness, and the implications for them of coping with this in the world of the healthy, are discussed in Chapter 7. Chapter 8 examines the concepts of stress and of social support as matters that are often suggested as important, both in developing disease and in the recovery from illness. The final chapter takes a critical look at some of the consequences of current advice to individuals to look after their health, and more broadly at the role of social science in the promotion of good health and in the prevention of disease.

Before this, it is necessary to examine the historical background to our everyday ideas about illness, doctors and patients. The purpose of beginning with this question is to help loosen some of the assumptions that the reader, probably steeped in a Western medical way of thinking, will inevitably bring to the topic. It also raises, all at once, many of the questions that we shall want to examine more closely in the course of the discussion to follow.

Chapter summary

- People's experience of health and illness involves both their social context and their body.
- It is useful to distinguish between *disease* as referring to pathology defined by medicine, *illness* as the experience of the patient or sufferer, and *sickness* as the social status of the afflicted person concerned.
- Health and illness are not equal opposites – illness is the more definite, marked term in our thinking. We often only know about health in terms of its disruption by illness, and medicine's clinical applications.
- There are three different approaches to studying health and illness within the human sciences, defined by the relationship of each perspective to biomedicine: the *behavioural* perspective focuses upon the individual, the *societal* perspective upon different social groups, and the *cultural* perspective upon the relationship of health beliefs to everyday understanding and action.
- This book examines how people, individually and collectively, *make*

sense of health and illness; these experiences are significant because they involve people's *bodies* and their *relationship to society*.

Further reading

Eisenberg, L. (1977) Disease and illness: distinctions between professional and popular ideas of sickness, *Culture, Medicine and Psychiatry*, 1, 9–23.

Engel, G.L. (1977) The need for a new medical model: a challenge for biomedicine, *Science*, 196, 129–36.

Gerhardt, U. (1989) *Ideas about Illness: An intellectual and political history of medical sociology*. Basingstoke: Macmillan.

Scheper-Hughes, N. and Lock, M.M. (1987) The mindful body: a prolegomenon to future work in medical anthropology, *Medical Anthropology Quarterly*, 1, 6–41.

Weinman, J. (1990) 'Health psychology: progress, perspective and prospects', in P. Bennett, J. Weinman and P. Spurgeon (eds) *Current Developments in Health Psychology*. Chur: Harwood.

2
Illness, the Patient and Society

This chapter examines the historical background to our everyday ideas about illness, disease and medicine. It makes a brief survey of people's experience of illness in the past, and relates this to the development of modern medicine. The chapter's purpose is to show that ideas about illness and disease are part of social change. For this reason, we need to reassess some of our assumptions concerning health and illness, many of which we are likely to take for granted.

Much of this book will be concerned with examples of health and illness that are familiar to many readers, including such things as visiting the doctor for everyday aches and pains. However, health and illness are also dependent upon the social context in which sickness occurs and in which it is treated. We cannot assume that words like 'ache', 'pain' or 'doctor' – or even 'health' and 'illness' for that matter – refer to things that remain the same wherever and whenever they are applied. This is true of the experiences of the sick as well as of the practices of the physicians and nurses who attend to them.

This concern about not taking our modern, medically dominated situation as a given is more than a matter of wanting to be broad-minded for the sake of it. It has important implications for the way in which we approach questions about health matters. For example, the use of the word 'patient' is based upon a number of assumptions about how people experience their illness and expect to be treated. These assumptions are to do with how ailing individuals seek medical help; how doctors make treatment decisions; and how generally held views about disease influence both of these matters. To understand what particular patients do, or how some respond to treatment, we need to review what it means to be a patient in modern Western society.

Looking at the place of the sick person in society also has implications for how we study this field. By giving aspects of health and illness an objective existence, we can measure them and perhaps make predictive judgements. Conclusions can then be drawn, say, about which patients respond best to particular treatments for a specified disease. This is very useful in the context of modern medical practice and, when it involves a behavioural inter-vention, is counted a creditable contribution of psychology to medicine. However, this approach separates 'patients', 'treatment' and 'disease' into relatively independent terms, while also assuming that they do not change. It also involves an equalization of the social significance of the human body (Manning and Fabrega, 1973). This assumes that, since the body is composed of universal features, it will be subject to a set of common diseases

experienced in a universal way. Manning and Fabrega (1973) set out the
implications of this 'biologistic' view as follows:

1   In any culture the body can be described in terms of identifiable organs,
    physiological systems and relationships, such as are found described in
    Gray's Anatomy.
2   Unless diseased, the body functions 'normally', and is experienced in a
    broadly similar way by all people.
3   The senses are universal; for example, everybody hears, sees and
    touches in the same way.
4   Diseases know no cultural boundaries; influenza is influenza wherever
    it occurs.
5   The body is, at base, a natural, objective, neutral entity.

They go on to challenge these assumptions by showing that for the Mayan
people of southern Mexico illness is understood in terms of problems in their
social relationships. This does not rely upon detailed knowledge of the body
as an organ system, for it is seen as a receptacle for evil that is being worked
in the social system. For that reason, curing involves making repairs within
society, not attending to the individual body as the source of disease.

This example shows that the biomedical viewpoint, into which industrialized peoples are socialized, is not universal. An immediate response to this
claim might be that this is interesting as a description of a pre-industrial
culture. It can have little bearing upon modern Western medicine, with its
extensive array of techniques for diagnosing and treating disease. Arguably,
what is enlightening about Manning and Fabrega's report is not just the
establishment of a cultural difference, but also its account of what happens
when these Indian peoples migrate to the city and attend Western-style
medical clinics. This reveals how the technology of modern medicine, in its
attempts to alleviate suffering, can undermine the legitimacy of the Mayan
culture. It does this by separating out body parts, fluids, emanations
(sputum, faeces, sperm, urine) so that each loses its sacred and cultural
meaning. This abstraction of the body's functions is partly responsible for
Mayan Indians feeling their original culture to be displaced by the ideas and
practices of Western industrial society.

We can take two important points from Manning and Fabrega's study:

1   Having an illness is social because of people's shared experience of their
    bodies, both when well and when sick; these are the general features of
    illness.
2   Having an illness is social because of the way it reflects the relationship
    of the sick individual to the cultural context. For any particular person
    at any particular time, these are its special features.

This suggests that medicine, and patients' experiences of treatment, are very
much involved in either confirming or challenging people's assumptions
about their bodies and themselves as members of society. For many people
in Western culture, the ideas and practices of biomedicine have quite a

different effect to that which they have on the Mexican Indian. As well as bringing about physical relief, they make a special kind of sense. They do this by organizing our bodily experience and by restoring a sense of value to our lives. Medical knowledge harmonizes with our assumptions about the world and our place within it. Because of this, terms like 'disease', 'patient' and 'doctor' do have a universal feeling to them; they do feel as if they are real and distinct variables for study.

However, should we assume that this transition from everyday idea to scientific belief is warranted? One way of addressing this question is by making a brief survey of how health and illness have been experienced and responded to in the past. If these topics have been understood differently in previous times, then this has important implications. Trying to deduce general laws of behaviour, based only upon present practice, is likely to confirm current preconceptions. On the other hand, if we can say something about how the experience of health and illness has changed, then we have a basis for seeing them as being open to continuing reconstruction in the contemporary world (Gergen, 1973).

The experience of illness in other ages

Prior to the emergence of modern medical knowledge in Europe, the significant diseases of the past were those of epidemic proportions. While we know little of what it felt like for the individuals concerned, there are reports about what effects it had on the people in general. Descriptions of the effects of plague give a sense of how illness was conceived in society at that time. Above all, there are descriptions of the 'crowds' of corpses, so that during the cholera epidemic of 1832 in Marseilles it was written:

> . . . street corners that were covered with sick and dying people spread out on rotten mattresses and abandoned without assistance. Half-rotten carcases in tattered clothes were lying covered with mud. Others were upright against walls in the positions in which they had expired. (Chateaubriand, quoted in Herzlich and Pierret, 1985: 147)

Because cholera spread so quickly, and because its progress was remorseless and its grip ultimately fatal, it caused panic and disorder among the people. The rich and educated could flee, as Newton did from plague-ridden London, to the safety of the countryside. The poor, however, generally remained to face what would come. While other ailments existed, it was the epidemics that defined disease for the people of the time. Plague was an affliction of the masses, to which there was no effective response by the individuals whom it touched. They generally saw their illness as fate, one that removed them into the mass of the sick and the dying, to which their fellows and family abandoned them. This fatalism was not misplaced, for it seems that there could be a very short period between the discovery of symptoms and the body's transformation into a horrible instance of the dread condition of disease.

What can be concluded from this picture of mass disease as social disorder? It shows that the meaning of disease, at the time of the epidemics, related primarily to the collectivity, not to the individual. However, it is worth noting that this idea of a collectivity should not be confused with our modern notion of the crowd. In the Middle Ages society had a hierarchical structure, in which there was a certain organic unity to relationships within guilds and institutions. It was this order that epidemics disrupted, so that while the plague may have shown itself on the streets, it struck at more than the 'mob' or the 'masses'. Indeed, the idea of the collective as a crowd 'on the fringe of the establishment' really only becomes possible once society is thought of as being comprised of citizens who are, first and foremost, individuals (Moscovici, 1990).

For disease to be thought of in individual terms, three main changes had to occur (Herzlich and Pierret, 1985, 1987):

(a) the survival of the afflicted person had to be seen as being more important than his or her dying a contrite sinner;
(b) medicine had to become capable of providing effective treatment;
(c) the linking of health with the production process gave sickness a meaning in relation to work, and the sick a new reason to 'get better'.

The first two changes are linked in the way that medical treatment developed towards the end of the eighteenth century. Prior to that time, doctors were available for people who could afford their services. However, as Duden (1985) explains in her study of German doctors in the 1700s, people often consulted their physician as a last resort. This was partly because he offered little in the way of effective treatment. Instead, the consultation held out a way of helping patients to *bear their ailments*. This confirmed why they had become ill and showed how, through this almost confessional act, they could regain the strength to carry on. These reasons were approached through the accounts that they gave of their lives and how they had lived them. The person's body was, therefore, very much part of his or her personal biography and social condition.

An examination of a physician's diary from this period shows, first, that he mentions the appearance of his women patients, then the humoural character that he attributes to them (e.g. phlegmatic, sanguine), then their husband's social status. Duden remarks that there is very little evidence of his carrying out a physical examination of his patients. In this, the era of what Jewson (1976) called 'Bedside Medicine', the doctor attempted to divine what was wrong with the whole body-person, not to isolate pathology in one particular organ or tissue.

Up until the end of the eighteenth century, physicians saw all elements of the person's emotional and spiritual life as relevant to the functioning of their patients' constitution. However, this focus upon personal experience meant that the physician did not – indeed, could not – differentiate the sick person from his or her condition (Jewson, 1976). Of course, particular afflictions (e.g. leprosy) and temporary bouts of sickness (e.g. fever) could be separately identified. But these were conditions of the person, not recognized as symptomatic of general classes of disease. It would only be later, with the new knowledge of anatomy and how it could be related to symptoms, that the sick body would become a system of synchronized organs. Then, as part of this shift in perspective, personal feelings and experiences would be irrelevant to the diagnosis.

In a later section, we shall explore further the changes in medical knowledge and practice that occurred at this time. For the moment, it is useful to return to the experiences of the sick to understand some of the changes that took place.

Tuberculosis was the disease that epitomized the transition from sickness as a 'way of dying' to becoming a 'way of living' (Herzlich and Pierret, 1987). In spite of the fact that the bacillus which causes the condition was discovered in 1882, tuberculosis (or consumption, as it was often called) continued to be a major cause of death in Europe until well into the twentieth century. The apparent contradiction in calling it a 'way of living' lies in the duration of the disease prior to its terminal phase.

For middle-class sufferers, being ill meant journeys to a sanatorium in the countryside, or even abroad. There was a romantic vision of the educated or wealthy tubercular patients, which focused attention upon the way that they bore their illness as individuals. The stereotype of someone with this disease was that of an interesting, aesthetic person, whose pale and thin demeanour came to be identified with a distinctive, almost aristocratic appearance. This romanticizing of TB is an early example of the promotion of the self as having an image (Sontag, 1991). This image was not shared by the working class, however, who were seen as the repository of the 'germs' (a new term) that caused disease, and for whom public health measures were seen to be more appropriate. But for those at the sanatoria, there emerged a world of illness that was distinct from that of health, that had its own institutions, its own privileges and its own relationship to medical knowledge and treatment.

The emergence of the individual patient also depended upon a changing view of what it meant to be a responsible and effective individual in society. In eighteenth-century Britain robust physical health was an egalitarian ideal, something to which everyone should aspire. This also meant that keeping well was something potentially in the hands of all individuals (though, in practice, poverty would deny this to the masses). From available written accounts it seems that middle-class Georgians pursued their health with care, using the doctors as auxiliaries rather than as undeniable experts (Porter and Porter, 1988).

The notion of duty to keep well was strengthened by the linking of health to work. By the middle of the twentieth century, laws had been passed relating to sickness benefit, and pressure continued to be applied for compensation for work-related accidents. Alongside this, the development of technological medicine meant that the doctor became instrumental in diagnosing the patient as someone either 'fit' or 'not fit' for work. This, as discussed in Chapter 1, has become a major conception of illness for many people today. Many of us see our ailments in terms of their effects on our working lives. The continuation of the work ethic in Western society has meant that joining and leaving the world of the sick (the sick role) is tied up with ideas of rights and obligations concerning one's duties in the workplace (Parsons, 1951a).

This brief overview of the experience of illness over the past two to three hundred years shows considerable changes in the ways that people have suffered illness and thought about disease. On the one hand, the role of patient emerged in relation to changes both in medicine and in society. On the other, the role of the doctor altered with the development of new clinical techniques, and because of the emergence of medicine as a profession. Perhaps most important to note at this point is that the place of the sick changed in relation to society. From being predominantly a mass phenomenon, sickness underwent a double movement. First, it became something that the individual lived with, and, second, it became a distinct social category occupied by those individuals when diagnosed as sick (Herzlich and Pierret, 1987).

This change has both a subjective and an objective reality: people experience disease differently, and society organizes the treatment of illness in new ways. Therefore, to become ill today is to experience a change in one's relationship to society that involves the distinct features of modern medicine. To be socialized into this way of thinking is to take on assumptions about 'disease', 'the sick' and 'the doctor' that often make them appear as absolutes. In the next section we shall take up the question of how this experience has been maintained, and examine its implications for our study of health and illness. As a way of doing this, it is possible to examine people's contemporary conceptions about ill-health as if they are part of continuing historical change. This does not mean that we give up social science for history. It does mean relinquishing the idea that we can study the elements of this problem as if they had always existed in this way, and must continue to do so.

The new anatomy and the problem of medical knowledge

Prior to the emergence of modern medicine, the body and its workings were often understood in terms of analogies that emphasized, for example, its growth and decay as a microcosm of the larger workings of the physical universe. Today we have different metaphors for the body, usually couched in mechanistic terms. The power of these metaphors is no less now than it was previously, so that our ways of thinking about the body do more than give it a sense of reality. They are part of its solidity, defying the idea that it could be anything less. Indeed, medical knowledge is, in everyday terms, treated in just this way, as the hard-won foundation upon which the expertise of practising doctors is based. To take the perspective of modern medicine is to look back over years of progress, moving from times of relative ignorance to relative enlightenment. What makes biomedicine different from earlier beliefs is that it is held to be scientific; it is built on facts.

An example (taken from Romanyshyn, 1982) will show that this is, if not an oversimplified view, then certainly a partial one. Arguably, it gives away too much to the scientific tradition that this perspective seeks to uphold.

Until the time of the Enlightenment, the idea of the body as a microcosm of the world included the notion that the blood ebbed and flowed, rather like the tides. By the seventeenth century, although it was known that there is arterial (oxygenated) blood and venous (de-oxygenated) blood, it was believed that oxygen transfer was achieved in the heart itself, through processes presumed special to this part of the body. As part of this function, it was thought that blood had to mix inside the heart, and the septal walls that divide its chambers had, therefore, to be penetrated by tiny holes (pores) through which the blood could pass. However, in 1616 William Harvey announced that the purpose of the heart was to displace blood, not to transform it. The means by which it does this is to act as a pump, by means of chambers divided from one another.

An important part of Harvey's findings was that there were no septal pores to be seen; nor could there be any holes in the chamber walls if the heart is to pump blood effectively. His critics, holding on to their beliefs in the heart as a vital, living organ, denied this. They said that only in a dying heart (such as Harvey had dissected) did the pores close up. It seems that, for some time after Harvey's discovery, anatomists who opposed his work still saw holes in the septal walls. From the standpoint of a cosmology that needed the blood to ebb and flow, if humanity was to keep its place in the universe, indentations in the septal walls had to appear as pores.

In his analysis of Harvey's discovery, Romanyshyn (1982) sets up the question 'Were there holes in the human heart before the seventeenth century?', to which the scientific answer must be 'No'. And yet he cautions us that what mattered prior to the scientific age is different to what matters now. To dismiss the earlier way of seeing as simply wrong is to lose sight of how people understood the world at that time. For social scientists to make that dismissal is to risk making an expensive choice indeed. Following that line makes it impossible to understand why, over one hundred years later, a German doctor who acknowledges Harvey's discovery is still engaged in attempting to make the blood of his women patients ebb and flow, at the rhythm that befits each of them individually (Duden, 1985).

Such questions as this, posed about either the past or the present, are at the centre of interest for this book. What this illustration teaches us is that, by remaining wholly within the natural science perspective, we make certain scientific observations appear as facts, while simultaneously making people's beliefs and experiences into error or mere fiction.

The argument that a new way of looking at the world emerged at the end of the eighteenth century is often derived from the writings of the French scholar Michel Foucault (1973). He proposed that a focus on the individual body emerged as a point for the deployment of power and control in society.

Outside of the anatomy laboratory there was a movement to separate and to classify people – the criminal, the insane and the sick. This movement was not restricted to particular political parties or causes, but was a pervasive way of ordering, classifying and knowing the world, including the human body and its workings. Medicine had a key role in this, through the introduction of new clinical techniques used by the doctor to investigate his patients. It also played an important role in the way that diagnosing and treating disease became organized in the community.

Both of these points are held together under a more general principle that Foucault put forward, that of the 'clinical gaze' (Armstrong, 1983). The ordering of bodies required that they be subject to inspection and open to scrutiny. It is easy to appreciate how the new science of anatomy, as demonstrated in the work of people like Harvey, would become part of this way of inquiry. More relevant was the way in which the practising doctor began to employ techniques that could relate this new way of seeing to the signs on the patient's body. Instead of asking for the person's own interpretation, or their life story, the doctor now asked about their bodily feelings. He inspected for specific signs of disease and he felt with his hand for changes and abnormalities. The connection of specific bodily changes to the diagnosis of disease meant that closer scrutiny of the body became imperative. For example, the invention of the stethoscope made it possible for the doctor to listen to the body's inner workings, while the patient lay quietly impassive.

These clinical techniques were, literally, instrumental in focusing the medical gaze upon the individual body. This helped to crystallize the relationship of doctor, patient and disease to each other. This might be why the stethoscope has come to symbolize the doctor as expert, as an authority in matters concerning ill-health (Armstrong, 1987).

The emergence of the modern medical view

Modern medical practice was able to do what the earlier physicians could not do (nor sought to do) – separate the sick person from the disease. Where previously the illness was perceived as part of the (rich) person's biography, relating to his or her constitution, now it was seen to be the result of a disease process understood in terms of the physiology of any-body. The patient 'as a person' retired into the background, allowing the doctor to be active in linking the signs of physical disturbance to the abstract classification of diseases.

This meant that the patient's body also mattered in a different way. Ordinary people began to think of it according to the new perspective, so that eventually most would take it for granted that the body is a machine-like entity, containing a pump for a heart. Today, as then, this is especially true for those who are formally educated in its workings. Medical students are educated in anatomy by having their attention directed (by means of an anatomical atlas) to certain structural similarities and differences, which make the inside of the body comprehensible. It has been said that although students understand the atlas as representing the body, in effect they are learning to see the body as a representation of the atlas (Armstrong, 1983). The belief in the reality of the body's structure goes hand in hand with the power to make effective interventions in its pathology.

Relevant to this point, Abercrombie (1960) has reported her experience of teaching medical students about how interpretations are made on the basis of clinical data. Asked to compare X-ray radiograms and to discuss common terms like 'classification' and 'average', some of the students found it disquieting not to have reliable access to the 'objective facts'. They said that questioning the objectivity of the body's anatomy made them uneasy, because it implied a threat to their expertise and authority as physicians. That is to say, they confirmed that knowledge is not neutral: it also serves the purpose of maintaining one's particular view of the world as 'real' and 'proper'.

The new anatomical knowledge grasped the body as a system of synchronized organs, so that the study of their pathology became of paramount importance. This was facilitated by the organization of medicine within hospitals and dispensaries in which the diagnosis and treatment of specific diseases could take place. The old 'Bedside Medicine' of the past was gradually replaced by 'Hospital Medicine', which operated with reference to the authority of doctors who specialized in the pathology of various organ systems (Jewson, 1976). In its new form, the dispensary did more than relieve the suffering of the sick: it also acted as a centre from which the prevalence and patterning of disease in the community could be mapped.

By the end of the nineteenth century the various strands of medical knowledge, clinical practice and professional organization had come together. This meant that, for people in general, being sick was synonymous with being treated by a doctor or in a hospital (Herzlich and Pierret, 1987). From this point on, individuals may feel unwell by their own account, but they can only become sick through the diagnostic attentions of a doctor. The considerable progress of medicine in technological intervention, in the control of infectious disease through vaccination, and in pharmacological treatment has meant that people in Western society think about illness in relation to these matters. The 'medical model', with its view of the body as machine, is now generally shared by many in the population, even if at times this knowledge remains sketchy and fused with other beliefs. The extension of its inquiries into various aspects of everyday life has meant that medicine now recommends how people should live a healthy existence, as well as how they should avoid disease (Zola, 1972).

Given this background, it is perhaps not surprising if there is a general belief in the efficacy of medicine and in its power to eradicate disease. Indeed, in the cases of the infectious diseases like cholera, scarlet fever and typhoid, Western medicine would appear to have completed this task already. However, a study of the decline in mortality rates in Britain over the last two hundred years makes it clear that this does not represent the whole picture, nor even the correct one (McKeown, 1976). Far from immunization of the population being the sole cause of mortality decline, the fall in the rate of deaths had been largely achieved prior to this time. This fall can be attributed to improved nutrition and hygiene, as well as to other environmental influences that were conducive to better health.

These ideas about the emergence of modern medicine are important to our study, because they bring into question the relationships between doctor, patient and disease as these are assumed today. If we take for granted that the body is nothing but a machine, then we forgo the possibility of understanding how it could seem otherwise to people, and how this matters in questions of being ill and staying well. Equally, we are then limited in our understanding of how people use this belief to make sense of their situation. For example, what does it mean when a man says that he has no fear of undergoing major heart surgery because, as when he takes his car to a good garage to be serviced, he is 'in professional hands'? By likening surgery to car maintenance, he implies something about the nature of his illness, about the surgeon's expertise, and about his own role in the treatment that is to come.

The conclusion of this section is not that medicine is unscientific. Rather, it emerged out of a more context-dependent way of viewing the world, of how people saw their bodies and their illnesses. In the course of developing as a social institution, it contributed to these changes in a way that has made its viewpoint dominant in Western society. This is not to say that medicine has replaced social interests in health and illness. These still remain, and a similar 'historical' approach has been used to investigate their relationship with medicine. The next section looks briefly at how this approach can be used to consider disease in contemporary society.

Disease and medicine in contemporary society

The point of view implicit in the previous section is termed *social constructionism* (Wright and Treacher, 1982). This perspective rejects the assumptions made by those who see social life as something best investigated by the methods of natural science. The latter approach, sometimes called 'positivism', assumes that the human world is like the inanimate one. This means that once we discover the laws to which it is subject, we can then predict events in a way that allows us to control it. Actually, the likening of the human to the inanimate world gives away more than many social constructionists would wish. For it suggests that there is a universe of 'things' governed by science, and a world of people following some other pattern of existence altogether. In matters to do with health, this would acknowledge that, while we might produce explanations of a constructionist kind when talking about doctors and patients, we would have to revert to a positivist (natural science) way of talking about disease and the body in general.

This way of thinking is not unlike the position that Romanyshyn described concerning the heart, prior to Harvey's account of the circulatory system. If we think of the heart strictly in (modern) scientific terms, then it is there, in its timeless form, waiting for Harvey to discover its true nature. The same would be true of the remainder of the body, and of the many and varied diseases that afflict it. Following this line of thinking, an account of health and illness would be about all those things that people do when they become ill or try to stay well, assuming that they had the disease in the first place. It is this assumption, the prior reality of disease, that social constructionism challenges. In Chapter 1, we separated our subject matter into sickness, illness and disease precisely in order to divide the social from the psychological, and from the biological. Having done that, and shown why it was important for social science to stand apart from the assumptions of medical science, we now appear to be retracing our steps. Why?

The constructionists would argue that this time we are coming at the question of ill-health from a different direction, so that matters which previously were taken for granted can now be seen to be the products of social change. Just as the anatomy of the body was discerned through social practices, so its diseases were established by a science that worked in a social context. To justify this argument, it is necessary not only to show how this occurred, but also to demonstrate that it is still occurring.

One example of the production of new medical knowledge, if not a new disease, is the case of hormone replacement therapy. This involves the prescription of oestrogen to post-menopausal women to lessen the likelihood of their developing osteoporosis (brittle-bone condition). This 'deficiency disease' can be seen to be the product of medical definitions, and of certain social assumptions. These suggest that women's biological condition associated with ovulation is linked to their youthfulness, attractiveness and hence their social worth. For example, one physician declared that 'in a family situation, oestrogen makes women adaptable, even-tempered, and generally easy to live with' (McCrea, 1983: 113). However, the initial case for oestrogen therapy was based upon its known effects on bone condition and the possibilities of it preventing atherosclerosis ('furring' of the arteries). Kaufert and McKinlay (1985) point to this as implying that once women had passed through the menopause, and produced less oestrogen, they were then considered to be in a state of oestrogen deficiency. This effectively turned the menopause into (i.e. constructed it as) as a 'deficiency disease', and hence into something that physicians are obligated to treat. The development of replacement therapy was the necessary condition for this to occur, tying it into a conception of the menopause as a reduction in women's psychological and social worth. This was required to justify its use, in spite of several contrary indications about the treatment's long-term effects. That is to say, the isolation of a reduction in oestrogen among women after the menopause is not enough to make this variation into a disease. By pointing to the possible harmful effects of this deficiency, and by linking it to beliefs about women at this stage of life, there can be superimposed on to a continuous variation a binary division separating 'health' from 'disease'.

Unlike oestrogen deficiency, coronary artery disease is one of the major causes of death in the industrialized world. In what sense could this, the condition underlying heart attacks, be considered a 'socially constructed' disease? Even by the beginning of the twentieth century it was believed that the modern pace of life had something to do with the occurrence of angina (chest pains) that are symptomatic of coronary disease. It was also assumed that those especially prone to these stresses of life were the educated male section of the community. It was clear, at least to one physician, that this did not apply to everybody in the community:

> Not all temperaments are susceptible to this modern stress. Women are almost immune. It belongs to the office and the technician's bench, not to the kitchen or the Labour Exchange. For all sorts of women there is perhaps no greater anxiety than that of too often repeated pregnancies. The haunting possibility of what seems an almost intolerable burden is seldom far from the thoughts of the average housewife. Yet should her fears be realised she is usually ready to accept what appears to be inevitable. No mental conflict develops. (Stewart, 1950: 869)

The same argument was applied to manual workers, about whom it was said:

> Today, more than ever before, the intuition of the manual labourer is to put his trust in collective action and wait for something to turn up. . . . He is content, if not with his lot, at least with himself. No sentiment of self-reproach assails his peace of mind. Neither is he troubled by ambition. He wants neither more nor less than his fellows. . . . All his problems are laid upon the altar of this restricted solidarity. (Stewart, 1950: 869)

The conclusion to this examination of coronary disease in British society in 1950 is that it is only 'the few' who suffer stress, so that it is 'from them [that it] exact[s] its fatal tribute'.

What are we to make of this account? First, the prevalence of coronary disease is linked to modern life, so that something about society is itself presumed to be pathogenic. Second, there are groups of people who, because of their own psychological shortcomings, are relatively immune to the disease. The ground is then laid for analyses based upon an acceptance of the two distinct realms – the 'natural' and the 'social'. These can then be investigated to find out how one affects the other. It is assumed that the disease is somehow triggered by social change, which makes its first appearance within the upper echelons of society. What, though, of coronary disease itself? One recent paper attempted to be reassuring about this by saying: 'A cultural approach does not deny the importance of somatic factors since it acknowledges that coronary heart disease has always existed and always will' (Appels, 1986: 480). This image of coronary disease as 'always existing' is similar to the example of the heart that was always really a pump. It places the disease, like the heart itself, firmly within a body that has its existence prior to social action and thought. In fact, coronary disease, considered as a diagnostic category, does have a history. This shows that in Britain it was only in the 1920s that heart disease appears as a cause of death about which there is concern in the official statistics (Bartley, 1985). This was partly to do with changes in the way that doctors completed death certificates, preferring to record heart disease over other possible causes. It was also a result of the movement away from coding death as due to arteriosclerosis of the body's blood vessels *generally*, to degeneration of the coronary arteries *specifically*.

This classifying of death, the way that doctors saw the clinical presentation of the patient, meant that rises in the mortality figures could be linked directly to a specific pathology of the coronary arteries (the atheroma, or 'furring'). As Bartley (1985) points out, this then allowed for theories about how diet, physical activity and lifestyle are causally related to raised blood cholesterol and narrowing of the coronary arteries. The belief that these risk-factors are more typical of the middle classes led precisely to the kinds of view set out earlier.

This view is at odds with data obtained since that time which show the economically disadvantaged to be most at risk of suffering chronic ailments, including heart disease (OPCS, 1988). As a result of these figures, there is a new emphasis upon changing the lifestyle of the working class, in addition to the middle classes. The point is that the way heart disease is conceived, including the significance given to specific parts of the cardiovascular system, is still supported by value judgements about how certain sections of the population live their lives.

Probably the best example of a 'disease' that is undergoing formulation in the present time is AIDS. There is a question whether AIDS should be called a disease at all, for it is the name given to a syndrome, a cluster of symptoms. The person suffers and eventually dies from various infections and malignancies which the immune system cannot resist. In the years since AIDS was first established as a distinct condition, and the HIV virus was isolated, the determination of what AIDS is has been inseparable from the discussion about who gets it and how. Deaths from AIDS, and subsequent reports of HIV infection among the male homosexual communities in the USA, meant that the social implications of this syndrome have been debated from the beginning. As with other diseases related to sexual behaviour, the definition of AIDS is inseparable from people's beliefs about how it is transmitted, and their attitudes towards the groups of people involved (Patton, 1985). Because of HIV being infectious, and because the end result of AIDS is death, it has been perceived in ways reminiscent of conceptions of epidemics, the just retribution for a sinful life. And by a process of inversion, the identification of groups as being 'at risk' of contracting AIDS means that they are seen as unclean, in a way similar to how the poor were perceived as germ-ridden in the nineteenth century (Herzlich and Pierret, 1987).

Establishing the biography of AIDS has involved a search for its origin. This, too, has been carried on within a discourse of prejudice, so that at various times separate nationalities (e.g. Haitians), whole continents (Africa) as well as races (blacks, Hispanics) have been blamed for bringing the AIDS epidemic to the rest of the world (Sabatier, 1988). These explanations have ranged from the idea that certain peoples have, albeit unwittingly, harboured the virus, to suggestions that it was contracted by certain of their members engaging in intercourse with animals. These beliefs, though without foundation, serve to colour the syndrome with metaphors that act to keep the disease at a distance from the majority in Western society (Sontag, 1991). Or rather, they serve to place the blame for the condition on certain groups or peoples, even if it is not possible to contain the infection wholly within these communities.

The debate about whether there will be an epidemic of AIDS within the heterosexual population in Western countries continues. Some have argued that the moral panic created around the syndrome has been fuelled by members of the 'New Right' exploiting the disease to proscribe sexual promiscuity. Others have said that homosexual groups have sought to escape blame by fostering the idea that it is a problem for everyone in society (Sabatier, 1988). The intensity of this debate has provided the rationale for trying to establish a definite link in the progression from being HIV positive to developing full-blown AIDS. On this point, it has been argued that no convincing evidence for such a link exists (Duesberg, 1988). However, it has been reported that medical authorities in the USA are seeking to rename the disease, de-emphasizing the final AIDS syndrome and placing greater accent upon what is believed to be the continuity of the progressive effects of HIV virus infection (Sontag, 1991). That is to say, determining what AIDS/HIV 'is' is a classificatory activity that continues to be influenced by beliefs about who is at risk and how the virus is transmitted in society.

The three conditions that have been discussed in this section – hormone deficiency, coronary heart disease and AIDS/HIV – are very different in their symptoms, treatment and prognosis. However, it has been shown that the determination of what kind of condition each is (indeed whether it is a disease at all) is a matter of categorization. This categorization is no mere classification, but involves conceiving bodily changes in a way that reflects their surrounding conditions as 'sensible'. It 'makes sense' that eating fatty foods and leading a sedentary lifestyle leads to occluded coronary arteries, just as it 'makes sense' that women's lowered quality of life after the menopause results from oestrogen deficiency. The argument concerning the link between AIDS and HIV also 'makes sense' of the behaviours believed to spread the disease. Because the construction of disease involves debate between experts and laypeople, it is more than just a background issue. It affects how, in this book, we approach questions concerning individuals and their illness.

The social constructionist perspective: some implications for explaining health and illness

The purpose of examining the historical and social context of health and illness has been to place a question mark against the relationship of social science to medicine. We have seen that, rather than there being a ready-made subject matter to which theories can be directly applied, these problems are themselves subject to construction. People's everyday ideas about health and illness are an example of what Berger and Luckmann (1971) have described as objectifications of the social world. Through language and social practice the world is ordered into objects that are apprehended as reality, and then internalized again as objective truth. In this way knowledge has a double aspect: it is both the means of producing the world and the way of knowing what it is that has been produced (and, one must add, what kind of people could have produced it).

For Berger and Luckmann this double process involves knowledge being institutionalized. With regard to health and illness, this concerns the institution of medicine. It means that there are social definitions about what constitutes 'medical knowledge', who can exercise it, and the procedures for passing it on to the next generation. Not all of these social definitions are available to everyone in society. In the case of medicine, there are strict limits placed upon who should or should not have access to information, even concerning the state of their own bodies. The point is that these limitations, among other things, lead to people experiencing this knowledge not as constructed, but as objective, as if it came from elsewhere than the social world. Berger and Luckmann refer to this experience as *reification*, a condition that is inevitable in an institutionalized world, and arguably essential for everyday life to go on.

For the purposes of this book, the social constructionist argument provides a way of freeing ourselves from the everyday assumptions (reifications) of medicine. However, it should not be inferred from this discussion that bodily afflictions 'do not exist'. This inference is sometimes mistakenly drawn, once it is proposed that bodily processes are not the essential things modern science says they are. What is being suggested is that while bodily growth, decay and death can be considered organismic processes, they are also something else. These changes are matters that people suffer, try to explain and attempt to influence. Therefore, we can accept that, while the organism sets limits upon what can be done with the body (e.g. women suckle children, in old age people become frail, severe pain incapacitates), society penetrates the organism by defining, regulating and valuing its functions (e.g. when to eat, how long to sleep, whether to breast- or bottle-feed).

This argument shows that modern medicine, even when considered as a belief system, remains powerful and important. This is because its procedures for verifying its 'truths' (i.e. its scientific and clinical effectiveness) are part of the perspective by which it makes the body into a 'thing'. And because this perspective can operate relatively independently of context, it has been able to attain a global presence. This is the basis upon which critics of constructionism have argued that medicine is not just one view among many. On the contrary, it has attained a qualitatively different position, in being able to define, for industrialized peoples, the reality of disease and the physical body (Bury, 1986).

What has this excursion into the social construction of health and illness provided? It has sketched out how, on the broad canvas of history, illness, disease and sickness emerged as separate categories. This provides a basis upon which to ask how these things relate in the everyday experience of people who are unwell, and of those who are healthy. Not to have made that separation would have meant trying to relate aspects of individual patients (e.g. social support, motives, personality) to criteria laid down by bio-medicine (e.g. diagnosis, or some physiological measure). We have seen that this approach is limited in its view of how health and illness are fashioned in society. It would also add to the individualism that has been seen as a major weakness of current social psychology (Moscovici, 1990). This individualism, and the picture of society that underpins it, relate to the early development of medicine that has been described. The emergence of an abstract classification of disease, together with the view of the body as a machine, is consistent with a psychological approach based upon individuals. Perhaps the greatest limitation of social psychology is that it is based upon a conception of a society that, '[h]aving taken science as a model, is conceived as increasingly divested of specific qualities, like a space in which things are expressed only quantitatively or in terms of material relations' (Moscovici, 1990: 84). This social space is the direct correlate, the supporting reflection, of the body that we saw emptied of its 'constitution'. Once turned into a container of organs, it can be treated quantitatively in terms of material relations.

Instead of this, we can turn to questions about how health and illness are conceived in society, and what these conditions mean for the social standing of sick individuals. What happens when we become unwell, and how do the healthy in society regard the sick? The separation of illness from disease means that questions can be asked about the way that symptoms are experienced by people in their daily lives, how they decide about possible courses of action, and whether they should seek medical advice. Also, once medicine is seen as a belief system (albeit a key one), it is possible to ask how doctors make decisions about people's ailments, and how patients make use of this knowledge in their own lives.

Chapter summary

- The assumptions of modern medicine underlie much of our everyday thinking about health and illness, making it appear that words like 'doctor', 'patient' and 'the body' have a fixed meaning, when arguably they do not.
- Taking the view that cultures are relative, and that society undergoes historical change, means that medicine, too, can be seen as a product of social life; this perspective is known as *social constructionism*.
- From the time of the plague, when sickness was a condition of the masses and more a way of dying, ideas of health and illness have become linked with the survival of the individual through the provision of effective treatment, and reflect people's fitness to fulfil social duties.

- Prior to the emergence of modern medicine, the doctor could not distinguish the person from the ailment. The development of new clinical techniques allowed the pathology to be perceived in terms of the classification of disease. The modern relationship of doctor and patient, and the idea of the body as a machine, are products of this medical gaze.
- Seeing medicine as a process of social construction means that contemporary diseases can be understood in terms of their linkage to social categories – the establishment of labels such as oestrogen deficiency, AIDS and even coronary heart disease can be comprehended in these terms.
- The idea that the body is a container of organs parallels that of society being a container of individuals; this view is inconsistent with a socio-psychological approach to studying health and illness in everyday life.

Further reading

Armstrong, D. (1983) *Political Anatomy of the Body: Medical knowledge in Britain in the twentieth century*. Cambridge: Cambridge University Press.

Berger, P. and Luckmann, T. (1971) *The Social Construction of Reality*. Harmondsworth: Penguin.

Herzlich, C. and Pierret, J. (1985) The social construction of the patient: patients and illnesses in other ages, *Social Science and Medicine*, 20, 145–51.

Herzlich, C. and Pierret, J. (1987) *Illness and Self in Society*, trans. E. Forster. Baltimore: Johns Hopkins University Press.

Jewson, N.D. (1976) The disappearance of the sick-man from medical cosmology, 1770–1870, *Sociology*, 10, 225–44.

3

Ideas about Health and Staying Healthy

This and the next two chapters follow the course from health, via the appearance of symptoms, to the medical consultation and the treatment context. As we have seen, questions of health go beyond the medical consultation. People may think about their state of health when feeling well, and before they consult a doctor. This chapter is the first that will look in some detail at the topic of everyday health and illness. It will focus upon people's *ideas about health* and about what it means to be healthy. It will also examine individuals' reports telling how they avoid illness. Its purpose is, therefore, to present some examples of what people say about these matters, and to point up the main issues for further discussion. This will allow us to see, not only what people think about health, but also its relationship to illness and to other aspects of everyday life. It will also provide a basis for discussing what social scientists can deduce from accounts that individuals give about their state of health. Is 'health' just a bodily condition about which the individual can give a privileged account? Or is it something wider, and yet more elusive than this, taking in questions of social values and how people judge one another?

What does 'being healthy' mean?

The first chapter briefly described Apple's (1960) study of how people define illness. This was done in order to introduce the idea that becoming ill is socially and psychologically defined. In fact, the approach that Apple took was to select three criteria that she believed to be important in illness definition (interference with usual activities, recent onset, and ambiguity of symptoms). The problem with this approach is that it limits what people say to these three criteria, which might not be the ones they would wish to use if allowed a free reply. On the face of it, the simplest way to find out what people think 'being healthy' means is to ask them. In an early study that did just this, Baumann (1961) reported that people make three main types of response: (a) that health means 'a general sense of well-being'; (b) that it is identified with 'the absence of symptoms of disease'; and (c) that it can be seen in 'the things that a person who is physically fit is able to do'. She argued that these three types of response reveal health to be related to (a) feeling, (b) symptom-orientation and (c) performance. Rather than her respondents falling into discrete categories, nearly half of them used two, and 12 per cent of them three types of definition together.

Baumann's study provides a simple beginning, as much for the questions it raises as for what it tells us about how people view health. The people she spoke to were all patients attending an out-patient clinic of a general hospital in New York, and had already been given diagnoses of quite serious diseases. Also, they were only eligible for attendance at this clinic because they were on low incomes. This means that these ideas about health, though spontaneous, were provided by a specific group of people whose experience and background were likely to have shaped their views. We can take this as a warning that the study of health beliefs must be representative if it is to be applied generally. Alternatively, we can view it as a recommendation that health beliefs be studied in the context of particular social groups. Both of these cautions have been heeded in subsequent research, the results of which will be revealed in the discussion to follow.

There is one other implication that follows from this brief critique. It is that ideas about health are likely to be fashioned, if not change, in the context of people's experience of illness. It is one thing to talk about health when hale and hearty, another thing to give one's views when suffering a serious illness. Similarly, what health means to a person with well-paid employment, a family and access to medical facilities is likely to be different from the meaning it has for someone who is unemployed and homeless. Health and illness are not wholly separate categories; nor are they merely opposites that are mutually exclusive.

One biographical situation that puts these ideas to test is childhood. It is to be expected that children's ideas about health and illness will reflect something of their developmental capacity and their experience of illness. While over half of a group of British 6-year olds could not say what it means to be healthy, every one of a group of 11-year olds could do so (Eiser et al., 1983). In this study, children saw health primarily in terms of taking exercise and being energetic. This confirms the results of research in the USA that showed 'being able to participate in desired activities' is most important in children's views of health (Natapoff, 1978). The idea that health means being fit for work (schoolwork, household chores) is not common among children, suggesting that the connection of health with role performance and social obligation is something acquired through socialization (Campbell, 1975; Pratt, 1973). This involves specific instruction by parents about such things as teeth-cleaning, but it is also gained through more varied experience. The ways that children are treated when ill, and how they see adults in the family behave when they have symptoms, provide such experiences.

As we shall see below and in the chapter to follow, it is often through episodes of illness, and their consequences for social life, that people's ideas of health are given further shape. These episodes need not be personal, in spite of the reasonable assumption that we will draw the clearest lessons from our own experience of being ill. Television and films, as well as books, provide us with instances of sickness, both in the home and in hospital. These are often moral tales, about fortitude as well as misfortune, so that when one becomes ill oneself it is possible to draw upon these images from the media. As Frankenberg put it, 'as a member of society visiting hospital, I understand the symbolic significance of the screens round the patient's bed because of the many beds I have seen on the screen' (1986: 624).

At this point we need to review what people have said about health in general and their own health in particular. The remainder of this section concentrates upon two studies that provide this information. One is a recent survey carried out on a national sample in the UK; the other involved a number of in-depth interviews conducted in France, mainly with people in Paris as well as in rural Normandy.

The *Health and Lifestyles Survey*, addressed to 9,000 individuals, included two key questions about health (the reader might like to jot down an answer to each one before proceeding):

(1) Think of someone you know who is very healthy. Who are you thinking of? How old are they? What makes you call them healthy?
(2) At times people are healthier than at other times. What is it like when you are healthy? (Blaxter, 1990: 16)

Coding the replies produced a range of categories, including mention of lack of symptoms, ability to perform duties and physical fitness. In reply to the question about what it was like for her own health, one 20-year-old nursing assistant is quoted as saying:

> I feel alert and can always think of lots to do. No aches or pains – nothing wrong with me – and I can go out and jog. I suppose I have more energy, I can get up and do such a lot rather than staying in bed and cutting myself off from people. (Blaxter, 1990: 19)

This explanation of what it is like to be healthy contains all three types isolated earlier by Baumann (1961) – that of bodily feeling, freedom from symptoms and ability to perform duties. The survey data also showed that about 15 per cent of the respondents could not think of anyone who was 'very healthy', and about 10 per cent could not describe what it was like for them to 'feel healthy'. (This is a point worth remembering as we go on to discuss the detail of health beliefs.) Among the latter group, it was the younger male respondents who found difficulty expressing their view of health. For them it was a norm, a background condition so taken for granted that they could not put it into words. By comparison a smaller group, mostly of older women, could not answer for precisely the opposite reason. They had been in poor health for so long that, either they could not remember what it was like to feel well, or they were expressing a pessimism about their condition to the interviewer.

Analysis of the responses concerning health showed a number of different categories:

1   *Health as not-ill* – in which health is defined by the absence of illness, whether in terms of symptoms (e.g. 'he's got no aches or pains') or visits to the doctor (e.g. 'she hasn't been to the doctor in years').
2   *Health as reserve* – where someone is perceived as healthy because 'she

has got over her operation very quickly' or 'he comes from a family with strong constitutions'.

3   *Health as behaviour* – usually applied to others rather than to oneself. This is where people are defined as healthy because they 'look after themselves', take exercise, diet or generally take other precautions to avoid disease.

4   *Health as physical fitness and as vitality* – fitness was a definition often cited by younger respondents, for whom weight-lifting or playing sports was seen as a proof of good health. Blaxter notes that these descriptions usually applied to a man, and it was among men that the idea of being healthy because one 'feels fit' was most prevalent. Among women the concept of 'feeling full of energy' was a positive one, and often related to a willingness to undertake household jobs.

5   *Health as psycho-social well-being* – this involved defining health in terms of a person's mental state (e.g. 'feeling proud', 'being in harmony'), or else, more specifically, in terms of an enjoyment of other people's company.

6   *Health as function* – this is the idea of health as ability to perform one's duties. It might be applied to a man in relation to his ability to do hard manual work, or to an elderly person who is able to look after his or her own garden. It implies that you are healthy when 'you can do what you want, when you want'.

On the basis of these definitions, Blaxter concluded that when people talk and think about health they do not use a single concept. There are various ways of conceiving of good health, and individuals are able to use them in different combinations, at different times. Notably, people who are diagnosed as having a serious disease will sometimes say that 'apart from having . . .' they are in good health. As will be seen in the next chapter, the idea that the absence of symptoms may be a condition for someone to say that they are healthy often proves to be an ideal scenario. Normal health can accommodate a number of 'ordinary' ailments, so that someone with a toothache will not necessarily report that their health is bad. Finally, good health has positive qualities that go beyond the notion of it being just an absence of illness. This concept might not be used by all in the community, but where it is, it is likely to have certain implications; this includes what individuals see as being lost at times when they suffer from disease or injury.

The *Health and Lifestyles Survey* also examined what people do to maintain good health (e.g. diet, exercise), some of which we shall examine in a later section. However, at this point, a more detailed picture of people's health beliefs can be obtained by reviewing what individuals say when allowed to talk at length about these things in the context of everyday life.

One of the most influential studies in this field was conducted by Herzlich (1973), who interviewed 80 people, most of whom lived in Paris. The work was guided by the argument that health, as an idea that individuals hold, is a *social representation*. This is a concept that encapsulates a particular approach to social psychology: the way that individuals perceive and know the world forms part of more extensive 'systems of knowledge' that are shared in society. Hence, to study health beliefs from this perspective is to do more than record the aggregate of separate individual views. It is to tap into a collective way of understanding health and disease. This gives direction not just to specific matters concerning health and illness, but also to the individual's wider relationship to society.

Herzlich's findings confirm that people do not think of health and illness as simple opposites. Health, for her respondents, was sometimes an absence of symptoms and sometimes a presence – a positive feeling of freedom and well-being. Illness was also seen by people to have many forms. However, the state that many people found most common to them is neither of these conditions alone. Instead, it is an intermediate one in which one is aware of small troubles – headache, indigestion, an aching knee – which mean that the person is not exactly ill but nor is he or she in the best of health.

Herzlich pointed to three conceptions of health as being important – *health-in-a-vacuum*, *reserve of health* and *equilibrium*. The first, 'health-in-a-vacuum', refers to the absence of illness. One only knows one has good health when illness strikes, and then that something has been lost. It is, in a sense, independent of the person. By comparison, 'reserve of health' is more characteristic of the individual, in that people can feel themselves to have either more or less of this capacity. Some of Herzlich's respondents spoke of this reserve as a quality that they had inherited; others said that it was the outcome of a favourable childhood. It appears as an important bastion against the onslaughts of disease and as a key feature in resisting illness when one becomes sick. It is something that individuals deduce by comparing themselves with others ('I'm not like my wife, she's always catching colds'), and from how they cope with periods of illness in their lives. Although one's 'reserve of health' may be depleted, it always remains, even though (like a container) it might be emptied; one does not lose it altogether when one falls ill.

The third conception of health is different from the previous two in this latter regard. Herzlich found that when people spoke of health as a state of 'equilibrium', it was something that they could lose or regain. Where 'health-in-a-vacuum' is an absence, and 'reserve of health' a presence, 'equilibrium' is contingent upon events in the person's life. So, when things are going well, one might feel that it is there. It can be experienced, as one of Herzlich's interviewees said, through having 'sparkling eyes, a good colour, to feel at ease when you meet up with friends and not to be on edge' (1973: 58). Unlike the 'reserve of health', which varies in degree, 'equilibrium' is either there or it is not.

These conceptions can be summarized in the following way: 'Health-in-a-vacuum' is only a fact, an impersonal condition; the 'reserve of health' is a value, a stock that can be built up or depleted; 'equilibrium' is a norm, against which individuals compare themselves at different times and against other people. (This second basis of comparison links the conception of health as equilibrium to other areas of people's lives, and opens up the possibility of the positive aspects of health – as freedom to do things – that has been mentioned already.) By ordering the conceptions in this way, Herzlich offers three potential movements in how people think about health – from absence to presence, from impersonal to personal and from fact to norm. This does not suggest that one alternative is better than another, or that there is an inevitable progression from one to another in people's thinking. It is well to remember that Herzlich's respondents, like those in the *Health and Lifestyles Survey*, sometimes expressed several ideas together in their statements.

What, then, does this study tell us? First, it suggests that people's ideas about health are more than beliefs, if by this we mean a set of fixed attitudes about something. This is revealed in the demonstration that the object of these conceptions – 'health itself' – is not a simple, unchanging entity. Second, it confirms that health is logically independent of illness, so that it cannot be studied as 'the opposite of being ill', or be assumed to be the condition of someone not carrying a medical diagnosis. Instead, concepts of health – as reserve or equilibrium – connect with other areas of life, giving it meaning in terms of feelings and capacities involving activities and other people.

These conclusions are supported by the results of another qualitative study that examined the health beliefs of a sample of older people (aged over 60) in Aberdeen (Williams, 1983, 1990). This was a quite different group of individuals to the mainly professional people who formed the core of Herzlich's respondents. In spite of that, Williams (1983) identified three main conceptions that closely parallel those identified in Herzlich's study. He noted *health-as-absence of disease*, *health as a continuum of strength* and its corollary, *weakness*, and *health as being fit for work*. The appearance of weakness alongside the concept of strength reflects the concerns of an older group of informants. For these individuals, the reserve of health had been largely drained by repeated illnesses, and by what they saw as the irreversible problems of ageing. The idea of 'fitness for work', rather than 'equilibrium', might be due to a cultural difference, though other studies focusing upon class differences suggest an alternative explanation. (We shall return to this last point later on in this chapter, when we examine health beliefs in relation to social class.)

One aspect of life that the older Aberdonians mentioned, and this related to all three conceptions of health, was the positive effects of continued normal living. So someone might say 'I'm always on the go and that keeps me going', implying that normal, everyday activity is somehow health-generating. As Williams (1990) argues, it was the involvement in everyday social life, things like pensioners' clubs, gardening, discussing baking recipes, that these informants believed generated good health. Seen in this way, activity is not just an index of sound health, but also a medium through which it may be built up and sustained.

Health and illness as social representations

So far, little has been said about people's representations of *illness*. This is because it is necessary to establish, first, the independence of health as a concept. In a later section to do with health practices (how people keep well), and in the chapter to follow, we shall examine in detail questions to do with becoming ill and taking action to remedy it. At this point, it is necessary to say something about how illness forms part of people's representations of health. For while these two terms are logically distinct, they are often brought together in how people talk about each one. To return to the metaphor with which we began the book, the image that the healthy have of their own domain owes much to the view that they hold of that other kingdom, and how one becomes a citizen of the state of sickness.

When introducing Herzlich's study, it was pointed out that social representations have an orienting function, in that they express a relationship of the individual to society. This suggests that how people think about their health is not something limited to their own bodies or individual experience. Instead, it is affected by the way in which health is understood as part of a wider representation of society, and the individual's place within it. This is consistent with the idea that health beliefs are associated with other areas of life and that, for some people, social activity is itself seen as encouraging good health.

On the basis of her qualitative study, Herzlich (1973) proposed how social representations of health and illness might be structured. She had noted the opposition between the individual and the 'reserve of health', on the one hand, and society and the 'way of life', on the other. ('Way of life', for her respondents, summarized modern society's 'wear and tear' that leads to fatigue and ultimately to a likelihood of falling ill.) She represented the formal relationship between these concepts as follows:

[society = illness] as [individual = health]. (Herzlich, 1973: 92)

The important idea to grasp here is that to think of oneself as healthy is to think oneself in a particular relationship to society. The conflict between health and illness, Herzlich argues, reproduces that between the individual and society, from which it is derived. While health always somehow belongs to the individual, it is something that is exercised and proved in the person's active involvement in society. This 'proof' of one's good health is therefore parallel to the 'proof' that one is a worthy and responsible citizen within society. This gives the individual's state of health a value-laden or moral aspect, because a person's 'healthiness' may be read by others as expressive of his or her social attitude in general.

This point is illustrated in the accounts given by a group of middle-aged, mainly working-class women in a Scottish city, interviewed about the causes of disease (Blaxter, 1983). The causes that they cited were dominated by things outside of their control (e.g. germs in the environment, family weaknesses, poor working and living conditions). Explaining what she believed to be the cause of her arthritis, one woman said:

Well, put it like this, when you've got young family you've got a lot of hard work. More so when you have five. It's nae easy work. And we'd nae washing machines, nae hot water, nae sink – well we had a cold sink in the corner . . . there was a lot of hard work, there was stone floors. (Blaxter, 1983: 65)

Although, when talking of the past, the women said that they might have looked after their health better, they were at pains to point out that in such circumstances no-one could have acted differently. These circumstances related to an upbringing in relative poverty, and to a family life in which their responsibility to their own health had come second to the duty of raising their children. These accounts illustrate the point that the relationship of health to illness parallels that of the individual to society. What these women offered were explanations that not only made sense of health as a concept, but also made their lives sensible given the social setting in which they lived.

This discussion has shown that people's health beliefs are not reducible to their beliefs about illness; these are not the same thing at all. Instead, health is often understood in relation to illness, but this relationship is asymmetrical. Chapter 1 referred to this as an imbalance in the polar relationship of the two terms. Now we see that this is not merely a feature of grammar, but something to do with how health and illness are experienced alongside people's involvement in society.

This points up some further issues for our attention. These are related matters, concerning (a) the way that health appears as a background to normal life, (b) what happens to health beliefs when people become ill, and (c) the way that health is understood by individuals in different social and biographical circumstances. Each of these issues will be addressed in the following sections, where we shall focus upon the variation in health beliefs across different sections of society, and upon their relationship to beliefs about the causes of illness.

The causes of illness in self and others

This section extends the discussion to ideas about how illnesses are caused, and the implications of this for beliefs about health in general. Given that most people do have ideas about how illness occurs, it seems very likely that these will, in turn, shape their views about health and how to maintain it. Apart from the question of health as something that might stand on its own (a positive 'reserve'), the notion of maintaining health involves taking a view on the avoidance of disease. Chapter 2 showed that, with the emergence of modern medicine and the ability to counter infection, there was a corresponding change in the public understanding of disease and of its place in everyday life.

The middle-aged Aberdonian women whom Blaxter (1983) studied mentioned a number of causes of illness. The main ones among these were infection, family background and the environment. Much lower down the list was 'own behaviour', such as eating a poor diet or not taking care when symptoms first appear. At about the same time, another study was carried out with a group of working-class women in Wales (Pill and Stott, 1982). This aimed to discover the extent to which individuals hold their own behaviour as responsible for their state of health. It is worth noting that, where Blaxter's respondents were grandmothers (average age 51 years), Pill and Stott's interviewees were mothers (aged between 30 and 35), all with young children. This meant that they not only had a different cultural background, with a childhood after the Second World War, but were likely to have daily experience of childhood diseases among members of their immediate family.

To the question, 'What do you think are the main reasons for illness?', these mothers gave a range of answers, the most frequent being germs, being 'run down', and environmental factors. Over the interview as a whole, mention of heredity also appeared as an important perceived cause. Pill and Stott found that their sample could be divided into those who only mentioned things like germs, environment or heredity – the external factors that one cannot control – and those who mentioned their own behaviour (lifestyle) as contributing to their becoming ill. These individual factors, which included such things as eating the right foods, taking exercise and not 'abusing' their bodies, would place them (they believed) in a better position to fight off infection and resist disease. This notion of resistance, and of its depletion in becoming 'run down', is supportive of the concept of 'reserve of health' that was described in the previous section. Among these women were those who saw resistance as being a constitutional matter, something that the individual had either more or less of. Others saw it as something that could also be affected by what the individual did. This meant that if a woman did not look after her resistance, then she was placing her health at risk.

Pill and Stott drew upon Herzlich's (1973) account to underline this important point. *People do not feel responsible for catching disease; they feel guilty about having allowed their health to have become impaired.* Across their respondents in general, illness was perceived to be caused mainly by external agents for which the women did not feel responsible. However, among the sample there was one group of mothers who did feel that their behaviour was health-determining. This meant that failures to look after health (e.g. eating convenience foods, wearing clothes inappropriate for the weather, having insufficient sleep) meant that blame could be attributed to them by others. This also had an important correlate; for if they could be held responsible in this way, then in turn they could use these criteria to evaluate the behaviour of others.

This introduces into the discussion an important element that has been missing so far. The possibility of avoiding disease creates not only the potential for individual action (preventive health behaviour), but also a *moral requirement* that people act in this way. Of course, this will only happen if there are shared cultural expectations about health and its preservation, which then points up the question of the degree to which these beliefs are shared by all in the community.

At this point we can signal some concerns for future chapters of this book.

If people are judged in terms of whether they keep well and fall ill, then these become important social issues. This would include such things as going to the doctor, reducing work levels or taking early retirement due to poor health. As long as people see themselves as having some responsibility for their health, then all of these matters have implications for how we account for our ailments and present ourselves when ill. And of course, this is given particular emphasis in the construction of social programmes designed to make individuals more health-conscious.

When speaking of the causes of illness, it is important to be aware of distinctions that people make between different categories of disease. In general, infections are things that one just 'catches', while serious diseases such as cancer are seen as frightening because of the way in which they strike without warning, and seemingly without pattern. One exception to the general rule that disease is unavoidable is 'mental illness', which is doubted because there remains the suspicion that it might be self-motivated. In a series of interviews with 'healthy' families and with families who had a member suffering from either multiple sclerosis or schizophrenia, Pollock (1993) found that conditions such as 'nervous breakdown' were understood to be an expression of personal weakness. Central to this belief was the notion of 'attitude of mind'; this carried connotations of strength of will in the face of adversity. In general, these families expressed the view that attitude of mind makes little difference as to whether one contracts a physical disease, but it is a significant factor in how one copes with it. Applied to mental illness the opposite case was made. While attitude of mind would not help a person to cope with mental illness, its onset might be something that the person could have controlled. This reciprocal effect involving physical and mental illness is interesting, suggesting that the relationship between health and illness involves not only impersonal states, but also, in cases where these are deemed to be relevant, the actions of individuals themselves.

We have already seen how the parallel of society-to-individual and illness-to-health brings together the person's physical condition with his or her relationship to society. Differing conceptions – concerning individual responsibility, social setting and the varieties of disease – mean that there are various ways in which people express their beliefs about health and illness. We can examine this idea using Herzlich's (1973) theory of social representations. She suggested that illness can be regarded (a) as a state of the individual, (b) as an object external to people or (c) as the conduct of the sick person. (References above to 'attitude of mind' would be included in this last category.) Health, because it belongs only to the individual, relates to the first and to the third of these categories, but not to the second. Where health is a state of the person and illness is an external object, these terms appear in a rather static relationship. This associates the former with the individual, and the latter with society and its way of life.

It is only when we consider people falling ill that a more complex and dynamic relationship between the terms can be discerned. Illness then ceases to be something quite outside the individual, becoming instead the behaviour of the sick person. Health, on the other hand, is that which still binds us to the social world. We are sick and yet well, insofar as we can still relate to society. We do not lose our social identity entirely when sick; people call, and urgent notes are sent from the workplace.

When people become sick there is a change in the polar relationship of the two terms. Health and illness are transformed, becoming 'two poles of individual experience' (Herzlich, 1973). What these terms mean has now changed because, quite simply, the grounds of experience have altered. Beforehand, the health that was taken for granted as one's own was difficult to describe; the illness that lay far away (in others or in the environment) was a distant concern, perhaps to be discussed in the abstract. Now, when illness strikes, the conduct of the sick person involves both a way of resisting what was formerly outside, and coping with what defines him or her as sick. It provides, in the everyday experience of being unwell, a way of knowing health and illness that affects both terms. For illness, it becomes more particular and personal. Health, on the other hand, becomes tangible in being breached, where beforehand it might have been just an absence of bodily symptoms.

This summary of Herzlich's ideas might seem to have shifted the ground away from distinct 'beliefs' to the apparently fuzzier realm of 'experience'. However, as a theoretical contribution these ideas are indispensable if we are to understand how people organize their accounts of illness causation. The difference between health and illness as states, and their relationship within the personal experience of sickness, was noted by Pill and Stott (1982) in their description of the Welsh mothers' accounts. They reported that many of the women were less articulate when discussing the causes of illness in general, and more fluent when talking about their own last episode of sickness. Here, for example, is a section from one of their transcripts, in which the tentative suggestions relating to illness in general are underscored by a reference to an incident in the woman's own life:

> Well, my ideas . . . I think, as I say like, if it's chicken-pox or anything like that it more or less gets passed around and colds could be through what may not be dressed right the same day or the cold weather and rain and all things like this, you know. Then there's something like my little boy with the eczema and asthma is a thing, well, he hasn't had it from birth but it's something that just occurred like, you know . . . (Pill and Stott, 1982: 46)

It is not suggested that the general sections of accounts are more accurate than the personal ones, or vice versa. The point is that health beliefs are infused with the experience that people have of their own illness episodes (and those of family members). This means that these beliefs not only have different contents, in the variety of types of definition that people employ, but also a heterogeneous structure. One of the main findings of the *Health and Lifestyles Survey* was that individuals give different sorts of explanations depending upon context. These might be different for illness and for health; different for health as a generalized concept and 'my own health'; different for generalized 'illness' and for specific disease, depending upon the person's own experience. This conclusion bears upon the point made by Herzlich: that we think about health and illness both through shared representations and through their transformation in our own experience.

Reading or listening to people's accounts of their health changes can often be to discern a 'chain of cause'. In a further discussion of her study of Scottish women, Blaxter (1993) says that careful analysis of a transcript often shows people to be trying out various alternative ways to explain their illness history. She contrasts this search for 'experiential coherence' with the provision of 'theoretical coherence' that might be expected if people were giving a logical account. Summarizing sections from such a transcript, Blaxter annotates what the women said, and demonstrates the sequence of 'causes' that are offered, strung together in a single account. One account proceeds from mention of 'change of life' (life stage), continues via 'took on an old house' (social circumstances), and 'had a bout of pneumonia but never gave in to illness' (self-neglect), to 'I'm nae gaun to bed, I've a' these bairns at hame' (life-stage, not giving in). Blaxter points out that the presentation of a chain of cause meant that there was often a fondness for connecting the sickness events of members of different generations. This provided an account that did more than give a definition of health and illness in the abstract; it provided a history, an accommodation of these experiences within the women's family identity.

In the light of this overview, it is clearly a mistake to assume that all individuals not only have, but express their health beliefs as, a logical system. This view can lead researchers to impose a rationality on their respondents' thinking which is simply not warranted (Young, 1981). To understand the importance of taking this suggestion seriously, we need to look in more detail at two other explanations of how health beliefs vary. These concern group differences, on the one hand, and the context of research, on the other.

Social class differences in beliefs about health and illness

Interest in the health beliefs of poorer people and those in manual occupations originated in the concern that they do not avail themselves of the benefits of modern medicine. For example, in the USA, research was aimed at finding out whether the rational and bureaucratic organization of modern medicine would be a barrier to individuals who, it was assumed, led a more personal, family-oriented and 'folk-type' way of life (Rosenblatt and Suchman, 1964). Much of this research centred upon comparing social groups in terms of the accuracy of their medical knowledge and views of medical care. Comparing groups in this way was termed, in Chapter 1, 'taking a societal perspective' on health and illness. The problem with this approach is that it tends to be grounded in a questionable assumption – that the views of workers and the poor fall short of the rational knowledge of professionals. Therefore, it fails to comprehend that such views might make sense within the fabric of these people's lives, and that this fabric is in part supported by the way that health care is itself organized (Dingwall, 1976).

Inquiries into the structure of health beliefs have led to other studies attempting to compare the views of different sections of the population. This has been carried out (in the UK at least) against the background of a greater prevalence of disease and self-reported sickness among manual and unskilled groups, as compared with professional and middle-class people (Macintyre, 1986). Results from the *Health and Lifestyles Survey* confirm that these differences are particularly marked in the middle years of life (ages 40 to 70), implying that views on health matters are shaped by very different experiences, not just of disease, but of illness in specific contexts (Blaxter, 1990).

One study that examined responses to the question, 'What is, according to you, the best definition of health?' was carried out in France, using 4,000 informants and content-analysing the free responses to this question (d'Houtaud and Field, 1984). These researchers organized the answers into 41 different themes, which they clustered in association with the social class groups considered. For the 'higher' and 'middle classes' health meant such things as 'life without constraints', 'good physical equilibrium', 'personal unfolding' and 'dynamism'. To a group termed 'employees', health also meant 'good equilibrium', but also 'watching oneself', 'being in a good mood', 'sleeping well' and 'living as long as possible'. For 'urban workers', to these latter meanings were added such things as 'engage in sports', 'have a good appetite' and 'rest'. 'Rural workers' saw health as 'avoiding excesses', 'be able to work' and 'be under regular medical supervision'.

D'Houtaud and Field summarized their findings in terms of a particular distinction. Health is, on the one hand, *utilitarian* (it is a means to do other things); on the other, it is *of value in itself*, something to be sought and cultivated. It is the higher and middle classes who, because they manage social tasks, can appropriate health as value and norm (e.g. feel in equilibrium). In contrast, those who must labour with their bodies to carry out these tasks (the urban and rural workers) find physical fitness and ability to be key criteria of good health (e.g. to be able to work). This means that social representations of health, while expressing something of the individual's relationship to society as a whole, more directly express that person's location (degree of privilege) relative to others. Confirmation of these findings has been provided recently by Pierret (1993), who underlined the way in which, for French manual workers and small farmers, work imposes a sense of duty that illness threatens through bodily incapacity.

A British study along similar lines has revealed findings consistent with the research carried out in France. This focused upon people's recent health experience to obtain interview material that could be coded for its linguistic structure (Blair, 1993). The basis for this study was Bernstein's (1971) proposal that class experience is formed through differences in language use. This theory argues that middle-class children are encouraged to articulate their 'inner' experience so as to elaborate an individual point of view. By comparison, traditional working-class culture does not make this demand, leaving experience to be communicated either through restricted verbal expressions or by means of the body. By coding his informants' speech according to this distinction, Blair found that the middle-class respondents used more person-centred (*mentalistic*) terms when discussing their health, while the working-class respondents referred more to their bodies (*physicalistic* terminology). This difference extended to the references that members of the two classes made to treatment. For example, the middle classes saw attitude of mind and therapy as of possible help in treating cancer, while the working class made more mention of bodily interventions, such as drugs or surgery.

This focus upon language raises questions about the effects of the interview setting. Might the observed class differences be a function of the interview situation, as well as a characteristic of the individuals themselves? Middle-class people are more used to speaking in public, with individuals who have a wider vocabulary, or who have expert knowledge. In contrast, people from working-class backgrounds can often feel that it is difficult to find the 'right' words, or say the 'right' things, when speaking with individuals with expert knowledge – be they doctors or social scientists.

Reporting an ethnographic study of a group of working-class families in the East End of London, Cornwell (1984) noted that these individuals would put on their 'best face' in such situations by repeating what they believed to be the commonly accepted view on the matter. These *public accounts* are representations of the social world that, it is assumed, are widely shared. For that reason, they can be used to make the speaker acceptable in the eyes of a knowledgeable or influential stranger. Cornwell found that her respondents would often answer questions such as 'What is your health like?' with accounts of this kind. The overriding issue in giving a public account is to reveal oneself as a worthy individual. This is someone who cannot be 'caught out' or found wanting by a more powerful person, or someone 'in the know'. In this study, this meant a concern by the interviewees to show that health was something upon which 'they, personally', did not dwell. Others might moan and groan, and give in to illness, but 'I could never be called a hypochondriac'. Cornwell argued that this public view of health is tied in with a class ethos about work: that one's place on the social ladder is given, but one has a duty to work hard and to avoid illness. This view, paralleled in the accounts given by elderly people in the Aberdeen study (Williams, 1990), is consistent with the idea that for working people the fitness of one's body defines health and commitment to work at the same time.

The feeling that one has a duty to work hard extends to the idea that one is responsible for 'not being off ill'. (Note that this is not the same as feeling that one is responsible for one's health, by doing things like jogging or dieting.) While it has been found repeatedly that people cite external factors (germs, way of life) as the major causes of disease, there are differences between the social classes in the extent to which individuals are felt to be responsible for their own health.

In the *Health and Lifestyles Survey*, standard of living and poverty were
both mentioned when discussing health *in general*, but were less likely to be
so when respondents were talking about their *own health* (Blaxter, 1990). In
fact, those on higher incomes were twice as likely to cite poverty as a cause of
ill-health as those on low incomes. The moral imperative to avoid illness
would seem to explain, in part, the tendency for some working-class
respondents to blame themselves for illness. This blame is worked out in two
ways: first by a denial of social inequality, and second by an emphasis on
being a responsible patient.

An example of the first would include references to a hard rural
upbringing as being 'healthier' because of the fresh air and simple living
(Blaxter, 1993); or to office workers getting bad backs through too much
'lazing about in an office', compared with the factory workers whose activity
protects them (Calnan, 1987). An example of the second is provided by
working-class women who, in spite of excluding individual behaviour as a
cause of disease, direct blame at others who do not follow traditional
recommendations (e.g. let children sit around in wet clothes), or fail to take
medicine prescribed by the doctor (Calnan, 1987; Pill and Stott, 1982).

Private and public accounts

These attributions of blame are consistent with the need for respondents to
legitimate their position (and that of their family) to an 'expert' interviewer.
This *public accounting* often occurs as a response to abstract questions about
health, and it is to be expected that class differences in health beliefs might
occur in this context. This is precisely what Calnan (1987) found when he
interviewed samples of working-class and of middle-class women. While the
working-class women used more functional definitions, the middle-class
respondents used a wider range of definitions. However, when the women
were allowed to talk about their own illness episodes, no such class
differences were apparent. Why might this be?

One explanation can be found in Cornwell's (1984) concept of the *private
account*. These were stories told by her informants about their life
circumstances, in which illness episodes were revealed alongside other
aspects of their biographies. (This is similar to the 'chains of cause' that
Blaxter [1993] reports when people are trying to make sense of their life
through their illness biography.) Cornwell mentioned that this way of
talking came later in her meetings with the families, when they had accepted
her, and trusted her with information about their lives. She made the point
that there were no private accounts of health; people did not speak in this
way about times when they felt well. There were only private accounts of
illness, and these invariably involved individuals' employment position,
their place as a man or woman in everyday life, and their past experience of
health care.

Relating to the question of private accounts, Pill and Stott (1982) noted
the greater fluency of their women respondents when talking about their

own illness history. This fluency might derive from the absence of the need to give a proper (i.e. publicly agreed) account of oneself. It might also arise from the acceptability of speaking within a structure that is informal. Here, the speaker can make use of a 'restricted code' (Bernstein, 1971). In either case, what is apparent is that the health beliefs of social classes do differ, but only in certain respects, and only under specific circumstances. This does not diminish the importance of such differences, because they have implications for how people from different sectors of society become ill, and how they make use of health services. In subsequent chapters we shall want to refer back to these findings when discussing the interpretation of symptoms, how people seek medical aid, and how they cope with the burden of long term sickness.

Health beliefs and procedures for preventing disease

If people hold views about health and illness, then what difference do these views make to what they do to stay well and to avoid becoming sick? The question of the relation of health beliefs to action parallels the age-old problem in social psychology of the relationship of beliefs to behaviour. Partly for this reason, the following section makes a brief overview of an approach that has received much attention from psychologists working in the health field – the 'Health Belief Model'.

Before doing that, it is useful to clarify what is meant by 'things people do to stay well and avoid sickness'. It is useful to distinguish between *preventive procedures* (e.g. breast self-examination, dental check-up, attendance at vaccination) and *health practices* (e.g. the avoidance of smoking, taking exercise and diet) (Harris and Guten, 1979). Using this distinction, Pill and Stott (1985) set out to discover whether these two sets of practices were interrelated. Interviewing a group of working-class mothers, they asked the question, 'Do individuals who carry out one kind of behaviour carry out the other?' These researchers did not relate health beliefs to practices directly, though they did assess the degree to which the women thought that their lifestyle choices (their way of life) was relevant to their health status. This latter measure was shown to be strongly related to the adoption of a group of selected health practices. A cluster of socio-demographic variables (education level, marital status, employment) were associated with both procedures and practices, and showed that these behaviours are more likely to be carried out by people with social advantages. Preventive procedures, in particular, were carried out by women who had a greater belief in the personal control of their health. This suggests that staying healthy, and having a positive view on health, are different from the avoidance of specific illness conditions, as defined by things like check-ups and accepting vaccinations.

In a project that bears upon this issue, Calnan (1984) interviewed women who were to receive, one month later, invitations to participate in programmes to prevent breast cancer. The women were asked about their previous health practices and beliefs, including their intentions of future action. There were two conditions in the research. One group, in the English Midlands, were among women receiving an invitation to attend a breast self-examination class, in which they would be shown a film and participate in a discussion. The other group, in the South-East of England, were invited to attend for breast screening (mammography) at a local clinic. Follow-up data were gathered to see which women accepted the invitation in each case.

It was found that different features related to attendance for each group. For attendance at the breast screening clinic, 'intention to attend' was the best predictor, followed by the use of other preventive procedures such as dental check-ups and cervical smear tests. 'Intention to attend' the clinic was itself best predicted by 'perceived vulnerability to breast cancer'. By comparison, attendance at the class was related more to personal health practices, though perceived vulnerability to developing breast cancer was also important.

These results suggest that the reasons for practising a 'healthy lifestyle' and those for undertaking procedures designed to prevent a specific disease are not the same, although they might overlap. One area of overlap lies in the demographic advantage (higher social class, educational level, income, regional location) repeatedly shown for those who engage in more health-related behaviours. However, Blaxter (1990) cautions against drawing too simple a conclusion from this. Analysis of the *Health and Lifestyles Survey* showed that an inclination to drink alcohol, to smoke, eat a poor diet or not take exercise are not simply clustered together. For example, among males (smokers and non-smokers), drinkers had a *higher* probability of high exercise-levels than non-drinkers. Over the age of 60, smokers and drinkers with a good diet were more than twice as likely to take vigorous exercise as non-smokers and non-drinkers with a poor diet.

One contextual but important issue in this question of procedures and practices is how important health-in-general is held to be by the individuals concerned. The relative *un*importance of health has been remarked upon both for adults (Blaxter, 1990; Calnan and Williams, 1991) and for children (Gochman, 1971). What are regarded by professionals as unhealthy behaviours may have important roles to play in the life of the people concerned, and what are regarded publicly as being healthy actions may be practised by people for other than health reasons (e.g. young men rarely mention health as a reason for engaging in sport). To illustrate this argument with reference to diet, there are vegetarians whose food regime is motivated by a moral concern for animals. Though they recognize the health benefits of their diet, these individuals see this as a secondary gain of relatively minor importance. Beardsworth and Keil (1991) cite the case of a man aged 56 at interview, who had converted to vegetarianism at the age of 23, when the prevailing view among his family and friends was that such a move entailed serious health hazards. This example should serve as a caution: beware of attributing to individuals the motivations that professionals assume should be the background for behaviours seen as 'health protective'.

The 'Health Belief Model': scope and limitations

One approach that has been widely used by social psychologists studying health care has the label the 'Health Belief Model'. It gained its name from the attempt to identify those factors that influence individuals to act in a way that prevents disease, including the use of health services. The Health Belief Model (HBM) rests upon the assumption that whether a person will act depends upon (a) the value placed by someone on a certain goal (i.e. the desire to avoid illness), and (b) the belief that the specific action will achieve that goal (e.g. that dental examination will reduce the likelihood of dental caries) (Janz and Becker, 1984). The HBM takes the form of a set of variables that are presumed to be the dimensions on which people make their decisions about whether or not to practise some particular behaviour, like going to the dentist for a check-up or attending an ante-natal clinic. These variables, which are often measured by scaled, self-report questionnaires, include:

(a) perceived susceptibility (e.g. 'How likely do you think it is that you may get TB in the near future?');
(b) perceived severity (e.g. 'If any of these dental problems happened, how serious would it be?');
(c) perceived benefits (e.g. 'Suppose X-rays show that a person has TB, would it make any difference whether he starts treatment immediately or waits about six months to a year?');
(d) perceived barriers (e.g. 'What things might prevent you from undertaking a programme of regular exercise in the near future?').

In the original formulation, the first two features (perceived susceptibility and severity) were seen to provide the 'motive force' for action, while perceived benefits would determine whether that particular path was actually taken (Rosenstock, 1974). Later on, with the recognition that others serve as reference groups for individuals, either encouraging or hindering their efforts, the 'barriers' dimension was added to research.

We have already considered one study that used the HBM, which compared women's attitudes to attendance at classes or examinations for breast self-examination (Calnan, 1984). A more general, and perhaps typical, study was carried out in the USA using employees of a medical centre. They filled in questionnaires that asked about the likelihood of their suffering a number of common symptoms (susceptibility); the need for medical attention for each symptom (severity); the benefit that taking each symptom to the doctor might give, and that deriving from a number of health practices (benefit). No measure of 'barriers' was made in this study (Leavitt, 1979). Six months later there was a follow-up to find out about their use of health care services over the period. This showed that those who made greatest use were individuals who (a) saw themselves as susceptible, (b) saw diseases as potentially severe and (c) saw benefit in seeking medical advice for symptoms.

In their review of studies conducted over a 10-year period, Janz and Becker (1984) conclude that there is substantial empirical support for the HBM (i.e. that these same dimensions are related to health care behaviour). The HBM has frequently been used as an approach by many researchers in this area, although it is questionable whether they are all contributing to the same explanatory framework. It has been argued that there is a lack of consistency in the way that different researchers adopt questions supposed to measure the different dimensions. There is insufficient attention given to the specific populations used in the studies, and there is a lack of critical awareness about how beliefs might change after certain events have taken place (e.g. subsequent to being 'cleared' at a check-up [Shillitoe and Christie, 1989]). In effect, there is doubt whether the few dimensions that the HBM embraces could ever predict the variety of outcomes that occur in different social settings, and for individuals with different sickness biographies.

Some of these limitations were, in fact, spelled out in early presentations of the model. Rosenstock (1974) pointed to social pressure (e.g. legal compulsion, job requirements) as things that require people to undertake health checks, so that imagining individuals thinking about their health in splendid isolation is to assume a false set of circumstances. He also noted that the model might have greater application to middle-class rather than working-class groups, owing to the former subscribing to the assumptions that the (middle-class) researchers had built into the model in the first place. And finally, he wondered whether some behaviours are carried out not for health reasons (i.e. are decided upon), but through 'habit'. This touches on the point made above, concerning the relative independence of motives and behaviour, especially when viewed over time. It might well be that, for some people, cleaning one's teeth is a proper way of preparing oneself for others (to appear presentable, to avoid bad breath), not primarily a way of preventing tooth decay.

At least, these provisos should alert the reader to the fact that the HBM is limited to discovering what might immediately follow from holding certain attitudes, in terms of symptoms or practices. These caveats call into question the usefulness of trying to account for what people do by 'forcing' their experience into a pre-determined theory of the researcher's choosing. Fundamental criticism of the HBM is as old as the model itself. As long ago as 1970, Bloor (cited in Dingwall, 1976) pointed out that the perceptions of the actor are treated as independent variables, although they must be presumed to be socially generated. Abstracting the individual from his or her social setting simply pushes this socialization or normative constraint into the background, and leaves it mysterious. This is compounded by the person's experience of undertaking these behaviours, and the presumed effects of this upon attitudes, which creates a circular chain of influence.

Another criticism of the HBM is a general one, applying to all approaches of this kind. It is that the pre-specification by the researcher of what is to be included in the model makes his or her dimensions into a reality that hides the basis of its own creation (Stainton Rogers, 1991). What is left out is what people might say, if only they had been asked. This criticism applies equally to more elaborate models such as the 'Theory of Reasoned Action' (Fishbein and Ajzen, 1975), which has been found to be more useful than the older HBM in predicting health behaviour (Rutter, 1989). However, this theory is also based upon a model of social life that begins with the cognitions of the individual, so that researchers try to predict what people will do from a careful specification of their beliefs and intentions. The limitation of this approach is that it makes the understanding of health behaviour wholly contingent upon what people think immediately prior to their action. It loses sight of the social context in which such beliefs are fashioned, and the variety of relationships in which they might or might not be acted upon.

My own objection to the HBM is, on the face of it, a rather pedestrian one: it has a pretentious name. By calling itself the 'Health Belief Model', the approach commands a degree of attention, if not respect, out of all proportion to what it can ever tell us about people's beliefs concerning their health behaviour. Against the background of our previous considerations of the questions of health and illness, the limitations of this approach become clear. Having little in the way of an elaborated conceptual framework, it is more of an umbrella term under which a variety of data can be collected. These can then be used to try to predict the conditions under which people will use health services or comply with a medical regime. This general approach might be useful within the framework of certain health policies, but it is far too limited a basis upon which to construct a socio-psychological understanding of health and illness.

Health beliefs: some implications for the study of social attitudes

This final section takes up some of the ideas raised in our survey of beliefs about health and illness. It does this in order to draw out some of the implications of the work for the study of attitudes in general. One reason for focusing upon research describing people's views is to provide material against which one can judge the kinds of approach that will be most useful for social scientists to adopt.

Attitude study in social psychology is based upon the assumption that individuals make judgements about things that they hold in mind, as objects of thought (McGuire, 1985). Much research has been carried out to discover how individuals differ in the attitudes they hold, how these attitudes vary over time, and how they are open or resistant to being changed by persuasive communications (Eiser, 1986). In making these comparisons, this research tradition assumes that the objects of study (in this case 'health' and 'illness') remain as fixed entities in the minds of the people concerned. Making judgements about such things means that they will be compared, perhaps on a number of dimensions. The assumption is that an individual's attitudes will tend to be related, consistent and (it is also assumed) predictive of his or her behaviour. One problem with this approach is that it becomes difficult to know whether the beliefs that people express at any one time are their true ones. Another is that it has been shown to be difficult (though not impossible) to predict what people will do from a knowledge of the attitudes that they hold.

The picture of health beliefs that we gain from this chapter's overview suggests that attitudes are more complicated than the traditional view would suggest. Instead, it provides support for alternative theories, put forward in recent years, concerning not just the way that attitudes are assessed, but how they function in everyday life. In order to examine these ideas, three lines of criticism will be presented that have implications for understanding people's attitudes to health. These concern:

(a) the way that people discuss their ideas in interview situations, relating to the interviewer–interviewee relationship itself;
(b) the extent to which individuals hold shared ideas about health and illness, and how these originate and are maintained;
(c) the inconsistency in people's attitudes and what this implies about health in everyday life.

The first criticism raises the question of how individuals express their ideas. In several of the studies mentioned, health and illness were talked about in ways implying that the respondents felt they might be judged. In Cornwell's study, for example, some individuals were wary of being interviewed because they did not want to appear as people with poor health, nor as people who wanted to talk about their illnesses. The implication here was that 'going on about your illnesses' is likely to result in being seen, if not as a hypochondriac, then as a complainer. Health and illness are often discussed in terms of strength and weakness, inclusion and exclusion from social activity. Therefore, it is not surprising to find that when people talk about these matters they are careful in what they convey about themselves.

This means that *expressing* one's beliefs is not a matter of *exposing* them, as if they are inside one's head, ready-made. Instead, what people say also involves fashioning a context for their statements, something that is done within and alongside the things being said about health matters. Dingwall (1976) drew upon the work of Sacks (see Sacks, 1992) to show that, whether healthy or ill, people are concerned to establish the 'ordinariness' of their situation. In answer to Dingwall's question about the sorts of things that depressed her, a disabled girl said: '*Just simple everyday* things, *just* have arguments with people and *your* parents and . . . get bored with going to the same place and meeting the same people, *you know*' (Dingwall, 1976: 64, emphasis in original). The words in italics appeal to background knowledge shared by speaker and hearer, and set a context of 'ordinariness' or 'normality' within which the other things said can be taken. This is an example of justification or warranting, which has been demonstrated to occur across a range of beliefs that people express (Potter and Wetherell, 1987). One purpose of these justifications is to allow a person to discuss his or her illness in a way that will not make them seem 'different', so that whatever else they say will be judged acceptable by other people. This *legitimation of one's position* is constructed in the course of the interview, setting a context that helps to shape the meaning of what is said. For this reason, it has been argued that it is only through a study of discourse itself that beliefs can be investigated (Potter and Wetherell, 1987). From this position, there are no attitudes to be found 'behind' what people say, for what the beliefs 'are' is inseparable from the legitimation-work of the talk itself.

One dominant assumption in social psychology is that attitudes are held 'in mind' by people considered as separate individuals. This assumption is consistent with a culture that stresses personal choice, on the one hand, and individual compliance, on the other. In the context of health care it means the choice of how to view, say, eating a low-fat diet, or the likelihood that a person will comply with medical advice to attend a clinic for a health check. As a result, psychologists might be asked to measure attitudes to health practices or to medical prescriptions, on the assumption that they are finding out what makes people take or avoid a particular course of action.

An alternative position argues that how people understand the social world is not individual in essence, but social. The term 'social' here means ways of knowing that have their origin in society, collective representations that serve to make the world tangible. The theory of *social representations* is based upon the work of the French sociologist Émile Durkheim. It proposes that people's everyday views of the world are shaped by ideas that originate in the various spheres of modern life – e.g. science, politics, and religion (Moscovici, 1984). One of these spheres is medicine, and the work of Herzlich and Pierret (1987), considered in the last chapter, and of Herzlich (1973), in this one, illustrates how ideas of health and illness have been shaped by its concepts. Discussing Herzlich's work showed how the idea of social representations made possible an analysis of health and illness as conceptions that relate the individual to society. This, in turn, relied upon the assumption that illness and health are truly social conditions, in which people are either involved in social activity or, in their sickness, are withdrawn from it.

Social representations, like the traditional idea of attitudes, orient the person towards the world, which they also make sensible. To illustrate this, Moscovici (1984) uses Herzlich's (1973) analysis of 'fatigue' to show how a representation can give form to our experience, while also making it permissible for us to speak in its terms. Representations thus shape events by *anchoring* them (e.g. making feelings of tiredness, of headache, comprehensible as 'fatigue'). They are, in turn, *objectified* through their medicalization as diseases with diagnostic labels, or as quasi-illness conditions like 'fatigue'.

This theory has accumulated much support in recent years, but it has also

been criticized on a number of grounds. One of these relates to the problem of whether representations are shared by everybody, or even by everyone presumed to belong to a certain class or group. So, for example,
Herzlich's study of health and illness has been questioned for its conclusion
that all of the respondents necessarily shared representations that were expressed by only some individuals (Potter and Litton, 1985). The criticism is
that, by calling representations social, and by assuming that they are
common to people in society, the degree to which they are actually shared
is not tested.

A related point has been raised about how well the theory really explains
the relationship between the common sense of individuals and the ideas
gained from, say, medicine (Billig, 1988; McKinlay and Potter, 1987).
Studies of beliefs about health and illness have something to say on this
count. While the material that we have examined in this chapter can give
no definitive answers, the distinction made between public and private accounts is helpful (Cornwell, 1984). Both types of account involved medical
and common-sense knowledge, so it would seem that the origin of different
beliefs is important. However, as views that 'reproduce and legitimate the
assumptions people take for granted about the nature of social reality'
(Cornwell, 1984), public accounts were those in which medical concepts
(i.e. social representations) dominated. When it came to private accounts,
however, Cornwell reported that only illness was at issue, in stories where
preoccupations were more practical and pragmatic. The indication in other
studies, that middle- and working-class respondents differed mainly in
their public accounts shows that access to social representations (medical
knowledge) will differ according to social position. Taken together, these
findings suggest that the question is not primarily one of the degree of sharing of social representations, as much as of distinguishing between accounts in which they are either more or less in evidence. As Billig (1988)
points out, there is a need to describe socially shared beliefs that are *not*
social representations, in order to preserve a useful conception of what
social representations are. This work on health beliefs points to one area in
which this might be achieved.

Finally, we need to turn to the problem of consistency of attitudes. In
discussing individuals' descriptions of health and illness, it has been shown
that they often contain several different themes in one account. They are
not reflecting a systematic, unified view of a well-defined object or area of
experience. This is because, in their different ways, health and illness are
tied up with various areas of people's lives. In the absence of illness, health
has been shown to gain its meaning through what it makes it possible for
people to do. It makes a difference whether this possibility centres upon
feeding and caring for four small children, going to work or being able to
enjoy one's retirement. Therefore, it has been argued that it would be
wrong to impose an external logic on these beliefs. If allowed, people will
give varied accounts of what health means, as has been shown in recent
studies (Pierret, 1993; Stainton Rogers, 1991). The diversity of accounts

provides a means both of switching between themes to make particular points and of making other experiences in life sensible in terms of one's health.

The proposal that people construct differing accounts of health and illness suggests that these statements might express contrary themes in their thinking (Billig et al., 1988). This idea of contrary themes implies that thinking is less a predictive or representational activity than it is a kind of inner argument, in which the pros and cons of different points of view are put forward and countered. In the case of health and illness, we have seen that the two conceptions draw upon each other, so that they are not exclusive oppositions. In the context of the research interview, it has been shown that when people talk about illness, they must be careful not to prejudice their position as healthy individuals. The elements of the argument that would positively persuade someone that you have been 'really ill' also contain the seeds of the counter-position that you are someone who 'enjoys talking about their illness'. Showing, effectively, that you can do the former while disclaiming the latter depends upon the existence of this contradiction. As we shall see, these dilemmas are not restricted to the realm of thought and language, but can also be seen in the context of how people act when ill or when trying to regain their health. Indeed, it is in the way that people perceive and respond to the signs of disease, in what has been termed their 'illness behaviour', that we shall be able to see more of the interrelationship between the worlds of health and of illness.

Chapter summary

- Health and illness are not merely opposite terms, but stand in an unequal relationship to each other.
- They are not exclusive terms, because experience of one domain will be used to understand the other.
- Not every person has a clear concept of health, nor is keeping healthy a main priority for everyone.
- Individuals often have a variety of conceptions about health, which draw upon a range of life settings.
- There is a general feeling that, although one cannot be blamed for illness (being prey to disease), there are moral requirements to stay healthy where possible.
- Health beliefs can be seen as accounts that not only inform, but also legitimate the speaker's standing as an 'ordinary' and 'blameless' citizen.
- There are some differences in accounts given by members of different social classes, though these should be understood within the context of the ways that the views are sought.
- Accounts of health show the use of medical knowledge and of common-sense beliefs, although medical views are often taken as authoritative.
- Practices for promoting health and procedures for checking for signs of disease need to be distinguished. There is evidence that utilization of care

services varies with social class, with greater use being made by people with social advantages.

● The description of health beliefs obtained from accounts shows that these do not constitute a logically tight system, but often operate in an apparently inconsistent fashion.

Further reading

Blaxter, M. (1983) The causes of disease: women talking, *Social Science and Medicine*, 17, 59–69.

Blaxter, M. (1990) *Health and Lifestyles*. London: Tavistock.

Calnan, M. (1987) *Health and Illness: The lay perspective*. London: Tavistock.

Cornwell, J. (1984) *Hard-Earned Lives: Accounts of health and illness from East London*. London: Tavistock.

Herzlich, C. (1973) *Health and Illness: A social psychological analysis*, trans. D. Graham. London: Academic Press.

Stainton Rogers, W. (1991) *Explaining Health and Illness: An exploration of diversity*. Hemel Hempstead: Harvester Wheatsheaf.

4

Recognizing Symptoms and Falling Ill

When is one ill? If you feel unwell, how do you decide if you are really a sick person? How do you know when you should go to the doctor?

Immediate responses to these questions will probably depend upon the kind of illness the reader has in mind, and the point at which the symptoms are considered. For example, waking up with a thumping headache, dry throat and aching limbs might be a sufficient basis upon which to decide that one is ill. However, if the previous evening had been spent drinking rather too much alcohol after a hectic afternoon playing sport, then one might not be so sure. A different example might be the discovery that a mole on one's face appears to have grown in size. Here there are no feelings to guide you, but there is the possibility that a member of the family or a friend might offer an opinion. And finally, who has not known the indecision about whether or not to take some complaint to one's doctor. Is it worth it? Will it waste the doctor's time? Will you appear to be complaining about very little?

These are some of the questions that we shall be addressing in this chapter, which examines the experience of falling ill. In the previous chapter, the focus was on people's beliefs concerning their state of health. This surveyed what 'health and illness' look like from the position of 'the healthy', prior, as it were, to being ill. In fact, as was suggested there, this is an imaginary or ideal situation (Dingwall, 1976). People's views about health are shaped both by their previous experiences of sickness and by their understanding of medical knowledge, whether of an expert or lay kind. The point is that people fall ill against a background of beliefs about good and poor health. This means that questions of disease causation, of individual responsibility and of what it means to be a sick person are brought to bear upon any specific instance of symptom occurrence.

This chapter also raises some important questions about the relationship between social life and physical existence. As well as having a background of beliefs about health and other aspects of life, people's lives are also grounded in *activity*, in everyday conduct that depends upon the body (Radley, 1991). This can be instrumental, as in being able to hurry to answer the telephone; it can also be expressive, as in being able to appear youthful or attractive. One of the key distinctions that will be made in this discussion is between 'bodily sign' and 'symptom of disease'. We shall see that the recognition of signs and their interpretation as symptoms necessitates a closer look at physical existence than is usual in social and psychological studies.

The problem of symptom recognition has its roots in the question of why people who require treatment do not always see the need to seek medical advice. Mechanic (1962) gave the name *illness behaviour* to the ways in which symptoms may be differentially perceived, evaluated and acted upon. He saw it as having a place in what might be termed the stages of sickness, falling 'logically and chronologically' between the appearance of signs of disease and subsequent medical treatment. On a practical level, if one could establish which individuals or groups are likely to misinterpret symptoms, or delay seeking medical advice, then one might be able to formulate policies that could remedy this situation. This concern led to a study of the responses of individuals to their initial symptoms. It was found that people were more likely to take their symptoms seriously if they saw them as severe, as serious and as incapacitating. The problem of 'educating the public to behave rationally' was seen to derive from the individual's 'natural tendency' to underemphasize symptoms that are 'neither severe nor incapacitating' (Suchman, 1965). This, in turn, was seen to be important because many chronic diseases such as cancer begin insidiously, with relatively minor symptoms.

The question that this research left unanswered was 'How do people make judgements that a bodily disturbance is "severe", "serious" or "incapacitating"?' As we shall see, one way of approaching this problem is to look at how individuals perceive particular signs of disease in relation to medical categories. This has been the approach of social psychologists who have used the methods of cognitive psychology (e.g. Bishop and Converse, 1986; Lalljee et al., 1993). However, this does not address the issue of how people become aware of, and respond to, bodily feelings against the background of social norms and cultural practices. We saw in the previous chapter that people do not operate a unified health belief system, so we should not expect them to know that they are ill through a process of deduction or logical inference.

There is a further critical point to keep in mind. The early research mentioned above appeared to suggest that individuals who do not seek medical aid are not 'acting rationally'. This inference stems, in part, from the assumption that people think (or ought to think) in medical terms. This idea followed from the fact that because research into illness behaviour was medically led, it tended to see issues of illness definition as being defined by medical knowledge. One of the aims of this chapter is to put that claim to the test, for the important reason that it has implications for other arguments to be discussed in the remainder of the book.

Symptoms as marks of culture

Beliefs about health and illness are grounded in people's wider understanding of the world in which they live and their place within it. This means that they draw upon a stock of knowledge about sickness, and about its bodily signs, that owes much to their cultural setting. In subsequent sections we shall examine the meanings that people give to such signs, as well as how they are displayed for others, both in direct and in indirect ways. An example of a direct presentation might be a description of a pain, or showing someone an injury. An example of an indirect presentation would be intimating how difficult it is to reach for things, expressing discomfort associated with an injured back.

Symptoms are more than labels for the various changes that can happen to the body; they do not derive only from medical classifications of disease. Instead, bodily signs (which might not be symptomatic of disease) are often disclosed in people's everyday actions. Culture – in the sense of meanings placed upon symptoms – does not just arise once illness is present, but is there in the apprehension of bodily signs themselves.

This point can be illustrated with reference to a study of pain among a group of male patients in a New York hospital (Zborowski, 1952). The aim of the research was to explore the different reactions to pain among four ethno-cultural groups – drawn from Jewish, Italian, Irish and 'Old American' stock. It was stimulated, in part, by the impression of medical staff that Jews and Italians (meaning Americans raised within these sub-cultures) had a lower pain threshold. Zborowski found that while both groups of patients did express their pain readily, they differed in the aim of this expression. The Italians complained about the discomfort of the pain itself, while the Jewish patients typically expressed worries about the implications of the pain for their underlying state of health. As a consequence, where the Italian patient would trust the doctor and readily accept medication to ease pain, the Jewish patient was more circumspect about the doctor's skills and about whether pain-relieving medication would help cure the underlying condition.

Interviewing healthy men of each sub-culture revealed how their pain complaints made sense in terms of their role in the family. The Italian males, aware of their position as head of the family, felt a freedom to complain in hospital that was denied them at home. The Jewish males, by comparison, were allowed to be demanding and complaining at home, so that such complaints were not to be equated with weakness. Therefore, the presentation of pain symptoms had a different aim (gaining sympathy for the Italians, provoking the doctor's concern for the condition of the Jews) and a different basis. The pain that was displayed by the Italians was neither 'psychologically' nor 'culturally' the same as the pain displayed by the Jews.

This point can be clarified by comparing these patient groups with one other – the 'Old Americans'. Those men did not complain, nor did they display their feelings, but rather reported them in a factual way. Having views nearest to those of the medical staff, these men saw emotional expression as pointless, in a context where what was going to be effective was knowledge, skill and efficiency – not emotion. They minimized expressions of pain and, when it became too much to bear, would then withdraw from other people. In this case, pain is symptomatic of a body that works like a machine. Therefore, the situation requires an uncomplaining compliance that (these men believed) promotes effective treatment.

Zborowski explained these various pain behaviours in terms of different cultural attitudes that are learned during socialization. The general point is that culture shapes people's ideas of what is bearable in terms of pain. It also determines what is acceptable as a way of complaining and seeking help. Culture also embraces what have been defined as the three dimensions of adaptation to serious or chronic conditions, namely search for meaning, attribution of cause and social comparison (Mechanic, 1977). Understanding why this illness affected you, what might have caused it and how well you are coping with it are all matters that come within the bounds of one's cultural beliefs.

There is also a more specific point, worth emphasizing because it anticipates some of the discussion to follow. People's pain experience lies not only in what they think about or speak about their body, but in how they 'live out' their situation. To complain is not just to speak, but to demonstrate one's suffering. To 'bear up' is, similarly, not just to keep quiet but to compose one's behaviour against the background of actual or potential sickness. Although symptoms are the result of interpretations, they are also more than this. They are dramatized by individuals in the course of 'handling' or negotiating the transition from health to illness (Goffman, 1971).

This negotiation, bringing into play certain patterns of cultural behaviour, is not restricted to the patient alone. The differences between the cultural groups described above imply other variations, in the way that family members responded to the behaviour of the men in Zborowski's study. This refers to the fact that the men's expressions of complaint were seen very differently by the Italian, Jewish or 'Old American' wives when visiting their husbands in hospital. In the case of the Jewish men, their wives might understand their concern, and be sympathetic to their wish to give vent to their feelings. For the 'Old American' patients, however, emotional expressions might be seen by their wives as either embarrassing (breaching expected codes of conduct) or as signs that the men needed urgent and effective treatment.

Taken as a whole, the family does not just respond to symptoms once they appear, but plays an important part in shaping the way in which bodily signs are made real as symptoms requiring medical attention. This will, of course, vary with the culture concerned. In societies with a strong adherence to the extended family, its role in illness will be more evident. One example is the native-born Puerto Rican patient, described in the following episode:

> By the time one young woman was brought to the emergency room . . . she had already acquired her father's athletic socks, her sister's shawl, and her brother's army boots. This . . . conveyed a message . . . that all the members of the family loved the patient and that they had acted with great speed to rush [her] to the hospital. (Chesebro, 1982: 327)

Like the Italian patients studied by Zborowski, the Hispanic culture has strong gender-specific expectations that are brought to bear when people fall ill. While Puerto Rican men are normally expected to hide their emotions and to show control, during a medical emergency they are allowed to demonstrate great sorrow, joy or anger. The point is that these are not just individual responses to the onset of illness or to an injury. They are part of a collective activity that makes the ailing body sensible in terms of cultural practices and meanings.

From these examples we can see that symptoms are bodily signs that are given special, medical meaning. However, this meaning need not be arrived at just by diagnosis or some other mental judgement. The complaints of the Italian and Jewish men in pain, the stoic withdrawal of the 'Old American', and the accompanying concern of the Hispanic family show, in their different ways, that this meaning is also the product of a kind of bodily display. We shall have several opportunities to explore this notion of display in the context of the consultation and the situation of the chronically ill. The point here is that the designation of a symptom represents not only a pathology, a lesion applying to a bodily part, but also a *claim* by the sufferer (and perhaps others) that he or she be treated in a particular way (Goffman, 1971). At the risk of oversimplifying, we can say that the reaction to a bodily sign helps to produce the symptom's meaning. And because these reactions of concern, of fright, or of care are culturally based, they also constitute 'expected' ways of feeling.

From the social constructionist viewpoint, emotions like these are not inner reactions but socially patterned responses (Harré, 1986). In Western culture, when we are in pain we might not know exactly how to act, but we do have a notion of how we do *not* want to appear to others – as an embarrassment or a liability. In their turn, when others are ill, there are expectations that one will show feelings of concern, even if these are not 'felt' to a strong degree. All this means that deciding whether or not someone has a symptom of disease is more than a matter of material concern. It is also a matter of *symbolic status*, to do with how one is to be treated, both by one's fellows and by medical practitioners.

An example of this in British culture concerns the difference between having a 'cold' and having 'flu'. These are two common, and usually non-serious, conditions about which there are a number of everyday beliefs. These beliefs rest upon certain cultural assumptions involving, among other things, the relationship of the body to its environment (Helman, 1978). Within British folklore, colds are believed to result from sudden changes in the temperature or moisture level of one's physical environment. Getting one's feet wet, standing in the rain, moving from a hot room to somewhere cold are typical of the attributed causes of colds and chills. This is because (it is believed) the boundary of the person with the physical environment (the skin) is somehow penetrated by the cold/wet conditions. As a by-product of one's dealings with the environment, colds are one's own responsibility.

By comparison, fevers are believed to be the result of germs which originate outside of the individual but not outside of society. Because they are always transported by people, infection by germs implies a social relationship. Different types of relationship imply different kinds of risk, so that we deduce who the patient might have associated with according to the disease diagnosed (compare chicken-pox, flu, and HIV). Compared to catching colds, the person with a fever (influenza) is seen as blameless, a passive victim, who evokes in others the obligation of care (Helman, 1978).

This example from British folklore illustrates how the determination of whether one is suffering from a heavy cold or from flu can be more than a moot point of medical classification. It has implications for how readily the person can take up the sick role, and for the kind of care that might be given. For this reason, the extent to which it is believed that a person has good cause to be sick is likely to enter into expectations of how that individual might (or ought) to bear his or her symptoms – either with due suffering or with fortitude and good grace.

Symptoms and definitions of illness

In the first chapter we separated disease from illness, and both of these terms from the idea of sickness. This distinction is worth holding on to when discussing how people recognize bodily disturbance as symptoms. In the previous section it has been shown that although symptoms denote a specific disease to the doctor or knowledgeable layperson, they also exemplify (i.e. *portray*) a state of being (ill) for self and others. In terms of both of these conditions, symptoms are also symbolic of the individual's claim to be treated as a sick person. It is clear, then, that although there might be shared cultural meanings about illness, whether an actual instance of bodily disturbance is taken to be a symptom of disease is not necessarily a clear-cut matter.

In Western societies, one way of determining whether one is ill is to visit the doctor and obtain an expert opinion. While this might be regarded by many people as the best way to determine if one is 'really ill', it is clear that a large proportion of what would be regarded as illness never reaches the doctor's surgery (Chrisman, 1977). The possibility that this proportion of complaints, relating to symptoms in the population, is far greater than that presented to physicians has given rise to the concept of the *clinical iceberg* (Last, 1963). One study, of a sample drawn from the register of a health centre in the UK, found that 23 per cent of those interviewed admitted to medically defined symptoms in the previous two weeks, for which they did not seek medical advice (Hannay, 1980). Among those patients most likely to be part of this 'iceberg' were middle-aged women, the unemployed and those living in poor accommodation. (Other research has, however, challenged the assumption that the disadvantaged are necessarily those who make less use of physician services [Sharp, et al., 1983].)

From the standpoint of medicine, the 'clinical iceberg' reflects the problem of how to get people to go to the doctor when appropriate (as judged by experts). However, from a social scientific standpoint, it is yet further indication that the perception that bodily signs are symptoms of disease is neither automatic nor restricted to issues of classification.

If one compares what people say about whether they have been restricted by discomfort or injury with what they report about their visits to the doctor, then the differences mentioned above are confirmed. In one cross-cultural study involving British, European and American communities, between 39 and over 50 per cent of individuals who said that they had days when their activities were limited because of ill-health did not seek any form of medical treatment (Butler, 1970). On the other hand, in the British and American samples, fewer than a third of those who sought medical advice said that they had any days of health-limited activity in the previous two-week period.

This finding undermines the assumption that there is a close match between a particular experience of the body and the use of health services. The fact that people report frequent symptom occurrence makes little difference to the overall likelihood of their being a frequent visitor to the doctor's clinic (Blaxter, 1985). This might be because of the degree to which people treat their own ailments. It also disguises another reason: that some individuals (notably those from professional or 'white-collar' backgrounds) attend the doctor's surgery for checks about physical signs that do not limit their activities. These visits, and the reasons for making them, do not detract from these individuals' view of themselves as being basically in good health.

Clearly, whether signs of bodily disturbance are perceived as genuine symptoms will depend upon the perspective (medical and lay) from which they are perceived. The notion of the 'clinical iceberg' as a mass of unreported disease symptoms in the population is a judgement made from the medical perspective. From a different viewpoint, there is, in the community, a range of signs of bodily disturbance. Some of these are dismissed as 'normal', some are treated by the individual concerned, and some become matters for which medical advice is sought. What people think ails them, whether it calls for self- or medical treatment, and what it implies about 'becoming ill' are matters that need a more detailed examination of how individuals experience and recognize these signs of bodily disturbance.

The background of signs and symptoms

We can now consider the possibility that the 'symptom iceberg' it is not so much a matter of the *amount* of unreported symptoms as it is *a difference in response to bodily disturbance.* In an early paper Zola (1966) pointed out a number of examples of such differences. Among these is the frequently cited dismissal of back pain as illness among working-class women, for whom this condition is taken as part of everyday life (see also Blaxter, 1983). To take a more extreme example, Zola also mentions that, among the Mexican Indians of the Southwestern United States, diarrhoea, sweating and coughing are everyday experiences. The implication of this is that the people affected do not see these signs as symptoms requiring medical attention.

The above examples show that 'common occurrence' is one feature that might be involved in the recognition that a physical sign is either normal and to be expected, or is something requiring attention. However, this commonality is more than a statistical norm. It is a matter of agreed definition among those concerned, and is likely to vary from one situation to another. Even within a particular class or sub-culture, there are likely to be situations when a particular bodily sign is seen as expected, and other situations where it will be seen as unusual and potentially abnormal. Zola (1966) suggests another example to illustrate this point. Being among a group of students who stress hard work, even into the late hours, means that feelings of tiredness can be taken as proof positive that you are 'doing right'. In this setting, tiredness would rarely be a cause for concern. In contrast, where arduous work is not valued by the student group, and is not gratifying in itself, consequent tiredness is more likely to be seen as a problem, and perhaps even as something requiring medical attention.

Clearly, signs and symptoms need to be considered within the context of settings which are defined by shared expectations. These concern not only what we might do or say, but also how we might feel. The argument that we not only have but are bodies needs to be re-emphasized here (Berger and Luckmann, 1971). Different social situations involve different background expectancies of how we might use our bodies, act in an unencumbered way, be free or constrained in the degree to which we can communicate physically. There are cultural differences in the way that the body can be deployed in social life. The anthropologist Mary Douglas (1973) has suggested that the scope people have to communicate with the body is limited by controls exerted by the social system. In cultures which set high thresholds, there is relatively free use of the body. She cites the pygmies of the Kalahari desert who roll on the floor when they laugh, and the members of Haitian cults who hallucinate during worship. Compare this, for example, to the low threshold levels set by British culture; this emphasizes and values control, both in conduct and in the expression of emotion.

Set alongside this broad distinction in cultural controls, there are also more specific expectations about how we behave in social situations. 'Ourselves', here, includes our bodily selves. Goffman (1971) has argued that our claims to be worthy (or attractive) individuals depend upon an ability to manage our impressions. This means conducting our bodily selves in a manner expected of someone claiming this status. To drool, fall over, belch or doze off when in company is to risk falsifying this claim to be a self-controlled person. Of course, people do feel drunk, or tired, or need to belch, but it is expected that in public situations they can contain these as side-involvements (Goffman, 1990). The relevance of this for a consideration of symptom recognition is that in different situations, there will be different expectations about how much individuals need to contain their bodily feelings.

Let us return from this brief excursion into social theory to apply these ideas to symptom recognition. The key concepts of this *situational approach* are the degree of *tightness* or *looseness* of a situation, and the extent to which it produces bodily disturbance (Alonzo, 1979, 1984). We can set this out as in Table 4.1.

Table 4.1   *Limitations and opportunities for sign/symptom display in different situations*

		Production of bodily disturbance	
		High	Low
Requirement to contain signs	High	Engaging in sport	Attending a lecture
	Low	Giving birth	Watching TV

The table illustrates how bodily disturbances are interpreted differently in situations governed by dissimilar expectations of physical involvement. In these alternative situations, what would (from the medical perspective) be seen as the same *bodily disturbance* (e.g. raised pulse rate) will be experienced as a *different sign*. Therefore, its potential to be seen as a symptom of illness will vary. On the left-hand side of the table are shown two examples of situations in which bodily disturbance is to be expected. Playing sport often involves physical contact, and nearly always produces signs of high exercise levels. In quite different ways, giving birth also involves extremes of feeling and sensation. Both are examples of situations where bodily signs are not taken as symptomatic of illness, although these same sensations would be extraordinary in other settings. These two examples are distinguished by the degree to which it is legitimate to fail to contain these feelings. During sport, it is expected that accidental blows will be taken without complaint. In contrast, the woman giving birth is (according to cultural norms) allowed to give vent to her pain during delivery.

The right-hand side of the table shows situations where few bodily signs are normally produced. In these contexts indications of bodily disturbance may be viewed as unusual and possibly symptomatic unless they can be attributed to the situation itself. For example, a pain in the shoulder might be seen as the result of having occupied a seat at the theatre with a poor view, requiring the person to lean at an angle for a period of time.

The two settings on the right-hand side of the table are distinguished in terms of the different thresholds of containment required. This has implications for how the person will conceptualize this feeling. In a lecture or at a concert, for example, the audience is expected to contain coughs and to refrain from gross movements, so that (as with sport) one way of dealing with such feelings is to become engrossed in the activity. A slight headache can be forgotten in the course of watching an interesting play, just as the pain from a blow on the shin might not be realized until after the match is over. On the other hand, where the pain is so great that it interferes with our (and others') enjoyment of the play or concert, we might feel that we have to leave. The leaving, the admission that one can no longer contain these disturbances within the thresholds set for that situation, provides a context, a rationale for explaining our actions in terms of illness behaviour. Then we can say to others that we must go home early because of 'a dreadful headache'. The specification of the sign as a symptom concerns shared conceptions of what such bodily disturbances mean, the context in which they arise, and the person's way of accommodating to them.

In the light of this last statement, we need to make a critical point about the situationist approach described above. Emphasizing different kinds of episode risks what is surely an oversimple interpretation: that people just read off the meaning of bodily signs from the context they are in at the time. This proposal takes no account of the degree to which individuals might see the context as applying to them or to their group. Also, in its strong form, this approach turns the individual into a passive interpreter of signs. This overlooks the possibility that the situation is defined, and redefined, by the individual's approach to it.

Two further points can be drawn from this analysis of containment and bodily control. One concerns the implied circularity of commitment to action and severity of the sign (Twaddle, 1969). On the one hand, it can be said that the severity of the bodily disturbance is important for the person to be released from certain roles (e.g. your partner agreeing to leave the theatre early because of your 'bad' headache). On the other, the readiness with which others will exempt the person from social roles can be important in his or her assessment of the severity of the sign. If the people you are with have paid a lot of money for theatre tickets for your birthday, the obligation to contain the feelings, to try to ignore the headache and enjoy the performance, is altogether greater.

The second point is related to the first, and derives from the condition that Parsons applied to his analysis of the sick role. This concerns a change in the social status of the individual concerned. Here, the adoption of the sick role depends upon the acceptance of certain rights and obligations. Because health is 'the state of optimum *capacity* of an individual for the effective performance of roles and tasks' (Parsons, 1958: 100, emphasis in original), the move to the status 'sick' depends upon the person being deemed incapable of fulfilling these duties. Parsons emphasized that capacity is not to be confused with the commitment to *particular* tasks or roles. Whether a person cannot bear a concert any longer, or now finds playing a sport too tough, are not in themselves health problems. While questions of the containment of bodily signs are important in the consideration of whether one is ill, the claim to be a 'sick person' extends beyond the question of whether one had to leave the theatre with a bad headache. As we have seen already, people may acknowledge that they have symptoms but still not regard themselves as actually sick.

Recognizing illness and becoming sick

What is it that convinces us that we are sick? How we feel? Whether we can go to work? What we are told by the doctor? The question of whether people are or are not sick appears to follow the decision about whether they are suffering from symptoms associated with disease. In the previous section it was shown that symptoms do not have an independent existence. They are, instead, interpretations dependent upon the context in which bodily experiences occur. If becoming ill were a kind of logical decision process, then we might expect that the recognition that one has symptoms would be a sufficient condition for deciding that one is sick. This section questions that assumption, and puts forward an alternative idea. Symptoms do not necessarily precede sickness; instead, being deemed to be sick is an important element in appearing symptomatic.

The idea that one perceives one's body in terms of distinct signs is not supported by empirical studies. Research shows, instead, that individuals are aware of only gross changes in their physiological state, and that specific disturbances are subject to passing changes in context. For example, touching a vibrating board will be seen differently according to whether one has been told previously that one will experience a degree either of pleasure, or of pain (Anderson and Pennebaker, 1980). Similarly, whether one has been exercising hard only moments before completing a symptom check-list will affect one's bodily feelings. Then, for example, people are more likely to attribute these feelings to flu if they have been told that this disease is currently prevalent (Skelton and Pennebaker, 1982).

The experimental forerunner of this work is the study by Schachter and Singer (1962), in which they injected a stimulant drug into subjects who were given different information about its nature. They also arranged that the subjects would spend time either with a euphoric or with an angry confederate of the experimenter. It was found that subjects' interpretations of their body state (accelerated heart rate, faster breathing) depended upon the kind of person with whom they spent time. Their bodily change was understood according to the social situation with which it was associated. The conclusion is that we label our bodily states in the light of our understanding of the situation we are in at the time. This is consistent with the situationist approach described in the previous section.

These labels of body states can be thought of as patterned expectations, organized within a culture (Angel and Thoits, 1987). They can also be considered, within Western societies, as being formed by medical knowledge. This means that a knowledge of which bodily signs are associated with particular disease entities will allow people to understand what a specific disturbance might 'mean'. It also allows them to anticipate whether or not they ought to seek medical advice. It has been shown that where symptoms closely resemble the prototype for a specific disease, then people are more likely to recognize these as a set that unequivocally indicates that pathology (Bishop and Converse, 1986). What this suggests is that medical categories that have clear sign-sets (symptoms) associated with them are more likely to be easily recognized in self-diagnosis. For example, abdominal pains are generally thought to have a number of possible causes, some serious (inflamed appendix), some less so (indigestion). By comparison, a lump in the breast has a clear implication of breast cancer in the minds of many people, even though it need not be the sign of a malignant tumour. We can, therefore, expect that where sign-symptoms are clearly defined in relation to disease entities, people will be more likely either to be able to dismiss the problem, or else to see the need to seek medical advice. One study that examined such sign-symptom categories found that those individuals who held them to a strong degree were more likely to visit a doctor, both when feeling ill and for asymptomatic check-ups (Lau et al., 1989).

One recent study has extended the work on illness prototypes, exploring the possibility that individuals diagnose everyday diseases on the basis of the personal context in which symptoms occur (Lalljee et al., 1993). For example, mumps is associated with children, typhoid with those who have visited Third World countries, and stroke with older people. Using descriptions of imaginary cases, it was found that diagnoses of these conditions were more likely to be made where the typical symptoms related to the type of person usually associated with that particular disease. In effect, it was found that the layperson comprehends illness in terms of the personal contexts in which symptoms are normally thought to arise.

The views expressed in the previous paragraphs owe much to the *perceptual* or *cognitive* perspective in social psychology. This assumes that decisions about whether one is ill, whether to consult a doctor or to treat oneself, are made on the basis of individual judgements about one's own or other people's bodily experiences. It accords with the notion of a person isolated in his or her reflections about whether a particular sign does or does not mean illness. However, this is not typical of how people decide, in everyday life, whether they are sick. We have already made some points that lead us away from this individualist position: (a) bodily experience is embedded in social contexts, with differing, but often shared, expectations about what is a 'reasonable' amount of discomfort to put up with; (b) we use our relationships with others as ways of making our bodily experience sensible; and (c) feelings and discomforts are experienced differently according to our involvement, our committed engagement in what we are doing.

These ideas, along with that of the clinical iceberg, suggest that physical discomforts are part and parcel of everyday existence. This means that the question of becoming sick cannot involve only the perceptual recognition of a sign as a symptom of disease. It also rests upon a distinction between *states* where one can actively cope with discomfort, and those where one cannot. This idea of coping suggests that people often try to live with discomforts (e.g. headaches, strains and pains) in order to continue 'normally' for as long as possible.

On the basis of a series of interviews conducted in an out-patient clinic in the USA, Zola (1973) found that people explained their decision to visit the hospital in terms of a breakdown in their attempts to accommodate to their symptoms (i.e. to continue as normal). Although cultural groups varied in the way that they presented their complaints, it appeared that individuals did not seek aid at their 'physically sickest' point. Rather, it was when the symptoms interfered with their lives, in one way or another, that they went to the doctor. Zola identified five ways in which such breakdowns of accommodation could occur:

1   The occurrence of an interpersonal crisis, e.g. an argument with family about headaches that makes one 'irritable'.
2   Perceived interference in relationships with others, e.g. seeking advice about hearing loss, or about sudden bouts of 'flushing' of the face. (That the social obtrusiveness of symptoms can be more distressing to people than their physical discomfort is supported in another study, confirming embarrassment as a key meaning of symptoms [Jones et al., 1981].)
3   Sanctioning, meaning that the decision is taken by someone else on behalf of a reluctant patient, e.g. a wife rings the surgery to 'force' her husband to seek advice about chest pains that he insists are 'just indigestion'.
4   Perceived interference with vocational or physical activity, e.g. a woman secretary, noticing that her typing looks blurred, gets her vision checked in order to avoid making mistakes in her work. (I once interviewed a movie editor, diagnosed as suffering from an inherited brain disease [Huntington's chorea], who first sought advice when he began to tread upon the film on the cutting-room floor.)
5   The recurrence or existence of signs over a period of time, e.g. a pain in one's side, recurrent headaches, a lump that, though it doesn't hurt, 'is still there'.

Zola called these breakdown points *triggers*, meaning that they provide the reason for seeking medical help. Although this is a reasonable shorthand term to use, we should be cautious about adopting it in an uncritical way. This is because it suggests that something outside the person 'goes off', precipitating them into the illness condition. This gloss risks underplaying the role of the individual in defining when and how s/he is ill. In contrast, the trigger is something that is seen 'after the fact', a reconstruction of events that makes the seeking of medical care sensible in relation to the individual's social situation. Different signs will have importance depending upon their implications for how individuals see themselves. If we adopt the perspective of self-categorization theory (Turner, 1987), then the different situations that are affected by feelings of illness can be considered as shifts in how individuals define themselves in relation to others, e.g. as a student, as a woman, as a member of the family.

A recent study explored the possibility that the meaning of symptoms will change as a function of the importance of such different identities. In one experiment, physical education students were asked to rate a number of symptoms (e.g. a facial injury, a damaged knee, arthritis in the hand) with gender made salient (i.e. 'being a woman', 'being a man'). Others were asked to do this with sport/recreation made salient ('being a PE student'). It was found that for male students the identity shift made no difference, but for the women students it did. The same set of symptoms were rated differently by them depending upon whether the salient identity was gender or activity (Levine, 1992). When 'being a woman' was important, facial disfigurement was judged more significant; when 'being effective at sport' was important, a damaged knee took on an added significance.

Zola's study showed that individuals vary in terms of their reasons for visiting the doctor, but he also demonstrated that some of this variation could be understood in terms of patterns of cultural differences. Like Zborowski's (1952) finding concerning the 'Old American' patients, Zola found that his Anglo-Saxon group presented at the clinic for similar reasons. Their symptoms interfered with their work, or physical signs were considered to have been present for too long. Because they were members of a group with views near to those of the educated medical élite, they were more likely to bring that knowledge to bear upon their decision to seek medical aid.

The decision to visit the doctor is not necessarily an acceptance of the sick role. In fact, it might be an attempt to avoid being ill, hoping for 'some antibiotics to stave off this infection'. The choice to be sick, if one can call it that, is something rather different. It involves more an acceptance that one is 'not well', that one 'must go to bed', or at least 'take an aspirin and lie down'. Indeed, it is not necessary, or usual, for people to know precisely what is wrong with them (which disease is denoted by the sign-symptoms). Pains may be vague, refer to other areas of the body, or feelings of discomfort relate to a broad syndrome of fevers. In that sense, general feelings of being unwell may predominate (Telles and Pollack, 1981), suggesting that a cognitive determination of illness is an unlikely explanation of what occurs when someone becomes sick.

An alternative explanation has been offered by Herzlich (1973), who has argued that the key element to becoming sick is being reduced to *inactivity*. The prime example of inactivity is taking to one's bed. However, it also implies a 'giving up' of one's duties, whether these be at the workplace or in the home. It is the *experiential* aspect of this giving up that needs to be emphasized here. This (if the reader will reflect on own experience) involves a movement from the position where one has 'a bit of a headache and a sore throat' and an essay to complete, to one of pushing the essay to one side and saying, 'I'm going to bed, I think I've got flu.' Herzlich's argument is that the point of recourse to inactivity (abandoning the essay) is the moment on which the change in symptom-experience turns. The physical signs that were being contained ('a *bit* of a headache') as one tried to write the paper become constituted as symptoms of illness in the act of giving up. Because, from this point of view, inactivity integrates the physical signs and gives them meaning (as 'flu'), it implies a *reversal* of the process assumed by perceptual-cognitive theory. It is not the designation of a specific bodily sign as symptom that leads one to take the sick role. Instead, it is the behaviour of the person (considered as a unity) that transforms the specific signs into symptoms, and gives them a general and psychological, rather than merely a localized and physical, significance.

Having said that, we need to remind ourselves that it is, of course, possible to feel perfectly well, to continue one's activities without interruption, and still be diagnosed as having the symptoms of disease. However, as people in this situation will point out, they need not think of themselves as ill, even when the diagnosis relates to something potentially life-threatening like heart disease.

Symptoms and referrals: seeking advice from other people

Physical signs are often non-specific, so that the status of the individual as a well or sick person is uncertain. The scope for individual variation in this field of uncertainty is reflected in the different responses to minor symptoms. Of course, not all signs of disturbance are non-specific. If one cuts one's hand badly, leaving a deep gash from which it is difficult to stem the flow of blood, a decision to seek medical aid is usually made very quickly indeed (Calnan, 1983a). Nevertheless, in many cases where people have been asked about their symptoms, they report having first discussed these with at least one other person. In one study of working-class women, 71 per cent of the symptom episodes that led to a medical consultation were first discussed with a layperson, before a visit to the doctor was made (Scambler et al., 1981). There are good reasons why this should be the case. The sick role both involves the removal of social obligations and implies the need for care. The agreement of others is needed that one is sufficiently ill to warrant one or both of these privileges. If other people do not agree with the interpretation of your condition, then your claim to be a sick person will not be accepted, and your illness-behaviour might be disapproved of.

There are other times when people might want to discuss signs of their discomfort with others. These are typical of what has been called, more generally, a process of social comparison (Festinger, 1954). This allows people to evaluate their feelings of discomfort against the views of other people. Sometimes people wish for reassurance that the sign they have detected is not serious, does not signify disease and hence does not call for medical attention. This might occur when the problem is localized (e.g. 'I've got this lump on my arm, what do you think?'). It might also happen when the complaint is more general, when the person's feelings are used to legitimate their claim that something is wrong. Perhaps this is in anticipation of their needing to give up some activity (e.g. 'I feel dreadful, do you mind if I go and lie down?').

There is evidence that people use what has been called a *lay referral system* to establish whether they are 'really ill' and what they should do about it (Freidson, 1970). In one study, 220 students were asked how often they had suffered symptoms with no ready explanation in the preceding year, and whether they had sought advice about these from others (Sanders, 1982). It was found that, on average, approximately three non-experts (e.g. friends, family) were consulted, their advice being influential in 68 per cent of cases. These students also reported receiving medical advice from others without having asked for it. The majority (87 per cent) also said that they had acted as lay advisers to others in the preceding year.

The concept of the lay referral system relates to groups in society that 'operate to enforce particular views of illness and its treatment' (Freidson, 1970). This suggests something more than a network of mutual consultation or advice-giving. It allows for the social group to define someone as sick even though he or she does not feel ill (the example of mental illness is appropriate here). Indeed, because the idea of health-as-capacity is relative to people's position in the social order, it is possible for more powerful others in the group to declare that particular individuals must receive medical attention, or forgo desired social activities. In families, the elderly and children are more likely to be those taken to the doctor or told, for example, that they really are not well enough to go out.

Much of the research into lay referral systems has regarded them not as active in this way, but rather as social networks that individuals can use in time of need. Freidson (1970) identified referral systems in terms of (a) their size or complexity, and (b) how similar their culture is to that of professional medicine. He argued that the decision to seek medical aid (rather than use self-care or folk remedies) will be more likely where people belong to an extended system with beliefs similar to those of medical professionals. By the same token, individuals will be less likely to go to the doctor where they belong to an extended system with beliefs different to those of health professionals. In one study of health and welfare utilization in Aberdeen, it was found that those families who 'underutilized' were more likely to have relatives living in the same house, or living close by (McKinlay, 1973). Families who made more use of health services lived further away from their relatives, but nearer to friends, who tended to be of their own age. This pattern of health care utilization was confirmed in a study in the USA which found that the larger the network of friend relationships, the more ready were people to consult medical professionals. By comparison, the larger the network of family relationships, the more likely people were to delay using health services (Salloway and Dillon, 1973).

How are these findings to be interpreted? The suggestion is that families, partly because of their age-differentiated structure, provide immediate sources of advice and support. If the advice is drawn from folk beliefs, and if the support (e.g. a grandmother looking after her sick daughter's child) helps accommodate the physical discomfort, then help-seeking may be delayed. It might be, as we shall see below, that such offers of help oblige the ailing person to 'keep going' under a regime of family care. In contrast, where individuals draw upon the views of friends (peers), especially those who share the beliefs of medical professionals, they are perhaps more likely to comprehend their illness in medical terms. They might also feel obligated by this knowledge to use health services to avoid occupying the sick role.

The difference between these two kinds of referral system has been related to social class, where it has long been recognized that members of the working class use health services less, in spite of needing them more. The neat association of network, utilization and class is disrupted, however, by findings that among a sample of working-class women in Britain it was those who had large active kinship networks who used their general practitioner *more often* (Scambler et al., 1981). Again in contrast to other findings, large active friendship networks were associated with *low use* of the GP. How can this be explained? Clearly, one difference is that, because of the study's focus upon working-class women, the variation provided by class difference had been removed. Another, offered by the authors, is that women who have a high rate of contact with kin might have extensive discussions with them about health problems, leading to what Zola (1973) called 'sanctioning' taking place. Scambler et al. (1981) also wondered whether the friendship networks operated according to the social comparison process mentioned above, in which women used their friends to establish their discomforts as 'normal', and as less serious than they might have supposed.

The value of this contrary finding, for our discussion, is that it alerts us to problems of drawing premature conclusions about lay referral networks. More precisely, it shows that networks of different kinds do not have their functions built into them. It is possible for family relationships to offer immediate advice; this enables the person to make accommodations to discomfort and delay consulting a doctor. Subsequently, when the accommodation fails, it is these same relationships that are used to bring pressure upon that family member to seek medical attention. This shows the danger of thinking of networks as ready-made structures with distinct properties, when in fact they are theoretical constructs. Researchers use them to summarize people's actions once they have interpreted signs of discomfort and negotiated what should be done.

Rather than social networks channelling decisions and determining health status, the opposite case can be put forward. Manning (summarized in Dingwall, 1976: 39) has argued that the network of relationships is *created by the search, located by the searching* and *defined by the actions of the people concerned*. What this means is that the emergence of a sign (e.g. a lump in the breast, a partial loss of hearing) is the basis for a number of discussions that, taken together in retrospect, look like a 'lay referral network'. However, the network was not there waiting to be activated, (though of course family and friendship relationships are already established). It comes into being in the course of discussions between the person concerned and these significant others.

Uncertainty, obligation and bargaining in illness recognition

The significance of this point for the social constructionist position is that neither the ready-made symptom, on the one hand, nor ready-made social structure, on the other, are adequate explanations for what people do when feeling ill. This can be illuminated further by reference to one study of how families handled health-related events on a day-to-day basis. With reference to health diaries that they were asked to keep, Robinson (1971) noted that

signs of discomfort were often things that family members worried about
until a satisfactory outcome could be achieved. The uncertainty created by
children's complaints that they were 'sickening for something' eventually
'got on the parents' nerves'. That is to say, the uncertainty lay both in the
sign and in the relationships within the family. Resolving this uncertainty in
a satisfactory way simultaneously removed the worry and defined the
physical sign. For example, one woman who was seven months pregnant
listed in her diary a range of signs over a period of 12 days (nails splitting,
legs swelling, nerves bad, constipation). At the end of that time she visited
the ante-natal clinic, where the doctor commented that she was overweight
and must 'stop eating too much'. After this, the next seven days of the diary
contained no symptom entries at all. This was because the doctor's comment
'explained' her feelings, so that she was relieved of the worry (with its
consequences for her relationship with her husband), and rendered the signs
(swollen legs etc.) no longer worthy of note.

The question of uncertainty about signs – whether one is or is not 'really
ill' – is often a matter of social negotiation, not something for individuals to
contemplate in isolation. This means that explanations which rely upon
individual decision-making are actually missing crucial aspects of what
happens when people try to determine whether they are, or someone else is,
ill. In the case of others for whom one is responsible, such as parents for their
children, there is a moral dimension to the issue. This refers to the obligation
of parents to care for their children (or adults for their elderly parents), so
that deciding whether to call in the doctor has implications for the carer as
well as for the potential patient. The 'worry' expressed by the parents in
Robinson's study was of this kind. There may be a felt need to 'do
something', if necessary to treat the signs as symptoms of disease, in order to
justify calling upon the doctor's time and skills.

This moral concern is not restricted to the situation of family members. In
cases where a neighbour or stranger suffers an accident, even of a minor
kind, people are inclined not to take risks with someone else's health.
Instead, they are more likely to encourage them to seek advice, or to call for
help on their behalf. There is a dilemma here in the case of the bystander
observing an accident, for whom the presence of others will be important in
the decision about what to do. What has been termed the problem of
'bystander apathy' (Latané and Darley, 1970) has been shown to be
resolved, in the case of accidents, by people calling ambulances, and hence
being morally creditable, but insisting upon remaining anonymous and
thereby minimizing their involvement (Calnan, 1983b).

The moral issue in becoming ill extends beyond the question of whether
medical advice should be sought. This arises from the fact that the
determination of what physical signs mean involves, as Herzlich has argued,
the person in his or her totality. When somebody falls ill at home, others may
have to carry out household duties. When someone takes time off from
work, others might have to do his or her job, or else take on tasks that they
would not have had to do. The removal of obligations for the sick can often

mean the assumption of extra duties for the healthy. Whether in the home or in the workplace, the negotiation of sickness goes on in the context of relationships where individuals often have reciprocal claims upon each other.

In the work environment this can mean that the genuineness of sickness is a perennial issue for those concerned, management and workers alike. There may well be differences in expectation about men and women, and about younger and older workers, concerning whether their absences from work are genuinely caused by illness. The determination of whether a person is ill in the workplace (or from it) extends well beyond a discussion of the physical signs of discomfort. It often concerns the 'diffuse and particular relations' of gender, class and age (Bellaby, 1990). Absence from work is seen in the context of what others believe are the capacities, motivations and demands upon a person in that life-position. Deciding whether one is ill in one context might not be the same as determining whether one is ill in another.

A good comparison along these lines is that of the work setting with the home situation. Here gender and age differences will also work to distinguish the terms on which any particular member of the family can fall ill. For example, mothers with young children, who have little in the way of extended family support, may find it very difficult to adopt the sick role. This is because of the number of household duties which they must lay down (Geertsen and Gray, 1970; Parsons and Fox, 1952). This is made more difficult in the (many) cases where there is uncertainty regarding the meaning of the signs involved. In a series of case interviews with married couples, it was noted that there was a process of 'bargaining' over the definition of health status (Twaddle, 1969). While husband and wife might often agree about the need for a doctor to be consulted, in order to know what was 'really going on', such agreement could not be taken for granted. Where there were differences in the couple's views of the seriousness of the signs, then this allowed scope for a widened 'bargaining' about what the symptomatic person should or should not do, and at what cost or gain to the partner.

A general scheme has been put forward to explain how this might happen, based upon the concept of gift-exchange between husbands and wives (Robinson, 1971). For example, both parties might recognize that the husband is suffering from symptoms that should really be treated by his going to the doctor. Unfortunately, the couple had planned to go out that day. This provides the husband with the opportunity of 'offering a gift' to his wife, by putting off seeing the doctor until the day after. By acknowledging her husband's offer, the wife recognizes his 'selflessness', and the obligations that she owes towards him in the future.

In another condition, a husband might complain of 'feeling a cold coming on' and suggests to his wife that he might stay home 'to prevent it getting worse'. Both of them realize that his symptoms hardly merit his staying away from work, but the wife may use this opportunity of offering the 'gift' of the sick role to her husband, saying that if he stays home she will look after him. In this case it is the wife to whom a debt is owed, through her gift of care and consideration. In both of these examples (Robinson's scheme allows for many more), the person receiving the gift confers something upon the giver in return. This might be called a moral credit, or a change in status. However it is seen, the determination of whether one of the couple is 'ill' or 'not ill' takes place within a relationship that is more complex than an act of individual judgement about a specific symptom.

These examples underline the point that the determination of illness through inactivity is a conception involving the whole person (Herzlich, 1973). It also shows that the giving of meaning to bodily signs, and the legitimation of a person's claim to be sick, take place in the context of social relationships that are, in their turn, shaped by the person's transition from health to illness.

The sick role and its alternatives

In this final section of the chapter we shall examine the *sick role* as the outcome of being symptomatic. In doing so, special attention will be given to the concept as it was introduced by Parsons (1951a) and by Parsons and Fox (1952). One reason for doing this is to continue the overview of how people become ill, staying with our idealized notion of a linear progression from the world of health to the world of illness. We can appreciate that this is an idealized notion by mentioning some of the alternatives to the adoption of the sick role. It is not inevitable that a person either feeling discomfort or showing signs of possible disease will be diagnosed as such by a doctor, or accepted as sick by others. Among the other possibilities are self-treatment of symptoms with no change in role (e.g. take an aspirin); the designation of the person as a malingerer (e.g. as a result of the doctor finding no disease); obtaining advice about lifestyle changes to dissipate signs (e.g. take exercise, diet, don't overwork); seeking treatment within alternative medicine (e.g. homeopathy, chiropractic); and finally, ignoring signs and carrying on as normal.

We have already noted Parsons' (1958) definition of health as a state of optimum capacity for effective role performance. Illness, then, is a generalized disturbance of the person's role capacity. This leads to the individual being accorded a different status in society – that of the role of the sick person. This has four main features (Parsons and Fox, 1952).

First, sick people are exempted from the performance of their social duties. This is not a simple transition to make, unless the person has suffered some catastrophic event (e.g. a heart attack) or injury. It requires validation by others, and especially by medical practitioners, who are given special powers to determine (through the prescription and the 'sick note') the status of the claimant.

Second, the sick person is not held responsible for his or her state. That is, the sick cannot be asked to 'make an effort to be well'. Although people can be held responsible for not looking after their health, once they are sick it is no longer in their power alone to make themselves better.

Third, while the sick cannot make themselves better, they are obliged to remove themselves from situations in which they could make claims to the rights of healthy people. This is an important condition of the sick role, and one worth explaining in a little more detail. What Parsons meant is that being legitimately sick in the eyes of others (of society) is conditional upon the person being incapacitated. To be or to appear to be able to 'help oneself' is to risk losing the entitlement one has to the status 'sick'. That is why parents tell children who did not go to school that morning (perhaps because of stomach ache) that, now they feel better in the afternoon, they should not go to the cinema. We become sick at a price, and that price is giving up our claim to engage in activities that are the rightful dues of the healthy.

Finally, the sick are also obliged to seek qualified help where appropriate. So, complaining day after day about a symptom that prevents you doing something, yet refusing to go to the doctor about it, is one sure way of eroding other people's sympathy. While the relationship of the sick to the healthy places them in a position of dependency, of needing care, the transition to becoming a patient (a role played relative to medical personnel) incurs other obligations. Patients are expected, even required, to cooperate with medical staff in order to speed their recovery. Parsons emphasised that the sick role is *conditionally* legitimate, meaning that we are granted its rights provided that we follow the advice of doctors trying to make us better.

Parsons' concept of the sick role is, as mentioned in Chapter 1, important in sociological (and social psychological) analyses of health and illness. Its key contribution is to define sickness in terms of social rather than biomedical theory. However, within the social science perspective, this concept has been criticized for being too prescriptive about the illness experience. Specifically, critics have argued that Parsons placed too much emphasis upon the control function of the sick role (Idler, 1979), forcing the study of *illness experience* into the study of the *patient's behaviour*. Enough has been said in this chapter to show that illness is more than consulting the doctor. However, the legitimation of one's condition, turning upon the question, 'Am I really ill?', still involves considerations of whether one 'ought to', 'needs to' or 'must' consult a doctor. Inevitably, in Western societies, the dominance of medical thinking, and its authority in treatment, mean that questions of rights and obligations will enter into the determination of what it is that our bodily discomforts signify.

Another criticism of the sick role concept concerns its emphasis upon loss of capacity as a central feature. It has been argued that people often use their feelings of illness (rather than inability to do something) as their criterion for being sick (Telles and Pollack, 1981). This might be because, in Western societies, people explain illness in 'internal' terms (Young, 1976). This means that the decision whether one is 'really ill' or not depends upon the location of pathology in or on the body. It has been shown that people who consult their doctor more often (as compared with non-consulting controls) are more likely to attribute their symptoms to an internal cause (Ingham and Miller, 1986). It might be that reference to feelings becomes important in the way that patients talk to doctors, describing their problems in this way in order to have them diagnosed. The key difference here is between the time when, feeling unwell, the person is determining whether s/he is ill, and the point at which the individual moves into the status 'sick'. We need to remind ourselves of the distinction drawn at the outset: illness is usefully regarded as being the condition of the individual, while sickness is best seen as a social role.

Some help with this distinction can be gained from reconsidering Herzlich's (1973) suggestion that the significant feature of the transition from health to sickness is inactivity. It is this change in the conduct of the person, (e.g. leaving work and going home to bed) that reorganizes both bodily signs and social status together. For example, beforehand, when we struggled on with a headache and sore throat, there were feelings of discomfort and there were efforts to continue to fulfil tasks. Afterwards, when we have taken to bed, there are symptoms of our illness and clear evidence of our incapacity. In retrospect, it can be said that 'I struggled on all morning with flu'. In that phrase, the feelings of that earlier time are reconstructed from the position of being a sick person. The point is that feelings and incapacities are always potentially involved, but their relationship and contribution will change in our experience, as we make the transition from health to sickness.

Underlying the idea that sickness is a special form of deviance is the assumption that the sick should not enjoy (for too long) the benefits of their condition. Although rarely discussed in medical sociology (a notable exception is Gerhardt, 1989), Parsons suggested that, in the escape from the pressures of ordinary life, the sick role connects with what he termed 'the residua of childhood dependency' (Parsons and Fox, 1952). This means that sickness is motivated in ways that are unacceptable to society in its healthy aspect, the world of work and responsibility. It is for this reason that the sick need to be insulated from the healthy, because of the effects that they have upon the workings of everyday activities.

An example of this might be a student who, because of glandular fever, cannot participate effectively in tutorial discussions. Her tutor tells her to 'take time off and go home'. While this might be for reasons of sympathy, it is also in the cause of restoring the effective running of the tutorial. Parsons sums this up by saying that 'the essential reason for this insulation . . . is not the need of the sick for special "care" so much as it is that, motivationally as well as bacteriologically, illness may well be "contagious"' (1958: 108). What is contagious here is dependency, and it is this that must be overcome in the cause of getting well again.

We shall examine some of the implications of Parsons' ideas in the chapter to follow, when we discuss the sick person as patient in the medical setting. In the meanwhile, it is worth noting what the concept of the sick role adds to our analysis of symptom recognition. First, note how it links up with ideas about illness being defined in terms of inactivity, so that being ill is not just a matter of the determination of physical symptoms, but is a social condition. However, if one only considers the person once s/he occupies the sick role, then one can learn little about how people determine whether they are ill, or whether to consult a doctor. In that sense, the sick role concept, being defined at the point of seeking medical aid, 'comes after' many of the problems that we have addressed in the present chapter.

However, because of the issue of what bodily signs mean (including whether one should seek medical advice), the criteria attaching to the sick role are relevant to the question of how people think about their symptoms. Matters to do with dependency, with incapacity and responsibility attach even to the handling of non-scrious symptoms in the home or at work. We can guess the costs and benefits of becoming sick, and these include the advice or treatment that the doctor might give. Equally, we share in cultural norms about the sick and their treatment by others. The view that people begin with the recognition of a sign of illness, then discuss it with others, then go to the doctor, and finally adopt the sick role suggests an all-too linear path.

In fact, considerations of what it means to become sick often enter into the earliest stages of symptom recognition. This is especially true where the onset is catastrophic in the sense that *illness, sickness* and the diagnosis of *disease* all seemingly come at once. A major heart attack might be an example of this, where the person is simultaneously faced with the undeniably disabling nature and the medical meaning of the symptoms. The implications of sickness can also be evident where the symptoms of a past condition re-occur. In this case the individual might know the detailed implications of having this particular disease. Then the prospect of sickness might cast a particular light upon any symptoms, even if they are only of a minor nature. As we shall see, knowledge of a disease, especially where it is a chronic one, makes a great deal of difference to people's perceptions of their symptoms.

Bearing these points in mind, it can be seen that we have followed an idealized line of experience from initial bodily sign to the door of the doctor's surgery. In spite of that, we shall continue to follow this path one stage further, and examine what happens when, seeking medical advice or treatment from the doctor, the person becomes a patient.

Chapter summary

- We need to distinguish between bodily *signs* and *symptoms* of disease. There are cultural expectations about which bodily disturbances require medical attention and which ones are 'normal'.
- These cultural expectations extend to how to show illness and ask for treatment, as well as providing guidance as to when advice should be sought.

- The designation of signs as symptoms of disease involves interpretation. This is more than a matter of individual judgement, as it involves other people. Bearing symptoms constitutes *a moral claim* to be treated in a certain fashion by laypersons as well as by medical professionals.
- Many symptoms are never taken to the doctor and make up the so-called 'iceberg of illness'. The decision to seek medical advice is often *triggered by the breakdown of accommodations* that the individual has been making to bodily signs.
- The recognition of signs as symptoms depends upon the *situation* in which they are experienced and the role of the individual in producing them.
- People often use a *lay referral system* to determine the significance of their sign/symptoms. The seeking of lay advice has been shown to vary with age, gender and social class.
- The decision to go sick is often determined in relation to wider aspects of the person's social life, particularly those involving family and work relationships.
- The *sick role*, as defined by Parsons, is occupied by those people having a generalized disturbance of their role capacities. It is a status that is *conditionally legitimated*, meaning that the sick are granted certain rights provided they cooperate with medical professionals who try to make them well again.

Further reading

Alonzo, A.A. (1979) Everyday illness behavior: a situational approach to health status deviations, *Social Science and Medicine*, 13A, 397–404.

Freidson, E. (1970) *Profession of Medicine*. New York: Dodd, Mead.

Helman, C.G. (1978) 'Feed a cold, starve a fever' – folk models of infection in an English suburban community, and their relation to medical treatment, *Culture, Medicine and Psychiatry*, 2, 107–37.

Parsons, T. and Fox, R. (1952) Illness, therapy and the modern urban American family, *Journal of Social Issues*, 8, 31–44.

Zola, I.K. (1973) Pathways to the doctor – from person to patient, *Social Science and Medicine*, 7, 677–89.

5

The Healing Relationship: Doctors, Patients and Nurses

In the previous chapter we saw that the legitimate occupancy of the sick role demands that individuals (a) seek competent professional help and (b) do all that is required in order to make a recovery. This chapter discusses what this therapeutic relationship involves, and examines some of its main features.

From an everyday point of view, we are all acquainted with the medical consultation and the doctor–patient relationship. However, it is worth making a few general, if seemingly obvious, points before beginning our analysis. First, individuals are not patients except in relation to members of the medical professions. One becomes a patient – irrespective of one's symptoms – the moment one consults a doctor or nurse. Second, the possibility of referral to specialists, and of becoming a hospital in-patient, mean that one's experience will differ depending upon progress through the medical system. There are, therefore, aspects common to any doctor–patient encounter, as well as features that are peculiar to each alone. For example, we expect that undergoing invasive procedures in hospital prior to surgery will be different from being in a medical ward recovering from a broken leg. In turn, these are markedly different from seeing the family doctor, when s/he is checking if one has an ear infection following a bad cold.

The consequence of noting these differences is that we shall focus upon the *general* aspects of the medical relationship. This is partly because of shortage of space, but also because it is these features that need to be explored with reference to theory. We need a general perspective on these matters, not a mini-explanation for each and every different kind of consultation. Having said that, the discussion will concentrate mainly upon the relationships of patients with general practitioners, or with other medical and nursing staff in hospital settings. Following the (ideal) path set out at the beginning of the book, we want to see what happens when someone is ill and goes to seek help. What, in terms of experience and action, is involved in the procedures of diagnosis and treatment? What kind of relationship is that of doctor-to-patient, and what do we know about its different forms?

An example of a consultation

Here is an example of a consultation involving a woman patient who is visiting her general practitioner. The text is adapted from an illustration provided by Byrne and Long (1976: 12).

D: [1] Hello. Do come in. [2] How are you feeling today?

P: I feel terrible. Since I came to see you last week, and you said I needn't take those pills any more, I've felt really awful. Every morning when I get up I've got a dreadful headache, my eyes are sore and I've got a head like a rocking horse. And I'm all stuffed up with stuff running down the back of my throat.

D: [3] Are you coughing anything up?

P: No, I can't cough it up because I'm all blocked up.

D: Just lie back so that I can take a look – open your mouth wider . . . . . [4] It looks as if it's the cold that's affecting your sinuses.

P: Just here my throat feels so sore, and my head feels as if its going to fall off when I lean back.

D: [5] I'll change your tablets which will help that and you can go back on the capsules when you are over this.

P: Well, all the aches and pains have gone, apart from under my ribs.

D: Leave it a week and then come and see me again and I'll take another look at you. [6] Right, so a week from today.

P: Hope I will be alright then. Bye-bye now.

The numbers in the square brackets in the text refer to the beginning of phases that form a sequence in the consultation. The order is as follows (Byrne and Long, 1976). The doctor:

1   establishes a relationship with the patient;
2   attempts to discover the reason for the patient's attendance;
3   conducts a verbal or physical examination, or both;
4   alone, or with the patient, considers the condition;
5   perhaps with the patient, details treatment or further investigation;
6   terminates the consultation.

These phases do not form a rigid sequence, and there are consultations in which either the order changes or else some phases do not appear at all. For example, in the case of patients with chronic conditions who need regular medication, the patient may initiate phase [5] on entering the room, e.g. 'About these tablets you asked me to take . . .' (Johnson, 1986). The idea that the consultation has an ordered structure, even if this is not adhered to, is consistent with the everyday assumption that the doctor is there to find out what is wrong and to prescribe treatment. If this is a widely shared assumption, then social scientists might investigate how these beliefs affect communication and lead to effective treatment. In a moment we shall examine some work that proceeds on the basis of this supposition. First, however, it is useful to place the consultation in the context of our wider concern with health and illness.

From the text of the example it is clear that this patient is bringing some new symptoms to her doctor, although mention of previous medication suggests that she is also being treated for some other, perhaps long-standing condition. In the previous chapter it was said that the decision to consult a doctor is the pathway to becoming sick (in the sense of taking up the sick role). The doctor is a key person in this transition, because s/he has the power to legitimate the person's claim to be accorded the status of a sick person. In the above example, the patient expresses her feelings of illness by recounting a cluster of symptoms. These, taken together, constitute her claim to be in need of treatment. The statement that the symptoms are there 'every morning' underlines her assertion that they are sufficiently discomforting to disrupt daily life.

The idea that people make a claim to be ill is something over which we should pause for just a moment. It suggests that patients are not passive objects of medical attention but, in many cases where they bring minor complaints, are active in fashioning a picture of their situation. Because bodily feelings are private, we have to display or dramatize our situation in order that others may grasp our experience and credit us with having those feelings (Goffman, 1971). In cases of serious injury to the body, or of gross symptomatic change, simply pointing to the afflicted area will be enough to establish that one is in need of medical attention. In many cases, however, perhaps in the majority taken to the general practitioner, the issue will not be that clear cut. In these situations, the patient 'presents' (to use a medical term) in a manner that supports and confirms the 'self' that s/he wishes to put forward.

The text example above cannot show the way in which the patient acts in the course of presenting her symptoms to the doctor. It is the information that is 'given off', as well as that which is 'given' directly, which conveys the image that she wishes to put forward. How the patient walks into the room, how she speaks, with what difficulty she moves parts of her body or removes clothing – all these things will serve as information to communicate that she is feeling unwell. In these kinds of consultations, there is a dramatization of the signs in order to uphold this claim to being, if not 'a sick person', then at least someone who is making a legitimate demand upon the doctor's time. Therefore, the claim to sickness does not arise from the specification of symptoms alone but, as one doctor has put it, 'it is the act of asking, or in the case of those who cannot ask for themselves, of being presented to the doctor, that constitutes the relationship of which we call one half doctor and the other half patient' (Marinker, 1976; quoted in Helman, 1978: 128).

After the first three phases in this extract, the patient is (from her point of view) in a kind of limbo. This means that, having spelt out her symptoms and having staked her claim to sickness, she must await the doctor's diagnosis as to what, if anything, is *medically* wrong with her. This is a repeat of the dilemma mentioned previously, with regard to talking about one's health to other people. Then it was said that part of talking about one's health was to show, even when ill, that one remained an ordinary person – not altogether changed by one's disease or disability. In the same way, the patient has to steer a line between dramatizing her symptoms and yet conveying to the doctor that she is like everyone else. A failure to steer this line effectively – say by over-dramatization – would be to risk being seen by the doctor as 'a hypochondriac', 'a worrier' or 'an invalid'.

Each of these terms denotes a class of person who has fallen below the standards that are expected of the 'normal' individual. They derive from the expectation, on the doctor's part, that his prospective patients will be 'well-informed citizens', able to make reasonable judgements about when to seek medical aid. On the other hand, once a firm diagnosis has been made, the individual is expected to defer to the opinion of the doctor. When these two sets of expectations overlap, as they so often do, then the patient can be placed in a 'double-bind' situation (Bloor and Horobin, 1975). How many people have gone to the doctor only to be told either that their feelings of illness do not indicate disease, or else that they should have come earlier?

In the example of a consultation given above, the patient has received a diagnosis and treatment, and so we can say that her claim to sickness has been validated by the doctor. In cases where this does not happen (and here readers can resort to their own experience), the doctor's statement that there is 'really nothing much wrong', or that 'there are a lot of these colds about', undermines the patient's request for treatment. The resulting feelings of stupidity (that one has misjudged one's condition), or of guilt (that one has wasted the doctor's time), are evidence that one's claim to the sick role has been found wanting. In that instant we fall, so to speak, between two experiential stools. We are neither wholly well nor wholly ill, and probably wish we had never made the appointment in the first place.

What has been outlined here, on the patient's behalf, is a situation that involves a certain dilemma: how to present one's symptoms in a way that does justice to one's feelings, without prejudicing one's status as a responsible person (i.e. without being seen to be 'making a fuss'). Individuals have privileged access to their feelings, so that, when it comes to a diagnosis, patients have certain expectations about their entitlement to treatment. For example, being prescribed a sedative might be seen as an inappropriate response to asking the doctor for help for a recurrent headache. After such a diagnosis the dilemma might resolve itself into another form: whether the patient should insist on special attention or allow these feelings to be waived aside as ordinary and unimportant (Freidson, 1962).

Styles of consultation behaviour: the doctor's point of view

Let us now turn to the perspective of the doctor. It can be seen that Byrne and Long's (1976) six phases are actually defined from the doctor's point of view, in that it is the physician who opens and closes the transition from one phase to another. (Note in the text example how the bracketed numbers fall in the doctor's speech, not the patient's.) There are three features of the doctor's activity to which we might give special attention. The first concerns the location of pathology in or on the body of the patient; stage [3], for example, involves a physical examination. Asking the patient to 'lie back' and 'open her mouth' involves a special kind of access and privilege to the body that is granted to few (if any other) of the patient's family or close friends. This right of access is claimed on the grounds of the doctor's specialized knowledge, something which can only be applied through the inspection and palpation of the patient's body. The text example does not give any indication of how this is carried out, nor show the implications for

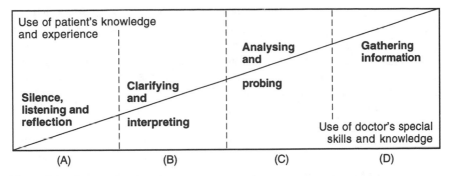

Figure 5.1 *Doctors' styles of communication during the consultation (adapted from Byrne and Long, 1976)*

the individuals involved. In a later section we shall examine this feature more carefully, and note its special relevance for the therapeutic relationship.

Throughout the consultation, the doctor is active in asking, informing and advising the patient what to do. The interaction appears to be one-sided, in that the physician has control of what happens in the meeting. This follows from his or her use of specialized clinical techniques to direct the course of the consultation. The most direct way this can be done is through questioning, or by requiring the patient to be passive and quiet during the physical examination. In this way, the doctor controls how much time is spent on each topic, and when to move on to the next. For this reason, it has been said that time patients spend in the consultation is not their time; it is at the doctor's disposal, and is granted to them on terms that s/he alone determines (Strong, 1977).

This interpretation sees the consultation as being largely one of interaction control. It has been criticized, however, on the grounds that it imputes to doctors, and patients, aims which they might not recognize, and powers which they might not claim (Sharrock, 1979). Are consultations so one-sided, with doctors directing patients who, in turn, feel cowed by their physicians? One should be cautious about reading into the doctor's questions intentions to control the patient. Part of the dynamics of the interaction comes from the patient's approach, because he or she wants to be treated and be made well. Where the authority of the doctor is *legitimate* in the eyes of the patient, questions of a struggle for control do not arise. (For a more general discussion of this question within social psychology, see Burke, 1973.)

It should also be noted that, on occasion where the accuracy of the doctor's interpretation is brought into question, the patient may attempt to steer the consultation in a different direction (Johnson, 1986). This might or might not be successful; but it shows that the location of control in the consultation is variable, as is its importance, as an issue, for both of the people concerned.

Byrne and Long (1976) suggested that the balance of doctor's specialized skill and use of the patient's own knowledge and experience could form a continuum on which different doctors' styles may be located. This is shown diagrammatically in Figure 5.1.

While much of the doctor's communication in the text example is to do with isolating the specific cause of distress, he does offer his diagnosis and place his suggested treatment in the context of the patient's longer term care. This might place him at the 'analysing and probing' point on the scale. Byrne and Long found that individual GPs tended to adopt and use a particular style with all of their patients, some exerting a greater control over their patients than others. To the extent that they applied their specialized knowledge only, then their patients were rendered more passive, in what has been called a 'parent–child' relationship (Szasz et al., 1958). If they listened a great deal to their patients' views, then they could be seen to be closing the distance between the professional and the layperson, in what is termed an 'adult–adult' relationship. (A recent study in the USA has shown that, compared to their male colleagues, women doctors conduct longer medical consultations, and engage in more positive talk and partnership-building [Roter et al., 1991].)

This issue of how doctors use their authority, and its implications for the relationship in the consultation, are matters to which we shall give special attention in a later section. For the moment, we can note that the doctor's routine of practice makes the variety of people's bodily experiences equivalent, or ordinary. This provides a means of rendering the consultation, which might be about very personal and delicate matters, into something impersonal and distant. While this measure facilitates the application of clinical techniques, it can also give rise to problems for the physician. Just as the patient has dilemmas about the significance of symptoms, so, argues Freidson (1962), the doctor has dilemmas about the extent to which s/he can adjust to the patient's expectations. This is a matter not just of meeting the patient's expectations about diagnosis and treatment, but also of acknowledging him or her as a person who has rights and a status outside of the medical setting.

In the remainder of this chapter we shall be looking at what is involved for the doctor in 'treating patients as people' and vice versa. If the patient is regarded as someone who is making a claim to be sick, then what kind of claim is made by the physician, and how is this substantiated? Parsons (1951b) was in no doubt that the special features of the doctor–patient relationship (including the rights to physical examination) depend upon the adoption of an impersonal 'matter of fact' attitude. By maintaining for the physician a position of authority, this attitude (or claim, in our terms) gives the doctor the right to expect that the patient will comply with his or her prescriptions. This can be illustrated with reference to the text example. The doctor's statements appear to be essentially descriptive, simply saying what the state of affairs is. However, phrases like 'Right, so a week from today', convey an expectation that the patient will comply with his recommended treatment and return for a further consultation.

How can we best summarize what this example has shown us? It suggests that the consultation often has a course or line. This is traced by the patient's claim to sickness, on the one hand, and the doctor's claim to special skills, on the other. However, because of patients' different histories and cultural backgrounds, on the one hand, and because of the different styles of physician communication, on the other, the particular pattern of each consultation is likely to vary.

These particular variations are not, however, our main concern. Instead, the example has raised important questions about how patients and doctors go about substantiating and maintaining their claims. Freidson (1962) has argued that the layperson and the professional are always in potential conflict with one another. In spite of this, there are occasions in the consultation when doctors and patients recognize these differences, and work to ensure that they do not disrupt the relationship. We shall examine this, first, in the context of research carried out into effective communications in the consultation. Subsequently, we shall take a closer look at how delicate procedures are managed in clinical settings, and at the hidden significance of speaking about doctors 'treating patients like children'.

The study of doctor–patient communication

This section will discuss how the issues surrounding the medical consultation became concentrated upon the question of communication between doctor and patient. If doctors have different styles of eliciting information, and patients, in their turn, come with differing expectations, then it is reasonable to suppose that the outcome of their meeting is something to do with the meshing of these various approaches. Approaching the consultation in this way turns out to be an exercise in answering questions about 'better' versus 'worse' communications.

So far we have discussed the patient's presentation of signs and the determination of these as symptoms by the doctor. The concern with doctor–patient communication began, and to a large extent remained, with what happens after the examination, with the prescribing of treatment. Early studies showed that patients often fail to cooperate with the doctor's advice. Typically, one-third to one half of out-patients either do not take medicines as prescribed, or do not follow dietary advice. Reviewing these studies, Ley and Spelman (1967) recounted the case of a diabetic patient who was found eating a large roast meal (with pudding). On being challenged, she said that she was indeed on a diet, but that she had had it for her elevenses. This story captures the notion of the patient who is not wilfully uncooperative, but who either does not comprehend or cannot remember the medical advice given during the consultation. It also carries, I think, something of the disparaging attitude towards patients adopted by this particular approach.

As a result of these findings, research was directed at identifying the characteristics of such patients, though without much success. Ley (1982), confirming the continuation of this pattern of non-compliance some years later, noted that about one-third of patients in Britain and in the USA said that they were dissatisfied with some element of the consultation. Moreover, there was an overall conclusion that satisfied patients are more likely to comply. The link between compliance and satisfaction is worthy of note, if only because it indicates a shift in the direction of the questions being asked. Whereas earlier research took it as given that failures in outcome lay with the patient, later work switched the focus on to the effectiveness of the doctor. Obeying the doctor's orders came to be seen as less a matter for compliance than of what the doctor had made it possible for the patient to understand (Stimson, 1974). The question now became: What kinds of communications between doctor and patient lead to desirable results, and hence to effective treatment?

Studies that have looked both at what people say about their doctors, and at what happens in the consultation, confirm that patients come to the surgery with views about what might be wrong with them. These expectations form both the context for comprehending the symptoms, and the basis of the claim that one should be treated by the doctor as an ill person. Individuals have views about their doctors, as well as about their own condition, and take these into account in dealing with the problem of how to present their symptoms (Stimson and Webb, 1975). On the matter of symptom presentation, it has been noted (in one American report) that patients will often discuss their bodily experience as an 'it', as something objective and separate from oneself (Cassell, 1976). There are two reasons for this that are relevant to our present discussion. One concerns the fact that depersonalizing the sign renders the patient less likely to be held responsible for what has gone wrong; the other arises from the taking on of the medical model by laypeople.

This adoption of the doctor's way of thinking can be seen, via the consultation, to be quite pragmatic. To the extent that the consultation is directed towards the determination of specific pathology, then the more precise and objective the patient can be in his or her presentation of the complaint, the more easily is that information assimilated into the biomedical way of thinking. The more diffuse the patient's presentation, the less likely is s/he to receive a specific diagnosis (Zola, 1973). On the other hand, where patients have clear and elaborated views about their illnesses, their expectations of the doctor may well be more extensive, and as a consequence their likelihood of being dissatisfied will increase (Fitzpatrick and Hopkins, 1981). Similarly, the more knowledgeable patients are about clinical techniques, the more is it possible that they will expect detailed questioning from the doctor and a lengthy physical examination. Where this is not forthcoming, patient dissatisfaction has been shown to result (Fitzpatrick et al., 1983).

As well as the effectiveness of clinical decision-making, the satisfaction of the patient has also been argued to depend upon the importance of 'good communication'. This concept describes, from the patient's point of view, the doctor listening well and giving explanations as required (Pendleton and Hasler, 1983). The study of doctor–patient communication becomes, therefore, the analysis of interactions in the consultation, noting both the doctor's and the patient's verbal contributions and non-verbal actions.

One study, for example, applied a modification of 'Interaction Process Analysis' technique (Bales, 1950) to a number of videotaped consultations. Use of this, or similar methods, is a way of quantifying the different kinds of statements or expressions that doctor and patient make. One finding was that reduction of patient concern (a measure of effectiveness) was strongly associated, not with what doctor and patient did, but with what they did *not* do. It seems that, whatever the kind of communication, there was *more* change in patient concern the *less* the doctor and patient talked together (Jaspars et al., 1983). Recognizing that amount of talk in the consultation varies with the seriousness of the condition, these researchers analysed their data further. As a result, they found that patient concern was reduced most when the doctor asked (relatively) many questions. They concluded that 'the doctor appears to be most effective psychologically when the problem that is presented to him is one with which he can easily cope, from a medical point of view' (1983: 147). The doctor knows what to ask, the interchange between them is, in consequence, brief, and (it is suggested) the patient's concern is reduced further.

By referring back to Figure 5.1, the reader will see that this is a description of the 'gathering information' style proposed by Byrne and Long (1976) where, basically, the doctor asks questions and the patient speaks only to answer medically pertinent questions. It seems odd, therefore, for these researchers to conclude that doctors are 'most effective *psychologically*' when they are acting in their most technical and impersonal manner.

We need to take a closer look at this interpretation in order to make a critical analysis of the doctor-patient relationship. Effectively, by focusing upon reduction in patient concern, Jaspars et al. make central the more technical aspects of the consultation. It is true that other studies have shown contact with experts (i.e. doctors employing specialized knowledge and techniques) is important in reducing patients' uncertainty about symptoms (Molleman et al., 1984). However, a heavy dependence upon quantified variables and correlational statistics means that the disturbances, the breakdowns and even the breakthroughs in the consultation are beyond consideration. One ends up by showing, in formal scientific terms, that when consultations involve the agreed presentation and diagnosis of a non-serious physical complaint, within the biomedical framework, then the patient is satisfactorily informed of his or her illness. This is nothing more than saying that, if all consultations could approximate closely to the ideal of expert–layperson, then patients (and, we presume, doctors) would be satisfied. But they do not; and, it would seem, they aren't.

In an important sense, analysing the consultation as a form of doctor–patient communication falls short of providing the kind of analysis that we require; that is, one for which social scientists should strive. The concept of 'communication' is too abstract, and too general, to do service to the range of different things that doctors and patients say and do. It also suggests that aiming for smoothness or economy in interaction will facilitate the exchange for all concerned. However, this assumes that doctors and patients always share an understanding of what is required, of what needs to be talked about, and what can safely be left on one side.

The reduction of the consultation to issues of compliance, cooperation and clarity is consistent with the acceptance of the medical aims embodied in the doctor's clinical skills and professional authority. It is, in terms of our definition, an example of 'behavioural medicine'. It accepts, uncritically, the medical definition of what is, or ought to be, happening in the exchange. By making social and personal experience into patterns of communication, these become reified into processes which can be discussed in terms of smoothness or effectiveness (Taussig, 1980). This has the effect of obscuring the various aims that doctors and patients might have, as well as the different scope available to them to secure these ends in the consultation.

From the patient's point of view

The question of patient compliance originated from what can be called the 'clinical content' of the consultation – whether patients actually follow the advice or instructions of the doctor. The change in focus to the doctor–patient relationship meant a concentration upon 'process', or the elements of control in this relationship. This focus upon communication processes, coupled with measures of patient satisfaction, opened the way for studies of what patients wanted from their doctors, and how they in turn might improve their consulting skills.

The question of how (and how much) the doctor–patient relationship should be 'improved' needs to be seen in the context of the role of the physician, and the sick role of the patient. Occupancy of the sick role places the patient in a deviant position, albeit one that is temporarily and conditionally legitimate. We have seen that the patient places pressure (information 'given off') on the doctor to be classed as sick. It is this pressure that the physician resists by use of an impersonal manner, holding back expressions of sympathy more usually associated with concerned family and friends. This concentration upon medical matters (conveying an impersonal manner) justifies the doctor's refusal to reciprocate what Parsons (1951b) calls 'the patient's deviant expectations'.

There are three reasons for making this link back to the sick role. First, it provides a critical reminder that it is not only patients who are subject to social scientific explanations; so, too, are doctors. Second, it raises the question of just how much one could expect doctors, within the present organization of Western medical care, to change their ways of relating to patients. And third, it signals that the very impersonal attitude that the physician adopts might have a therapeutic benefit as well as a control function in the relationship.

The remainder of this section will elaborate upon these three points, taking up the question of what it means to speak of the doctor 'taking the patient's point of view'. There is little doubt that control of the consultation lies mainly in the hands of the physician. In the clinic, doctors and other health professionals have various ways of ordering the exchange with patients. They can convey the need to be brief because of the short time available. For instance, they can break off conversation to write notes, consult a file or work with their desktop computer; they can instruct patients in the course of making a physical examination, or they can consult with another physician or nurse (Strong, 1979a).

One change that has happened in British general practice over the last fifty years has been the emergence of the patient's point of view as something that the doctor might legitimately take into consideration. It has been claimed that many patients come to the clinic not to ask 'Why have I got this particular disease?', but 'How have I come to be like this?' (Williams and Wood, 1986). Probably the most influential writer in this field was a psychoanalytically trained doctor, Michael Balint, who proposed that the focus upon the physical body did not meet the needs of many patients. Briefly, Balint (1964) proposed that when people go to the doctor they do more than specify a symptom: they 'offer' a range of possible 'illnesses' from which the doctor might choose. These 'illnesses' might include the person's worries, or problems with home or work, or even the illness of an ageing parent for whom they must care. (This is recognizable from Chapter 4 as Zola's [1973] 'breakdown of accommodation to symptoms'.) Balint's work set out how doctors might learn to accept the 'offers' that patients make, to listen to their concerns rather than just look at their bodily signs.

This immediately raises the question whether this kind of exchange is an alternative to the control often taken to define the therapeutic relationship. While it is accepted that individual doctors will vary in the degree to which they will listen and explain (Byrne and Long, 1976), the idea that the control available to physicians can be largely (if not completely) removed has been criticized. In terms of what doctors following Balint's method actually do (or say they do), it has been argued that their power is not diminished so much as altered (Herzlich, 1985). The fact that the patient now feels 'listened to', and that all aspects of his or her life can be brought to the doctor, does not diminish but arguably increases the doctor's expertise and control (Armstrong, 1984). Although the listening skills of the doctor, and the feelings of the patient, apparently become equal parts of a 'social relationship' in which both parties 'interact' (the communication model), in effect the professional authority of the doctor still remains intact.

The physician as healer: the placebo effect

While there is scope for doctors to adopt Byrne and Long's 'Silence, listening and reflective' mode (see Figure 5.1), the idea that they might be equal players with their patients in the relationship has been questioned on a number of grounds (Stone, 1979). Not least among these must be the continuing expectations of many people who present their problems as physical symptoms, and expect them to be treated as such. While there might be generally held beliefs about the role of lifestyle in illness causation, this does not necessarily mean that individuals want to hear advice of this kind from their doctors (Stott and Pill, 1990). One reason for this probably concerns individual privacy. However, a more powerful reason might lie in the patient's belief in the efficacy of the medical treatment that the doctor can provide.

Studies of the therapeutic effects of patients' beliefs are rare, although there is evidence that in cases where no definite diagnosis can be made, no treatment is just as effective as some treatment (Thomas, 1978). The situation of patients experiencing symptom relief, due to a treatment that they believe is helpful but for which there is no medical rationale, is termed the *placebo effect*. Although widely recognized as something that can happen in treatment, the placebo is rarely given central consideration in the literature (Cousins, 1976). In the main, the placebo (e.g. a neutral tablet) is understood from its use in medical trials. In this role it forms part of a control condition to ensure that scientifically reliable conclusions are drawn about the effectiveness of the drug under test. From the medical perspective, therefore, to refer to the placebo effect is to draw attention to a spurious outcome dependent upon people's 'magical' beliefs. In the extreme, placebos might be advocated for patients who, in the doctor's judgement, have nothing 'really' wrong with them but who might be 'made well' through the administration of a neutral substance.

However, as Thomas (1978) notes, the existence of a belief in the healing powers of *any* prescription by the doctor means that the *therapeutic illusion* has a widespread, if not universal, effect. To the extent that doctors believe that it is only the medication, in its chemico-physical form, that produces improvement in the patient, then they too participate in this illusion. Calling the placebo a 'psychological effect', or locating it in the minds of gullible patients, directs attention towards what doctors are convinced is happening when they give medication. Turning the phenomenon around, it is possible to ask about the therapeutic effects that arise directly from the role of the doctor as healer (Price, 1984). Parsons was clear that the effective use of the doctor's role works through, but is not reducible to, the technical means at his or her disposal. He argued that the fundamental psychological features of the doctor's role imply that, '[W]hether or not the physician knows it or wishes it, in practicing medicine skilfully he is always in fact exerting a therapeutic effect on his patients' (1951b: 458). This suggests that where doctor and patient both subscribe strongly to the belief system that we call modern medicine – and where their separate roles are clearly defined – then they are likely to give *more play* to these therapeutic powers. These matters are not easily amenable to experimental demonstration. Nevertheless, they allow a different interpretation of the finding of Jaspars et al. (1983) discussed above, where reduction in patient concern was related to brevity of conversation in the consultation.

It is possible that one element in this improvement (though undetected by the researchers) was the placebo effect. Their finding, that the doctor appears most effective *psychologically* when the patient's problem is one that s/he can cope with from a medical point of view, now makes a different kind of sense. It can be argued that these are also the consultations in which the doctor's clinical skills are the vehicle for maintaining the 'illusory powers' granted him or her by the patient. That is, the role of the physician as healer is strongly accentuated. For the patient, this means that, in addition to knowing what is wrong, the search for a positive slant to the question 'Why has this happened to me?' can result in him or her feeling 'good' once again. This ability to form and to maintain illusions is neither abnormal nor undesirable. It is arguably crucial to our taking a positive view upon events of significance for us, something that can deliver real psychological benefits in any sphere of life (Taylor, 1983).

Therefore, the conclusion to this discussion must be that the psychological effectiveness of the doctor is not some spin-off from clinical practice; *it is intrinsic to the role of the physician as healer.* The physician in Western medicine shares similar powers to those usually discussed only in relation to healers in traditional or non-literate societies (Helman, 1987).

These therapeutic effects are not, of course, restricted to conventional or orthodox medicine. Some people always seek help from healers in complementary medicine; others go to a chiropractor or to an osteopath for advice about specific complaints, and others only when the treatment they have received from their doctor has not helped (Thomas et al., 1991). It might be that some individuals use complementary medicine because they are dissatisfied with the way that they have been treated by their regular doctors. Indications are that people are quite sophisticated about their use of alternative healers. They appreciate the technical opportunities provided by modern medicine, yet value the relationship they can establish with a practitioner of alternative medicine (Sharma, 1992).

Where individuals adhere strongly to the beliefs of orthodox medicine, they might be more likely to seek help for specific complaints, accepting a different but still technically specific treatment. Where people hold different views, or where their faith in modern medicine is undermined, they might seek help through a healing relationship based upon a belief system to which they can subscribe more easily. One study found that, after eight weeks, 33 out of a total of 56 patients attending a centre for alternative medicine felt much better, although only 19 had completed their treatment at the time (Moore et al., 1985). Whether this can be taken as evidence for the kind of therapeutic effects we have been considering above is not certain. What is clear, however, is that both orthodox and alternative healing can be considered from the perspective of social science. Related to this, the role of the 'placebo effect' is not a side issue, but one that deserves more attention than it has received so far.

Physical examination and body care: embarrassment and healing

Most research into doctor–patient communication has approached the problem either from the perspective of efficient practice (e.g. getting the patient to comply), or from the standpoint of the patient as 'a person' (i.e. patient-centred consultations). Each of these approaches has the effect of trying to make one of the parties communicate in the other's terms. This means that doctors discuss patients' feelings, or patients learn to remember which pills to take with what frequency. This assumes (mistakenly) that doctor and patient each have only one standpoint: the 'voice of medicine' on one side and the 'voice of the lifeworld' on the other (Silverman, 1987). However, we have already seen that some patients, especially those nearest in socio-economic background to medical professionals, will express their illness to the physician in medical terms. There is also evidence that doctors will often use the everyday terms of their patients in the course of prescribing treatment for ordinary ailments (Helman, 1978). This suggests that medical encounters are more complex than the 'separate voice' model of events would suggest (Silverman, 1987).

The previous section's discussion of healing and the reduction of patient concern provides the context for seeing how these two 'voices' are used interchangeably by doctor and patient. The interesting thing about this context is that it is to do with an aspect of medical care that is central to the consultation but apparently distant to the concept of 'voice': the physical examination. The physical examination, and the body care that involves or follows treatment, is an essential part of the doctor's (and the nurse's) function. For the doctor, access to the patient's body is essential for the practice of clinical techniques, while for the nurse it is the locus of her caring work (Lawler, 1991). Exposing one's body to others, allowing them to touch it, press it and examine it internally are special privileges that most people will grant in no other situation. For that reason, the physical examination and care of the body give rise to issues of personal integrity as well as bodily inviolability (Parsons, 1951a). This is especially true when those involved are of a different sex, where the examination is of parts of the body normally regarded as private, or where the patient can no longer control his or her bodily functions. This means that there must be ways in which all of the individuals concerned act so as to avoid the embarrassment that threatens this part of the consultation or treatment process.

Examining how physical examinations and body care are managed is, however, only one aim of this section; the other relates to the question of healing. Earlier on in this chapter, when discussing the dilemmas of patients and doctors, it was said that one threat to the patient is that the doctor will find his or her complaint to be trivial. On the other hand, the discovery that one's symptoms are not life-threatening, that they are in a sense 'ordinary', can be a source of considerable relief for many attending the doctor's clinic. As Berger and Mohr (1967) put it, illness separates and encourages a distorted, fragmented form of self-consciousness. The doctor can compensate for these broken connections through his or her special relationship with the patient, a vital part of which is the special intimacy that s/he is allowed. The potential for healing lies, in no small part, in the physical examination and care of the patient. Certainly its special significance to this field far outweighs, so far, the research that has been conducted into it.

The physical examination can be considered to be an episode of non-vocal activity bounded by talk (Heath, 1986). Often, talk is suspended during the period when the doctor is inspecting a part of the body or, for example, sounding the patient's chest. As we shall see in a moment, this need not be the case. However, considering a prototypical case without speech directs attention to what the doctor and patient are doing regarding the patient's body. In his study of body movement during consultations, Heath (1986) noted that after gaining permission to make the examination, the doctor becomes engrossed in looking, listening or feeling. The patient rarely looks directly at the doctor, but directs his or her attention to one side, into the middle-distance, seemingly uninvolved in the proceedings. There are no responses to the doctor's actions, which are treated by the patient as if they do not quite involve his or her self. Sensations that would ordinarily call out a response of some kind – whether of pain, pleasure or challenge – are taken as directed for the while at the body which the patient 'has', rather than the body s/he 'is'.

This unflinching composure, and the holding of a middle-distance gaze, are things people do in the clinic to transform themselves into an object for medical examination. This does not mean that the patient abandons this body to the doctor. Instead, the holding of the middle-distance gaze allows the patient to monitor the requirements of the doctor as the examination proceeds, and to recognize when it is being terminated. In the context of the gynaecological examination, Emerson (1970) has pointed out that the patient is expected by staff to be 'in play', attentive to the situation to the degree that she can switch attention to the doctor's face if a verbal exchange is required.

The psychological significance of the physical examination lies both in what is being achieved in the sense of healing, and how this sensitive episode is managed by the parties involved. From research to date, we know more about the second than about the first. This is because the idea of social episodes being sustained through what people say and do has a general validity in sociological and social psychological theory. Using Goffman's (1972) approach, the consultation can be regarded as a well-defined episode, a realm that has special meaning, and in which a particular language of reality is binding. This frames the actions and events that take place, making some relevant and ruling out others as irrelevant to the consultation. This helps to sustain the encounter as a 'this' rather than a 'that' kind of occasion (Strong, 1979a).

In the case of the physical examination, this is extremely important if the situation is to be defined as one in which the doctor has legitimate access to the patient's body, and if it is not to threaten the integrity of the individual's sense of self. The reciprocal aspect of this requirement is that the patient should not call into question the doctors' and nurses' propriety regarding their actions. For the examination to take place we have seen that the person must 'yield up' his or her body to the physician. This involves a sense of displacement of oneself from one's body that is sustained by the attitude described by Heath (above). To the extent that there is a sense of loss of self – of discomfort in this – then patients may attempt to reconstitute themselves 'as persons' in the course of the examination.

One way in which the person can feel less of a patient, and more of an individual, is through interspersing parts of the examination with anecdotes or information about themselves. In a report of one such examination, Young (1989) explains how the patient (an elderly Jewish professor) tells the doctor a sequence of stories relating to the parts of his body being examined. Among these stories are accounts of how certain scars and past injuries relate to the period during which he was an internee in a Nazi concentration camp. Young argues that the stories are the professor's way of reinserting himself back into the consultation as a whole personality. He does this by placing the accounts at points where they do not disrupt the necessary distance between self and body that the examination demands. Instead, what these stories do is to reintegrate the professor's bodily experiences once they have been objectified and separated by the external gaze of the physician.

The therapeutic value of such stories is recognized by medical staff who are willing to listen to them. For nurses looking after patients in hospital, the apparently innocuous talk at the bedside can be of this kind. Here is another example, this time from a nurse in an Edinburgh hospital:

> Sister Hanna goes to give the . . . suppository to Mrs Prior, . . . who looks bright and says, 'I feel good'. She says she's been thinking about doing her laundry, and that she is concerned about her husband boiling it. As she gives the suppository, Sister Hanna listens and shares a story of when she was in hospital having her youngest baby and her husband boiled the jeans, long before boiled jeans were in style. (MacLeod, 1993: 186)

In order that medical staff can carry out their work in relation to the patient's body, it is also important that they are able to sustain the view of the situation as impersonal, i.e. one in which they do not have a personal interest. The latter refers to the need for what can be termed *medical gentility* (Strong, 1979a). This requires both doctor and patient to subscribe to the belief that medical staff bring an objective, unfeeling eye to the examination. (The word 'unfeeling' here is not meant to imply 'not caring'; it refers to the suspension of personal desires, interests and judgements that properly belong in the world of everyday relationships.) This is particularly marked in situations such as gynaecological examinations, where the possibility that this might be seen as something other than a medical situation is especially threatening – both to patients and to staff.

In her study of a gynaecology clinic, Emerson (1970) pointed out that the staff's demeanour toward the patient is one of: 'Of course, you take this as matter-of-factly as we do.' She underlines the point that the necessity of defining the patient as a technical object, in order that clinical procedures can be carried out, constitutes an indignity in itself. Therefore, work must be done simultaneously to acknowledge the patient as a person, taking care to modulate the instructions given. Emerson's study focused upon the way that the medical reality is sustained in this setting. She noted the depersonalization and desexualization of the encounter, so that parts of the body are either alluded to indirectly, or else given the definite article; the doctor might refer to 'the vagina' but never 'your vagina'. The patient adopts an attitude of what might be termed 'indirect attention', similar to that described by Heath (1986) in his study of general medical consultations. In this way – by an upward gaze into the middle-distance, a taut facial expression, a flat tone of voice – she conveys that she endorses the definition of this as a 'matter-of-fact' medical encounter.

The relevance of the gynaecological examination for our discussion is its precariousness. The looks, touch and verbal references of staff must avoid any suggestion that any one of them experiences personal pleasure or disgust in what they are doing. Should this happen there will likely be embarrassment on both sides, an indication that other identities of the person (e.g. as a sexually active woman) have been acknowledged. Embarrassment is avoided by the backgrounding of these other identities (Gross and Stone, 1964), and this is achieved by the careful attention given to fashioning particular selves for all concerned (Goffman, 1971).

The gynaecological examination is also special because it often involves the examination of a woman's sexual organs by a man, sometimes in the presence of other people watching. However, the problem of making the patient into an object, while simultaneously rescuing her (or his) sense of integrity and honour, is a more general one. In the hospital setting, it occurs for female nurses who must attend to the bodily needs of male patients. Sponging down a male patient for the first time can be a frightening prospect for many newly qualified young female nurses (Lawler, 1991). They are often taught to handle these situations by cultivating an emotional detachment, and by concentrating upon the procedures they must follow. This also serves to demonstrate to the patient what kind of encounter it is: clinical, impersonal, scrubbed of the sexual innuendos that would otherwise attach to these kind of actions. The nurse's uniform – like the white coat of the doctor – is intended to aid in this definition. (This, in spite of it having been eroticized in Western culture.) The clothes of medical personnel do not just inform us who is who in the hospital; they also act as 'props', defining the situation in terms to which staff should adhere, and patients be encouraged to subscribe.

We can now see that the significance of the physical examination and of bodily care is not just medical; it is also socio-psychological. The body is the site of care, but it is more than just the object of clinical attention. Through touch, especially, as well as through gaze, the doctor treads (if s/he is successful) a careful line. This is between, on the one hand, making the body an object and, on the other, recognizing that it belongs to an individual whose integrity is not to be compromised. This is what some refer to as the 'art of medicine'. In the case of nursing, it has been argued that caring – the melding of instrumental and expressive functions – needs to be understood as an expertise involving personal knowledge, 'knowing how' rather than 'knowing what' (Benner, 1984). This requires us to consider the body in ways that, so far, few social scientists have been willing to do.

'Good' patients, 'bad' patients and 'children'

Among the obligations imposed upon those taking up the sick role are the desire to get well and the acknowledgement that sickness is itself a deviant state. Parsons and Fox (1952) emphasized that the patient must relinquish, with the burdens of normal adulthood, the rights that go with it. This acceptance of what is a child-like status imposes a number of constraints upon the individual, either as an out-patient (e.g. forgoing an anticipated activity) or as an in-patient (e.g. staying in bed and doing what s/he is told by hospital staff). Where patients resist these expectations, or present with conditions that suggest they might do so, then they risk having negative judgements made about them by the medical staff concerned.

Patients in hospital are well aware that they should comply with what staff expect of a 'good' patient. This is true even when they are not sure exactly what they should do to fulfil those expectations. It is said that the 'good' patient is highly regarded by staff because s/he is compliant, non-complaining and generally passive (Taylor, 1979). The 'sensible' patient gets things in the proper context, doesn't worry and accepts his or her fate (Strong, 1979a). Whatever the staff's view, it has been shown in one study in the USA that hospital in-patients experience a certain conflict in their role. This arises from their acceptance of the need to follow medical orders, while also appearing neither demanding nor inconsiderate (Tagliacozzo and Mauksch, 1972). For example, patients might wait passively for a medication that is late, or watch a specimen get cold rather than point this out to the nurse. There is a feeling that one is helpless in hospital, although this does not mean that patients passively conform to what staff expect. Rather, their compliance is often a way of actively resolving dilemmas experienced in the course of wanting to 'be helped' and yet to 'be helpful'.

We have seen that in the setting of the GP consultation the very presentation of the person is nearly always taken as sufficient condition for him or her to be treated as a patient. This does not mean that s/he will always get treatment, or that s/he will be treated like someone who has what the doctor perceives to be a more genuine complaint. It should not surprise us to know that doctors (and nurses) have preferences and distastes for certain kinds of patient. Knowing what these are, and how they come about, is important for understanding the procedures by which patients are accepted into or steered away from the therapeutic relationship. This is not a matter of cataloguing the prejudices of medical staff; it is a concern with how patients appeal to doctors to be treated as legitimate recipients of their clinical skills, and as appropriate occupiers of the sick role.

Four criteria have been described as used by health professionals in their judgement of the prospective patient (Askham, 1982). These are: (a) the patient's motivation to get well: (b) the possible relationship between physician and patient (e.g. travellers or holiday-makers might be told to visit their own GP); (c) the simple demographic characteristics of the patient, such as gender, age and ethnicity (some members of minority groups in Britain experience difficulties in access to health care [MacCormack, 1980]); and (d) the awkwardness or troublesomeness of the patient. With regard to the last category, some doctors report difficulty dealing with three categories of patient: husband and wife attending together, adolescents and medically trained people (Bennett et al., 1978). Each of these conveys its own special difficulty, but all can be interpreted as presenting the doctor with a problem in sustaining a definition of the encounter. This definition is one in which s/he can operate as expert in relation to a patient who accepts his or her way of viewing the situation.

How the doctor views the patient, whether that individual is seen to be a member of certain groups that are negatively stereotyped, can have an effect on how (or whether) treatment is carried out. For example, alcoholics, the mentally retarded, vagrants and drug addicts are all people whom doctors perceive less favourably in the surgery (Najman et al., 1982). More generally, one study found that younger adult patients are preferred to older ones, middle-class to working-class patients, while men receive more extensive diagnostic efforts than women (Armitage et al., 1979). In terms of the different likes of doctors, Najman et al. (1982) report that while younger (American) doctors are likely to have negative feelings about patients presenting with headaches or obesity, their older colleagues dislike those with sexually transmitted diseases, those wanting immunizations and those they describe as 'vulgar, garrulous know-alls'.

Clearly, it is not just the particular group to which patients belong that marks them out, but the disease from which they suffer and the way that they conduct themselves in the consultation. Sometimes, as Freidson (1970) has pointed out, the illness might be condemned by the doctor though the patient be treated with sympathy (e.g. drug addiction). In spite of this, the person is expected to get rid of the disease and, to the extent that s/he bears its marks, s/he suffers the obligation to try even harder to remove it. The relationship between disease, group membership and conduct can be quite complex indeed. For example, Irish labouring men in the UK will sometimes visit the doctor for treatment to an injury. Whether or not this follows a fall or fight during a drinking bout, it carries the probability that they will be labelled either deviant, or drunk or both (MacCormack, 1980).

One group of individuals who avoid being categorized as 'bad' patients are children; this is in spite of their doing many of the things that are typical of those stereotyped in this way. For example, they are often *responsible* for their injuries (e.g. they fall off bikes, walls and ponies); their symptoms are often *not serious*; they may *complain out of all proportion* to their injury; and, most important of all, they are notoriously *uncooperative* (Dingwall and Murray, 1983). In spite of all these things, children are, in general,

Table 5.1   *Conditions for the labelling of patients by medical staff*

		Rule-breaking	
		(a) No excuse	(b) Has excuse
Responsibility	(c) Could have acted knowingly	'Bad'	'Inappropriate'
	(d) Could not have acted knowingly	'Children'	'Naïve'

treated quite differently from 'bad' patients, for the very good reason that they are not held responsible for their predicament.

What we have seen above are examples of patients who are categorized in different ways by medical staff according to the origins of their presenting symptoms. This matters for the patient, because the validation of his or her claim to the status 'sick' rests upon judgements made by the doctor about the legitimacy of the condition as presented.

On the basis of research in hospital accident departments, Dingwall and Murray (1983) put forward a general scheme to organize the conditions of presentation, and hence show which kind of patient is more or less likely to be seen as 'good' or 'bad' by medical staff. The scheme rests upon two basic distinctions. The first is between a situation (a) where the person has broken a rule where there is no excuse for breaking it, and (b) where the breaking of the rule is 'explained' by some appeal to other factors. The second distinction is between (c) individuals who can be held to have knowingly acted so as to break the rule, and (d) those who cannot be held so responsible. These conditions are set out in Table 5.1.

The table shows that 'bad' patients (who might include drunks, tramps and overdoses) are people who are held to be responsible for their predicament, in that they could have brought it about knowingly. Their breaking of rules (both everyday and those of the clinic) suggests that they are people who do not disavow their deviance, and hence are not likely to try to get well or to comply with treatment. They (or other adults) might be able to persuade staff that they could not help the situation they are in (e.g. a person who injured herself falling off a wall while trying to rescue a neighbour's cat). If this is the case, then they might be seen as 'inappropriate' patients who receive a more impersonal mode of treatment from staff. Individuals who break rules (e.g. fall off bikes, get their heads stuck in jars, superglue their fingers together), but who are not seen as responsible (i.e. capable), fall in the 'children' category. They are, therefore, treated in a special way by staff, depending upon their demographic characteristics. If they are young children, then there might be displays of friendliness, kindness or game-playing, which actions mark them out as different.

Non-compliance or complaints in the clinic are also more likely to be tolerated.

The difference between 'children' and *children* now needs to be made clear. Some patients who occupy this category are not children but adults. Often they are elderly individuals who are deemed to be no longer responsible for their actions (e.g. they might have Alzheimer's disease). However, it is not necessary that the elderly suffer from a disease for them to be treated in this way. In Western society there has been an 'infantilization' of older people that serves to make them out as dependent, and somehow less than responsible (Hockey and James, 1993). The general use of metaphors of childhood ('little old lady', 'old boy') structure their physical and social reality. Such metaphors are therefore double-edged in relation to the medical consultation. While the elderly patient might not be held responsible for his or her situation in the same way as a middle-aged adult, s/he might be placed in a similar position to that of a child when it comes to symptom reporting. Children are brought to the clinic by parents, and it is the latter to whom the doctor looks for a definitive explanation of the problem. To be cast in this category at any age means that other people have the key role of saying what one's problem is, and what must be done if one is to comply with medical advice.

Lastly, the category defined as 'naïve' requires a brief explanation. In their account, Dingwall and Murray (1983) suggest that this is rule-breaking without either knowledge or intention. They give the example of a toddler urinating in the lap of a consultant, or of a child who, on being asked the cause of his injury, said, 'Daddy hit me.' Such episodes often give rise to mirth, including when they are brought about by adults (e.g. stock jokes about foreign patients who take out their wallet or purse and offer to pay for treatment).

In summary, what this scheme suggests is that it is possible to set out the conditions under which different groups of patients are more or less likely to be seen as deviant by medical staff. In many ways it gives priority to the person rather than the disease, so that it is necessary to introduce into the framework the conditions that pertain to the presentation of symptoms. It is possible that while a child might be excused for bringing about one kind of self-inflicted injury, s/he might not be so readily excused another. However, what is important to see here is that it is the category of 'children' that is particularly important, and that this is one that is socially constructed. (It is constructed with reference to *children* too, although this question is outside of our consideration in this book; but see Hockey and James, 1993.)

Clearly, taking up the sick role via the consultation is not as straightforward as a reading of Parsons might have us suppose. True, obligations are placed upon the sick by the physician simultaneously with his or her acceptance that the patient is legitimately ill. However, this does not happen automatically. It is subject to meanings and practices that involve the doctor in judgements about the patient as an individual, and as a member of this or that social group. This does not mean that patients will be refused treatment should the doctor perceive them as less than worthy of sympathy. However, it might affect the way in which medical staff practise their clinical skills in that particular case.

Chapter summary

- The typical consultation with a general practitioner has been shown to go through *stages*. This progression is usually controlled by the doctor, who uses preferred styles of communication with patients.
- Early research described the consultation from the doctor's point of view. This approach saw it in terms of effective diagnosis and the conveyance of information to the patient, who was expected only to *comply* with medical advice.
- The social psychological perspective recovered the patient as a person who also has a point of view. The doctor–patient relationship was studied like other social relationships, and argued to require essentially smooth *communication* if it is to be effective.
- The medical consultation, and care of the sick in general, are not only interactions or exchanges; they also depend upon the *construction of negotiated meanings* and the agreement as to how the situation shall be defined.
- Patients must establish their claim to sickness through a *presentation* of their symptoms. The diagnosis and treatment of disease by the doctor constitutes a *legitimation of this claim*, possibly leading to the person being granted occupancy of the sick role.
- The effectiveness of the doctor lies both in his or her clinical skills, and in beliefs shared by doctor and patient alike concerning the efficacy of biomedicine. This, the *therapeutic illusion*, is central to the consultation being a healing relationship.
- There is a need for doctors to conduct their clinical practice without displacing (or disrupting) *the integrity of the patient as person*. The physical examination and the practice of bodily care provide an important medium through which this can take place.
- The likelihood of an individual's claim to sickness being validated depends upon views of medical staff. These concern the *worthiness* of the person, as well as the legitimacy of the complaint. Treatment can be understood in terms of the (perceived) deviance of prospective patients from social norms. Medical staff use these norms to determine whether people should be held responsible for the symptoms which they present.

Further reading

Benner, P. (1984) *From Novice to Expert: Excellence and power in clinical nursing practice*. Menlo Park, Calif.: Addison-Wesley.
Dingwall, R. and Murray, T. (1983) Categorization in accident departments: 'good' patients, 'bad' patients, and 'children', *Sociology of Health and Illness*, 5, 127–48.

Emerson, J.P. (1970) 'Behavior in private places: sustaining definitions of reality in gynecological examinations', in H.P. Drietzel (ed.) *Recent Sociology*. New York: Macmillan.

Heath, C. (1986) *Body Movement and Speech in Medical Interaction*. Cambridge: Cambridge University Press.

Lawler, J. (1991) *Behind the Screens: Nursing, somology, and the problem of the body*. Melbourne: Churchill Livingstone.

Ley, P. (1982) Satisfaction, compliance and communication, *British Journal of Social Psychology*, 21, 241–54.

Pendleton, D. and Hasler, J. (eds) (1983) *Doctor–Patient Communication*. London: Academic Press.

6

Illness and Gender: Studying Women's Health

The last three chapters examined what people think about health, what they do when they feel ill, and how they are treated when they attend the doctor's surgery. In each case, it was shown that people make sense of their experience in the context of relationships with others. This means that the transition from the world of health to that of illness is not automatic. It depends upon interpretations, claims and permissions that are sought and, for the most part, granted. In our treatment of this progression, the reader might have noticed a parallel shift in our concern from society (beliefs), via the individual (symptom experience), to the body (the physical examination). In Chapter 1, these terms were linked to the concepts of disease, illness and sickness, so that disease was said to refer to pathologies of the body, illness to the experience of the individual, and sickness to the person's place in society. Tracing the course from health to sickness (via illness) in this way has meant, in effect, that the initial concern with social beliefs gave way to an interest in the doctor's treatment of the symptomatic body.

An unintended consequence of this approach is the implication that the body only matters when it becomes diseased or injured. This, in turn, might be taken to imply that wider social concerns do not penetrate the privacy of the consultation between doctor and patient. An examination of issues surrounding women's health will show both of these suggestions to be untrue. The body matters before it is diseased, and the treatment of patients by doctors takes place in terms of their (i.e. physicians') beliefs about groups in society. Taking the first point, this refers to the fact that people do not suddenly acquire bodies only when they become ill. Judging by most books written by social psychologists and by sociologists, one might be forgiven for thinking that this was the case. This is somewhat surprising, given that many debates about the role of men and women in society have referred to anatomical differences between the sexes. The advocates of male superiority have often used biologistic thinking to point to the inherent weakness and unpredictability of the female body, a condition purported to make women unreliable and irresponsible (Ussher, 1989). By comparison, although men have located their masculinity in physical strength, their supposed social supremacy has often been claimed in terms of an ability to transcend their bodies, particularly through superior intellect. This has resulted in men feeling their bodies to be a means towards further ends (particularly work). Women, on the other hand, have been assigned roles in which the care of infant, elderly and male bodies is central, not to mention the obligation to focus their lives around reproduction (Smith, 1974).

For this reason, women – like the insane, crowds and the sick – have occupied an oddly marginal place in social and psychological theory. This is because the disciplines of psychology and sociology are based upon the assumptions of dominant groups in Western society – healthy, white, male individuals. And because the condition of these dominant individuals is one where the body can be, as it were, taken for granted, the physical experiences of disadvantaged groups is difficult, if not impossible, to explain. As a result, these experiences are sometimes turned into the 'emotionality' of women, the 'irrationality' of the crowd or the 'invalidism' of the sick, thus making them exceptional and open to dismissal by social science theory (Radley, 1991).

The reason for making these points is to show that there are two different perspectives that will become apparent in this chapter. One concerns the discussion of women's health as being different to that of men; here women are treated as exceptional to men, who are taken as the standard reference point. Researchers have emphasized the differences between men's and women's health, allowing us to make a commentary upon issues that we have already covered in the book. The other perspective explains men's and women's illness not as an inevitable opposition, but as part of the way that experience is gendered in society. From this position, other researchers have attempted to redefine the illness experience from the point of view of women. This gives us an opportunity to present and to discuss matters pertaining to the health of women as subjects in their own right. In the course of this chapter, we shall need to adopt each one of these different approaches.

The second perspective is a result of the emergence of the feminist movement in health studies. This rejected 'the stereotypical passive feminine role supporting the traditional authoritarian medical-professional model' (Ruzek, 1978: 9). As a result, awareness has been raised concerning the role of gender in health care, in particular regarding male-dominated medicine and its part in the designation of women's complaints as 'problems'. For example, it has been said that 'women do more than "enter" the health system through their reproductive organs; they often organize their health care around gynaecological care' (Ruzek, 1978: 11). This is a key example of how women's experience has been the basis for their being designated as particular kinds of patients. Taken at face value, however, it suggests that matters to do with reproduction are problems for women alone. This assumption tends to hide questions concerning the male reproductive system. These questions, it has been argued, are made invisible because men's reproductive processes are invariably presented in a positive way, free of the complications argued to affect women (Pfeffer, 1985). This is an example of the way in which social and psychological studies of 'the thinking male' depend upon obscuring the role of the body in everyday life.

Historically, women as mothers have been a continuing focus of concern for both medical practitioners and administrators alike. For example, early twentieth-century Britain was a place with high levels of infant and maternal mortality. In her account of how mothers were treated in this period, Lewis (1980) describes how medical (and political) authorities interpreted these high mortality rates in ways that ignored the women's social and environmental circumstances. Although infant mortality was highest among the urban working class, for whom sanitation was worst, some politicians and medical officers were reluctant to connect these two facts together. Instead, they argued that disease was caused through the 'ignorance and fecklessness of [individual] mothers', who should be persuaded to adopt clean and natural ways of feeding their children, i.e. breastfeeding. Those who chose not to, or could not do so, were condemned for their 'selfishness'.

This example shows how, in the everyday life of women as mothers and providers, issues of disease and of social concern have been brought together in beliefs about how they should use their bodies. It also shows, in line with the arguments made in Chapter 2, that views about childbed fever were not separated from the values of right and wrong as these are applied to particular social groups.

In terms of illness experience, and of decisions whether a bodily sign might be a symptom of disease, both menstruation and pregnancy have been, and continue to be, fields of ambiguity and conflict for women and doctors. In the case of pregnancy and childbirth, there is a long history of how a 'natural' event has been gradually taken over by medicine (Oakley, 1984). Compared to the medical view of childbirth as a separate event in the woman's life, the woman herself is likely to experience it more within the context of her own biography. From the obstetric point of view, childbirth concerns the external manipulations of a (machine-like) body, the key part of which (the uterus) contracts in an involuntary way (Martin, 1987). By involving an array of technological monitoring equipment in a hospital setting, medicine makes childbirth into an illness-type experience, with the woman taking the sick role as patient. Much of the debate about childbirth has centred upon women's dissent from this position, arguing that birth is not an illness but part of the world of health (Graham and Oakley, 1986).

This is an episode that typifies the situation discussed in Chapter 4, which analysed the problem of how bodily signs and changes come to signify illness. One argument made at that point was that illness can be defined in terms of feelings (Telles and Pollack, 1981). Certainly women report a range of feelings during pregnancy (e.g. tiredness, nausea, need to urinate frequently) that may be construed as illness. Childbirth, too, involves a whole range of unpleasant physical signs that may signal risk in medical terms. However, from another frame of reference, midwives can help the mother to interpret her feelings, to put her in touch with what is happening to her, and advise how she can participate in the event. Oakley

(1993) has argued that this can help the woman in labour to experience her feelings and reactions as legitimate, rather than as an emotional side-issue to an essentially medical episode.

As with the doctor–patient consultation, these frames of reference are not restricted to each of the parties taken separately. As far as women are concerned, they are often encouraged to view their labour in terms of the medical procedures to which they are subject, as passive patients. In addition, however, they are also expected by doctors to cooperate actively during the course of the birth. For example, later on in labour a woman may be encouraged to 'push'. This suggests that she is no longer a body-machine but someone who can voluntarily act (and, by the same token, should try, can fail, is responsible). This, however, can lead to a sense of confusion about what is required of her and of what is possible – is it the uterus as machine that is to produce the baby, or is it the woman as labourer who must make the birth happen (Martin, 1987)?

The question of the relationship between women and the medical profession is one that we shall take up in more detail later on in the chapter. In particular, we shall be concerned with the way that the healthy and the sick female body has been viewed by a profession dominated by men. It has been argued that from the late nineteenth to the early twentieth century doctors saw women as languid, weak creatures whose normal state was to be sick (Ehrenreich and English, 1978). For middle-class women this was set against a background of a sexuo-economic relationship with their menfolk, in which they were confined to the home and to rearing children. This social distinction came to be marked in terms of the respective anatomies of the sexes: men worked with their brains – making, writing, inventing – while women were urged to side with their uterus – their 'nature'. Ehrenreich and English argue that doctors were active in prescribing such things as rest cures for these middle-class women, treatments that underlined their frailty and their need to be confined within the domestic setting.

This example shows how the interpretation of women's illness takes place on the basis of assumptions about the place of men and women in society. While doctors may no longer prescribe rest cures for women, there are differences in their (and our) beliefs about men and women's health, their strength, their ability to withstand pain and their response to different kinds of treatment. When (as reported in Chapter 3) people interviewed for the *Health and Lifestyles Survey* (Blaxter, 1990) were asked to think of someone whom they knew who was very healthy, the majority (men and women) mentioned a man (see Miles, 1991: 39). This is consistent with reports that some GPs see typically troublesome patients as female, not employed, and having vague psychiatric symptoms (Stimson, cited in Oakley, 1993: 14).

Oakley (1993) makes the point that the two female conditions that are beyond men's understanding (menstruation and childbirth) each give rise to medical diagnoses of psychiatric illness (premenstrual tension and postpartum depression respectively). In the case of premenstrual tension, the contradiction that we saw in the case of childbirth re-occurs. Within the biomedical frame of reference, the woman's feelings are reduced to a matter of hormonal imbalance. This can mean that she is denied important responsibilities outside the home, since (it is believed) she does not retain complete control of her rational decision-making (Rodin, 1992). However, she may also be blamed for the impact that her emotional state has on others (notably her family), or for failing to seek appropriate medical treatment (Martin, 1987).

The reason for beginning with these conditions special to women is to alert us to issues that are somewhat obscured in the treatment of sex differences in health and illness. Much of this chapter will be concerned with evidence concerning the amounts of reported illness and the consulting rates of men and women. In that sense, we shall often be talking about these matters as if they were the same thing (a headache, an abdominal pain, a feeling of nausea) for members of either sex. Given the special conditions that affect women because of their reproductive capacities, this is not an assumption that one should make. This is not to say that women cannot have an 'ordinary' headache, or that all of women's illnesses are linked to their reproductive anatomy. (Who says this and when, is part of the problem that we shall be addressing.) It is rather that if we think of people having a health biography, a personal history of when and how they became ill and were made well, then what symptoms mean depends upon the personal context in which they arise. Blaxter put this nicely in the conclusion to her study of the health beliefs of middle-aged women:

> People have to inhabit their bodies, and their physical identity is part of themselves. Particularly as they grow older, they have a need to account for this identity, to draw together all that they have experienced. This body is their inheritance, it is the result of the events of their life, and it is their constraint. (1983:69)

With these points in mind we can proceed first to a review of the differences between men and women in their life expectancy and death rates (*mortality*). Then we can progress to the question of why women appear to fall ill more frequently than men, suffer from more symptoms and more often seek medical advice (*morbidity*). In both of these sections we shall begin by looking at data collected either from official statistics or gathered by means of social survey. This was termed in Chapter 1 the 'societal approach', to indicate its focus upon differences between social groups. As we proceed with our analysis, it will become clear that other kinds of data are also required if questions are to be answered about what men and women do to create these health distinctions.

Differences in male–female mortality

There is evidence from a number of sources that women in the Western world, particularly, have a higher life expectancy than men (see Kane, 1991, for a review). Table 6.1 shows this pattern quite clearly for a selection of European countries. In England and Wales, for example, a young woman

Table 6.1   *Trends in longevity: life expectation at birth in selected*
European countries around 1960, 1970 and 1980

| | Life expectation at birth | | | | | |
| | Males | | | Females | | |
Country	1960	1970	1980	1960	1970	1980
Belgium	66.3	67.3	69.0	72.2	73.5	75.6
Czechoslovakia	67.8	66.2	67.5	73.2	72.9	74.6
England & Wales	68.2	69.1	70.2	74.2	75.4	76.2
Finland	65.4	66.7	68.9	72.6	75.2	77.2
German Dem. Republic	66.5	68.1	68.7	71.4	73.3	74.8
Greece	67.3	70.1	72.9	70.4	73.6	77.6
Hungary	66.4	66.8	66.0	70.6	72.6	73.2
Netherlands	71.1	71.2	72.4	75.9	77.2	78.9
Norway	71.0	71.4	72.3	76.0	77.7	78.7
Portugal	61.6	64.6	67.3	67.3	71.0	74.2
Sweden	71.2	72.2	72.8	74.9	77.1	78.8

Source: Lopez, 1984

born around 1980 can expect to live until she is 76, six years longer than her male counterpart. However, even within this group of countries, there are differences in the pattern of mortality advantage for women. In Eastern European countries like Poland and Bulgaria, the excess of male over female deaths occurs at around age 40; for countries like Canada, the USA, Australia and Scandinavian countries, the excess is at age 20 and a smaller one at about 60; for Britain and the Netherlands, men show two equal 'peaks' of excess mortality over women, at age 20 and age 60. This may reflect differences both in health care provision and in the lifestyle of the sexes in these different communities. Whatever the case, in the developed world there is a tendency for men to die earlier than their female counterparts at *every age*; i.e. it is not that men and women have the same health until they reach about 70 years of age (Rodin and Ickovics, 1990).

This tendency for men to die younger than women (a mortality rate of about 1.7 times higher) has not always been of the order it is today (Kane, 1991). For example, taking Australia at the end of the nineteenth century, at no age group did men's mortality exceed that of women by more than 1.4. By 1980–2, however, no single age group had a ratio below 1.7. Over this period, health care has advanced in the developed world, and it might be that this has improved the lot of younger women who are at risk in their reproductive years. This suggests that the mortality ratios found in the Western world might not be typical of those in the developing countries. In Bangladesh, for example, female death rates exceed those of males at all ages between 1 and 39, most being due to problems in pregnancy and childbirth. Similar excesses in mortality rates for young girls are found in Pakistan, China and Thailand (Kane, 1991). In parts of northern India, girls

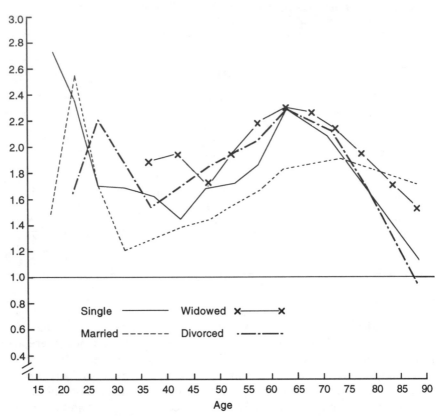

Figure 6.1   *Excess mortality of males over females by marital status:*
England and Wales, 1984 (Kane, 1991)

receive less adequate nutrition and health care, and in consequence they
have a higher mortality than boys in this region (Waldron, 1983).

How can the mortality advantage of women in countries with developed
medical services be explained? It has been mentioned that one 'peak' of the
ratio occurs at about age 20. This has been related to greater risk-taking by
males, who (in the USA) are five times more likely to die by drowning or
from a gun accident than are females (Waldron, 1983). Men also drink more
alcohol, smoke more cigarettes on average and take more illegal drugs than
women in the USA. Recent evidence from the UK shows that more men
smoke than do women, but this difference is not large (36 per cent compared
with 32 per cent) and is reducing. Men also drink more alcohol than do
women, although there are significant regional differences (Blaxter, 1990).

Attempts to apportion these health risks from mortality data have not
explained the sex differences regularly observed. The mortality ratio in
favour of women varies little when statistical procedures are used to remove
these risk factors, though it has been shown to drop more if physiological
factors are taken into account (Verbrugge, 1989). There remains the distinct

possibility that women do enjoy a <u>biological advantage</u> over men. This has been located in the positive effects provided by female sex hormones (e.g. the association between oestrogen level and lowered risk of heart disease in pre-menopausal women) and in genetic make-up. It could be that female chromosomes have a part to play in what appears to be women's greater resistance to infectious disease (Waldron, 1983). However, such physiological differences, though important, are beyond a social science approach to health and illness.

Although <u>variations in lifestyle</u> cannot account for the mortality difference between men and women, there are nevertheless important <u>social factors</u> that play some part, and need to be considered. One of these is <u>marital status</u>, as shown for England and Wales in Figure 6.1. The excess is smallest for married men, meaning that they have a death rate most similar to married women. Women who are single, widowed or divorced enjoy a greater advantage over men in a similar situation to their own. This implies either that marriage is beneficial to men, and/or that it is disadvantageous to women.

An analysis of data from the 1971 British census has shown that the inference of disadvantage is not true relative to other women (Moser et al., 1988). Data from this study are shown in Table 6.2, comparing women who were single with married women classed according to their own occupation and women who were not themselves employed (principally housewives and students).

Table 6.2 shows that, overall, the highest standardized mortality ratio (i.e. the worst incidence of death) attaches to single women (108), followed by married women without an occupation (101) and then married women in employment (88). Within the table it can be seen that women who (a) belong to a manual social class, (b) are in local authority rented accommodation and (c) have no car have higher ratios. These differences were particularly marked in the case of single women and married women without employment. They show that it is important to understand differences between women in different situations, just as it is to comprehend how women differ from men. The data also suggest that the lowered mortality ratio for married men might need to be interpreted differently, depending upon whether the wife is employed or works in the home. As the next section will show, we need to understand the role situations of men and women together, not just the differences between men and women taken as two homogeneous populations.

One feature that might promote women's mortality advantage is the possibility that they are more sensitive to illness, or look after themselves better once they become ill. After examining mortality data relating to both the occurrence and the progression of disease, Waldron (1983) concluded that there is no strong evidence for the latter hypothesis. An alternative case can be made for the possibility that disease in women might be diagnosed earlier, owing to the fact that women see doctors more often for check-ups. In the USA, estimates have been made of the number of visits by women for

Table 6.2 *Mortality among single and married women aged 15–59 at death: Great Britain, 1976–81 (numbers of observed deaths given in parentheses)*

	Single women		Married women			
			With occupational class		'Unoccupied'	
	Standardized mortality ratio	95% confidence interval	Standardized mortality ratio	95% confidence interval	Standardized mortality ratio	95% confidence interval
Own social class						
Non-manual	84 (68)	65–105	79 (262)	69–89	–	–
Manual	160 (62)	122–203	97 (310)	87–109	–	–
Husband's social class:						
Non-manual	–	–	72 (172)	62–84	71 (155)	60–83
Manual	–	–	96 (400)	87–106	121 (383)	109–134
Housing tenure						
Owner occupied	85 (48)	62–111	79 (269)	69–88	84 (258)	74–94
Privately rented			93 (79)	73–115	111 (75)	87–138
Local authority rented	129 (82)	102–159	99 (223)	86–113	130 (203)	112–148
Cars in household						
Car(s)	80 (44)	57–105	83 (394)	75–92	83 (312)	74–92
No car	133 (86)	106–163	99 (177)	85–115	144 (224)	125–164
All (as defined in this analysis)	108 (130)	90–128	88 (572)	80–95	101 (538)	92–110

Note: Discrepancies in some totals due to non-response.

Source: Moser et al., 1988

pregnancy, gynaecological or breast examination, or disease connected with the genitourinary system. These account for 79 per cent of the female excess visits (i.e. over men) between the ages of 15 and 24, and 60 per cent between the ages of 25 and 44 (Waldron, 1983).

On the point about sensitivity to illness, it has been suggested that women's greater experience of medical attention leads them to be more knowledgeable about their bodies (Umberson, 1992). This knowledge has a secondary benefit for married men (and, presumably, those co-habiting) who report that their spouse (partner) is likely to monitor their health and encourage them in positive health behaviour. After getting divorced or after the death of their wife, this support will be withdrawn, and men are then more likely to increase their tobacco and alcohol consumption (Umberson, 1992). This finding is consistent with the idea of a mortality advantage for married over single men, though it focuses only upon what is done for them by their wives, rather than what they might do for their own health, i.e. men benefit from the social support that marriage provides.

The matter of sensitivity to illness, and the greater use of physician services by women, are consistent with the notion that, overall, women might just *appear* to be more ill than men. This is the problem to which we now turn, and is one that lends itself to a fuller analysis than does the question of mortality differences. We have seen enough already – about culture and health beliefs, as well as about the designation and recognition of signs as symptoms – to expect that these social processes will be worked out differently, depending upon the gender of the person concerned.

Differences in morbidity between men and women

The term *morbidity* is used to refer to the extent or to the frequency of illness within a group or a population. What is meant by illness in this context is subject to definition. It might mean the presence of disease as diagnosed by a physician, so that the basis of measurement would be doctors' judgements given in medical records. However, in many research studies in this field, illness is assessed by asking individuals to give information about their own state of health. In Chapter 3, when discussing the 'illness iceberg', we discussed the reason why researchers might be loath to restrict their analyses only to people who take their symptoms to the clinic. Much illness never gets to the doctor, so that estimating how often a group of people feel unwell, or take time off work, must take account of what they themselves say about it.

There are three ways of measuring illness that have been regularly used in studies of morbidity. One is to ask people to say if they have *felt unwell* or had any symptoms in a stated recent period (e.g. the four weeks prior to the interview). Another is to ask if they have been *restricted in their normal activities* as a result of feeling unwell or through injury. The third measure asks if they have been *taking any prescribed medication* in the recent past, or have visited their doctor. Questions are often asked about whether any

Table 6.3   *Acute sickness: percentage who reported restricted activity in the 14 days before interview: Great Britain, 1991*

Economic activity status	Men (age)				Women (age)			
	16–44	45–64	65 and over	Total	16–44	45–64	65 and over	Total
Working	8	8	8	8	11	11	13	11
Unemployed	6	7	[0]	6	12	9	[0]	12
Economically inactive	18	28	16	19	13	17	18	17
All persons	9	12	15	11	12	13	18	14

Source: OPCS, 1993

illness reported is temporary (an acute condition, e.g. influenza) or whether it is of a chronic or long-standing nature (e.g. arthritis). Each of these questions taps something slightly different about illness and, for that reason, they are often used in combination. From the separation of disease and illness we know that it is possible to feel unwell without restriction or treatment; that one can take time off work but not see the doctor; and that people can take medicine for a condition that does not make them feel unwell (e.g. high blood pressure). To use one of these indices alone as the sole measure of morbidity would be to risk making a partial analysis of the problem as a whole.

In developed countries, in spite of women's advantage with regard to mortality, studies have repeatedly shown them to have a higher prevalence of morbidity than men (Rodin and Ickovics, 1990). This has been found in relation to numbers of symptoms reported, amount of restricted activity and amount of prescribed medication taken. Tables 6.3 and 6.4 show recent data from Great Britain (OPCS, 1993) indicating that, overall, women report more restricted activity due to acute illness than men, and report more frequent recent visits to an NHS general practitioner. The tables also show, however, that men who are economically inactive (classed as either not seeking or not wanting work) report high levels of illness on both measures, suggesting that there might be wide variations within the two gender populations.

Perhaps the clearest statement regarding why women have excess morbidity over men was made by Nathanson (1975), who first removed from her data all illness, disability and visits to doctors associated with pregnancy and childbirth. Expressing the rates of different measures of illness as a female/male ratio, she found that, without exception, these indicated that women report more illness than men (a ratio greater than 1). For acute conditions the ratio was 1:2; for days of restricted activity it was 1:3; and relating to visits to the physician it was 1:3.

Table 6.4   *(NHS) GP consultations: percentage who consulted a doctor in the 14 days before interview: Great Britain, 1991*

Economic activity status	Men (age)				Women (age)			
	16–44	45–64	65 and over	Total	16–44	45–64	65 and over	Total
Working	8	9	12	8	14	15	10	14
Unemployed	10	11	[0]	10	25	13	[0]	22
Economically inactive	18	22	19	20	20	20	19	20
All persons	9	11	18	11	17	17	19	17

Source: OPCS, 1993

Nathanson set out three *possible* explanations that might account for these results:

1   The findings depend upon people's *verbal reports*. These result from the fact that it is culturally *more* acceptable for women to say that they are ill. By the same token, it is culturally *less* acceptable for men to say that they are ill, because (it can be conjectured) this is paramount to an admission of weakness.
2   Because of the domestic situation of many women, it is *easier* for them *to take up the sick role*. However, because many men are in employment, they are less able to take time off to be sick.
3   Women's lives, and the roles that many of them occupy, give rise to *more stress* than do the life situations of men. Women are ill more often because their situation makes them so.

At the time Nathanson set out these hypotheses, there was insufficient evidence upon which to evaluate the alternative explanations. However, she did point to an important difference between the first two hypotheses and the third. Both explanations (1) and (2) involve women's *behaviour* in response to illness; that is, what they say or do in relation to cultural norms and roles. By comparison, the third possible explanation proposes a direct link between a woman's circumstances and her health status. It is, in essence, *a stress model* in which illness is 'caused' as a direct result of 'strains' endemic in women's life situations. It was the option Nathanson favoured least in her paper, not only because it seemed unable to explain certain data, but also because it stands in line with explanations of a reductionist kind, which locate women's problems in their essential make-up. By not allowing for a distinction between 'illness' and 'illness behaviour', the stress model detracts from an analysis of the differential scope that women and men might have to change their role situation in the pursuit of better health.

Since the publication of this article there has been a considerable amount of research carried out into women's health, both in terms of comparisons

with men and in terms of differences between women in various life settings. However, we can still use Nathanson's original three hypotheses as a
way of surveying these data, in order to evaluate once again their relative
merits.

1   *Illness as reported – the 'cultural acceptability' alternative*

This explanation was put forward by Phillips and Segal (1969), in the context of a study of sex differences in the reporting of psychiatric symptoms.
Comparing men and women who had similar levels of physical illness, they
found that, as the level of illness became more marked, so women were apt
to express more psychological difficulties than men. They interpreted this
to mean that women are more likely to express signs of emotional tension,
which might then be seen by health professionals as signs of psychological
disturbance. This is explained in terms of a basic difference in cultural expectations, embedded in the distinction drawn by social psychologists between the instrumental roles assumed to be played by men, and the
expressive roles assumed to be played by women (Zelditch, 1956).

Although they both report a similar number of complaints to their
doctor, American women report a greater *variety* of illnesses than do men,
and tend to combine physical and mental symptoms in their complaints
more than men do (Verbrugge, 1980a). Similar results have been found in
a recent British study showing that men's consulting is associated with the
presence of physical symptoms, while for women consulting is associated
with a need for 'psychological help-seeking' (Briscoe, 1987). (This does not
mean that women do not have physical symptoms, but rather that men and
women interpret, and therefore present, their complaints in different
ways.)

Verbrugge (1980a) also found that physicians are more likely to give
women an unclear diagnosis, or to assign them a diagnosis of mental disorder. This implies, as it must if we talk of cultural expectations, that doctors have different views about symptom reporting by men and women.
Indeed, they tend to feel that women are more emotional than men
(Bernstein and Kane, 1981). For that reason perhaps, physicians weight
the psychological component of the illness more heavily when the patient is
a woman, and have been found to be more pessimistic about women's
health in general (Wallen et al., 1979).

What does all of this suggest about the importance of illness reporting by
men and women? It has not been shown that the amount of difference in
reporting can explain women's excess morbidity. Instead, it suggests that
how men and women report their illness is different, and that this difference will matter both to doctors and to researchers too. As has been
pointed out, one cannot begin by assuming a common set of symptoms for
everybody and then looking to see how men and women report them, because *the definition of what is a medical problem is itself gendered* (Cleary et
al., 1982). For example, an abdominal pain experienced by a woman who

is menstruating will be perceived and acted upon by her in one way. This will be different from the response of a man suffering from an abdominal pain that he believes was caused by heavy lifting at work.

This last point was made some time ago by Phillips and Segal (1969), who noted that the items in their index (used to measure psychological disturbance) emphasized passive discomfort (e.g. feeling depressed). It did not contain a single item to do with expressing anger, losing one's temper or being irritable. If it is the cultural assumption that women are more likely to adopt the former ways of expression and men the latter, then men will fail to check items on this scale simply because they are less descriptive of their way of reacting to events. While it is possible to alter the scale to make it more applicable to both sexes, this misses the theoretical point. Symptoms do not objectively exist; they are made to appear in the context of a biographical situation, a key element of which is whether one is a woman or a man. In conclusion, it can be said that there are differences in the way that women and men report symptoms but, on the evidence available, this does not account for the observed excess morbidity of women.

2   The 'role compatibility/multiplicity' explanation

In her original paper, Nathanson (1975) concluded that women with a large number of obligations are less likely to adopt the sick role. This is somewhat different to the way that the argument was initially posed, i.e. that women are ill more than men because the structure of their life situation allows them to be so. In fact, the revised explanation was to become elaborated into a number of hypotheses, some of them focusing upon the possible benefits of having multiple roles. The original argument had been couched in terms of the controls that roles provide (e.g. the constraints of having to go to work). This derives from the writing of Parsons, who also saw controls as being exerted in the domestic setting. He had suggested that women with young children to look after would be less able to go sick, owing to the disruption to the family that this would cause (Parsons and Fox, 1952). Later on, however, explanations came to focus upon the benefits and costs that might attach to holding down several roles at one time. Therefore, whether women become ill more often is not only a matter of whether their domestic role 'allows' them to do so (a functional effect). It might also be because certain role combinations make positive or negative contributions to their sense of well-being (a symbolic effect).

Nathanson (1980) set out to test the hypothesis that women with heavy role obligations will be less likely to take action in response to symptoms. Also, that where they do take action, this will be in terms of visiting a physician rather than self-treatment at home. She used survey data to compare the self-ratings of health of employed women and housewives who were (a) married, (b) divorced or separated and (c) widowed. Table 6.5 shows the percentage of women in each of these groups who judged themselves to be in 'excellent' health.

Table 6.5 *Marital status, children, employment and subjective health appraisals among women, age 45–64; percentage with 'excellent' health; USA, 1974*

Presence or absence of children at home	Marital status and employment					
	Married		Divorced/separated		Widowed	
	Employed	Housewives	Employed	Housewives	Employed	Housewives
Children	36.8	30.5	36.4	13.0	38.0	21.2
(*N*)	(1,442)	(2,535)	(228)	(131)	(213)	(250)
No children	36.4	26.6	44.1	15.1	41.6	22.0
(*N*)	(1,791)	(2,881)	(396)	(199)	(531)	(514)

Source: Nathanson, 1980

Looking at the entries for married women, it is clear that employment makes relatively little difference to their subjective health status. In contrast, employment has marked effects on the health of both divorced/separated women and those who are widowed. Housewives in both groups report considerably worse health than women who are employed. In a further analysis, Nathanson examined the health ratings according to the women's highest level of education. It was found that only among those with less than high school education did employment have an effect on perceived health status. In this group, employed women had markedly higher self-ratings of 'excellent' health than did housewives.

The interpretation of these results is that employment has a positive effect on perceived health, *particularly for women lacking other means of establishing status in society* (i.e. divorced, widowed, those with little education). This has also been shown to be true for women's feelings of general well-being. Paid employment is particularly conducive to 'feeling good psychologically' among single women rather than the married, and among working-class rather than among middle-class women (Warr and Parry, 1982). However, one Scandinavian study showed that the increased life satisfaction and lower morbidity levels enjoyed by employed married women were offset by their reporting frequent symptoms of anxiety. These anxiety reports were higher than those given by married women who stayed at home (Haavio-Mannila, 1986).

How the positive health effect of employment is achieved is difficult to establish on the basis of these data alone. However, Nathanson (1980) found support for the idea of multiple roles helping to contain symptoms (similar to the 'high containment' situation shown in Table 4.1). Women with heavier obligations (employed and having young children) were more likely to visit a physician than restrict their activities at home. That is, family and work duties meant that these women perhaps needed to 'get some help quick' rather than take time out from everyday obligations. On the other hand, there is a strong indication here that work provides positive benefits, and that traditionally these have been enjoyed more by men than by women. The data also show, once more, the importance of considering the different situations of women (and men), rather than trying to compare them as homogeneous populations.

How do these findings stand up when men and women are compared with reference to their employment status? In one study examining the effects of multiple roles, it was found that the greater amount of women's self-reported illness disappeared if one statistically controlled for the effects of social roles such as employment (Verbrugge, 1983). When the health profiles of the sexes were examined, it was shown that those having the *best* health among men were employed, married fathers. Among women it was employed, married mothers (and employed non-married mothers as well). Defining the *worst* health for specific groups of men was difficult. However, women with the poorest health were those who were unemployed, not married and childless (often older widows).

It may be that the various social role features carry different significance for men and for women. In one reanalysis of British survey data, it was concluded that health inequalities for men are primarily associated with unemployment and occupational class, pointing to financial and material disadvantage as key variables. By comparison, health disadvantage for women was associated with non-employment (either being a housewife or unemployed), class, marital status (being separated or widowed) and not having dependent children (Arber, 1991). That is, the meaning of work – what it can provide and what it demands in terms of health – may be different for men and for women.

What these studies show is that observed sex differences in health status are not about men and women per se, but about the kinds of social roles that they tend to occupy in society. This is supported by cross-national evidence showing that when social policy is geared to helping women work outside the home, their health is favoured in comparison to that of men (Haavio-Mannila, 1986). However, why employment should have a beneficial effect on health is difficult to deduce from survey data alone. The original notion of role compatibility – that women's (domestic) role is more compatible with the sick role than men's (employment) role – receives some support from the studies cited here. However, in being expanded into a hypothesis about 'role enhancement', it proposes that occupying a number of roles is itself health enhancing. This is either because of some emotional benefit of social involvement, or because the threshold for perceiving symptoms is raised when one is a busy participant in life (Verbrugge, 1983).

However, there remains the problem for these studies of what has been termed 'the healthy worker effect'. This refers to the confounding of the data by the likelihood that women (and men) with poor health will fail to re-enter the labour force (Repetti et al., 1989). Unless one takes this into account (and many earlier studies did not), there is always the possibility that the findings we have reviewed reflect the fact that healthy women are able to find employment, while less healthy women must stay at home. This is, of course, to suggest a causal effect in the opposite direction to the one which nearly all researchers have been examining.

A recent British study, reanalysing data from the *Health and Lifestyles Survey*, did control for health status when examining symptom reporting by women in different social situations (Bartley et al., 1992). These researchers found that women in professional and managerial occupations had fewest symptoms when doing part-time paid work or no work at all. The women in manual occupations who reported they were healthiest were those working part-time; those least healthy were doing no paid work. This means that 'being a housewife' has different health implications for women from professional and from manual backgrounds. For women in the professional class, who have available a range of status-enhancing aspects to their lives, full-time work is unlikely to bring the advantages (financial and symbolic) that it gives to women from manual sectors of society. In fact, this study found some disadvantage in physical health, and no advantage in mental health for professional women who worked full-time. This conclusion has to be qualified, however; the reasons for doing work, the pleasantness of the work and other demands on time are also important matters. Data from two separate surveys in Britain suggest that, for working-class women up to the age of 30–40 with children, employment is associated with higher levels of illness. This is not true for women from professional and managerial backgrounds (Arber et al., 1985; Blaxter, 1990).

As this section has shown, there has been a shift in emphasis in the discussion of whether women report more illness because their roles allow them to 'go sick' more easily. In effect, this prediction rested upon assumptions about men and women being homogeneous groups, holding down traditional sex roles; the men being in employment and the women looking after the home. Closer analysis of the health of men and women in various life settings has exposed this as an oversimplification, a prediction too crude to yield a fruitful answer. It appears instead, on the basis of available evidence, that it is employment that has beneficial effects for both men and women. For women who have few opportunities to enhance their material and status levels (e.g. the poor, the separated/widowed, those without children), employment offers the best chance of health benefits. This, of course, still does not explain why women in these disadvantaged social settings are ill more often.

3   The 'nurturance/stress' explanation

Nathanson's third alternative explanation was that women's assigned social roles are essentially less satisfactory than those of men, with the result that they have more illness. On reflection, it can be seen that the first part of this statement is not incompatible with the studies that we have just reviewed above. Women whose economic and educational disadvantages restrict their life-opportunities, and limit them to traditional domestic roles, are those who *report* more illness. The key difference between this statement and the third explanation is the proposition that it is something about the traditional homemaker role *in itself* that makes women ill; they have more (real) illness. This view is identified with the work of Gove and Hughes (1979), who used measures of 'nurturant role demands' to show that, once these are statistically controlled, the sex difference in health status is removed. This, they argued, shows that the obligations of women to look after others in the family have a negative effect upon their own self-care. There are two aspects to these demands: (1) that women will find it more difficult to adopt the sick role, and (2) the excessive demands from other family members impair women's ability to rest and relax. Together these work to make women run down and eventually to become ill.

It is because of the imputed link between role-assignment and illness that this explanation has been called a 'stress model' (Nathanson, 1975). It has been criticized on several grounds concerning its methods of research (Marcus and Seeman, 1981; Verbrugge, 1980b). Perhaps the major criticism is the difficulty of separating out 'real illness' from 'illness behaviour'. For example, several studies have found that women with more nurturant roles (especially those with young children) report better health. This could mean that they have no symptoms, or it could mean that they interpret (i.e. ignore) bodily signs in the context of more pressing maternal duties. Which of these alternatives is 'true' is not identifiable from studies that cannot distinguish between a 'real' and a 'reported' symptom. In effect, this is a theoretical, not an empirical, distinction. The assertion of one condition (e.g. illness behaviour) also tacitly assumes the other (the illness itself). This might seem a rather abstract point to make, but it leads to an important conclusion. It is impossible to test which of these alternatives is 'true' within the kind of research designs typically used to address this problem. It is also a position challenged by the social constructionist viewpoint introduced in Chapter 2 and developed in our discussion of bodily (sign-to-symptom) experience. If people construct their reality, then there can be no objective or 'real' illness, only illness as it is experienced in the context of people's lives.

Some of the problems that surround the idea of illness resulting from stress will be discussed in detail in Chapter 8. With respect to women's health, we need to remind ourselves that illness is not a unitary concept. This means that bodily signs will be interpreted in different ways, so that being sick will be different for women and men according to their situation. The question that we have to ask ourselves in this chapter is: What is significant about these experiences for women and for men (in Western culture)?

To answer this question we shall need to move away from the kind of data that have held our attention in this section. While survey data can provide important bases for asking questions, and for preventing us making false generalizations on the basis of local observations, in the end they are limited by their distance from the problem. The categorization and quantification of people's experience renders it uniform, so that one speaks of 'employment' or 'being divorced' or 'having children' as if these things had the same meaning for all concerned. This is an assumption that has been challenged, not least by feminist social scientists working in the field of health care. We need to turn to this critique to see how it might help us appreciate what illness means to women, and through that to get a better grasp of what we mean by 'illness' as a concept (Clarke, 1983).

A 'methodological' note

One of the problems relating to the kind of survey data discussed in the previous section is that they rest upon the assumption that people will report their illness 'accurately'. We have already seen that this is quite a large, and probably an unwarranted, assumption to make, if researchers are looking to count episodes of 'real' illness. In comparisons of the sexes, it has been found that men and women do not report the same symptoms, perhaps because different signs mean different things to them (Waldron, 1983). Also, there is a belief that because women are at home more often when interviewers call, they provide data about their spouse or partner as well. Although it is unclear how widespread it is, this kind of proxy reporting might work to diminish men's apparent morbidity, as women respondents are more likely to remember (or indeed, know of) their own bodily discomfort, as compared with that of their partners.

Beyond these kinds of criticisms, however, is the fundamental one of whether objective, quantitative methods like the survey are suitable for getting at what 'we' want to know about health and illness of women. I have placed the word 'we' in inverted commas to draw attention to the fact that it assumes a commonality among readers (and investigators) that should be questioned. In an article discussing the assumptions behind interviewing as a research method, Oakley (1993) has examined what happens when women interview women. In the course of interviewing women about pregnancy, she found that they asked her questions, and made references to experiences that they assumed were common to them both. That is, because both interviewer and interviewee shared membership of the same (disadvantaged) group, this gave rise to common ground that enabled certain matters to be raised which might otherwise not have been broached. Oakley argues that for her to accept this basis of equality, this shared experience of womanhood, made it necessary for her to question, if not abandon, the guidelines of objectivity to which 'good interviewers' are expected to adhere. She concludes that the 'proper interview', conceived as a technical device for maintaining a psychological distance between interviewer and interviewee, is a 'masculine fiction' (1993: 240).

It is possible to relate this idea of the interview to the kind of survey data that we have been considering for much of this chapter. The interview's function is to act as the medium through which data from men and women become 'universalized', are organized into the same categories defined by dimensions assumed to cover the experience of both sexes. Oakley's experience, articulated into a critique, points to these categories and this kind of methodology having their source in men's ways of thinking, rather than women's.

We can relate this to the discussion in Chapter 3 concerning the difference between 'public' and 'private' accounts of health and illness. There it was suggested that formal questions invite people to take the perspective of the dominant ideology in society. While this is not restricted to a medical way of thinking, the views of a male-dominated medical hierarchy are important in fashioning the 'public' accounts that people give. For this reason, we can see why the interview appears to sustain a 'masculine' way of seeing the world, a way that turns people's subjectivity into 'sources of error'.

The importance of this critique for our discussion is twofold. First, it raises questions about the limits of survey studies on which most of the analysis has, so far, been based. One answer might be that, until now, this has been the main form of research into sex differences in health and illness. While this is true, it does not satisfy the criticism that such data do not allow the special experiences of women or men into the analysis. Statistical comparisons, when significant, call out for explanations that the data cannot provide, concerning the feelings and the values that underlie people's statements about their health and their way of life. In relation to women particularly, Martin has posed the questions, 'How do women react to their circumstances? . . . Do they find them acceptable and unquestionable but not changeable facts of life? Or do they find them outrageous and intolerable?' (1987: 22). We shall touch on some illustrative answers to these questions in the following chapter, when we look at how people live with chronic illness. For the moment, we shall examine the question of women's perspective in more general terms, and then relate this to gender, illness and the sick role.

Femininity, masculinity and health

The criticism relating to the masculine form of the interview is but one example of a larger concern. This has been articulated by feminist scholars as the way in which the world of men stands in authority over the world of women. In particular, the domestic world is subordinate to the sphere of work, which is dominated, in its higher echelons, by men. This has meant that, in the history of social science, women (in their domestic circumstances) have been made effectively invisible. (This is the general point already made, specifically, about survey interviews.)

Smith (1974) has argued that abstractions and objectivity are particular features of the world of men, who are enabled to enter this world fully by being liberated from having to attend to the mundane, bodily needs associated with the home. These needs are traditionally met by women, both in the home (in all aspects of housework and childcare) and in the workplace at points where the abstract world meets the mundane sphere. For example, (female) secretaries organize their boss's day; (female) nurses draw the blood sample from the patient; (female) interviewers collect the data for the survey. The consequence of this is not just that 'women's work' is undervalued, but that its form (being bound up with a bodily commitment to these kinds of tasks) is difficult to capture in abstract terms. Sociology and social psychology contribute to this situation by transposing all 'immediate and concrete features of experience' into abstract concepts (Smith, 1974). This is also true for women social scientists; women researchers who adopt the abstract, objective perspective of organized science must cross a 'gap' in their existence. What Smith is proposing is that the domestic sphere for women – changing nappies, cleaning up after other members of the family, and, indeed, caring for them when they are sick – is not well represented in our textbooks. This is because it is of a different form to activities that involve abstraction and technical procedures.

The relevance of this argument for our discussion should be apparent, if not altogether clear. The questions that arose in the survey of studies comparing the health of men and women all gravitated towards the issue of what is special about roles occupied by the sexes. What, for example, does it mean for a young woman to be married, with young children but need to go out to work? How does someone in this position put together these different demands, and does this affect the recognition of bodily signs and the action taken towards them? These questions call for a different kind of evidence from that provided by the sample survey, useful as this methodology is for disciplining the generalizations that we make. It is this kind of evidence that is being sought by feminist researchers who give full weight to the reported experiences of those to whom they speak (McBride and McBride, 1981; Martin, 1987; Oakley, 1993). For example, one study of women who had been forcibly made unemployed detailed the way in which their relegation to the home involved them in filling up the day with housework (Bloch, 1987). Their experiences of this time were matters that they could not easily articulate, but which found symptomatic expression in wordless feelings of 'fatigue' and 'heaviness'.

Clearly, not all experiences of working in the home are the same, nor all ways of acting when one becomes ill. When it comes to differences between the sexes, assumptions about 'going sick' have been shown to differ in a qualitative way. In her study of couples in East London, Cornwell (1984) reports that for the men the question was whether they were fit enough to go to work. If they were, then they spoke of 'working off' their symptoms. If they were not well enough for work, they stayed at home, where they expected their wives to look after them, and to show them sympathy. Cornwell says that this was something that the wives did, but not without some feeling of resentment. This resentment arose from contrasting their husbands' sickness experience to their own. When they were ill, the wives said, they had to carry on and do what they had to do, seeing a doctor if necessary in order to 'put them back on their feet looking after the children' (1984: 140).

Relevant to this point, it has been said that, in contrast to housework, employment possesses an all-or-none quality (Brown and Rawlinson, 1977).

The domestic situation is different because it is both the appropriate place for sick role enactment and it is (for women) the place of work. This means that, simultaneously, housewives may alternate between performing domestic tasks and engaging in sick role behaviours like bed rest. From the traditional perspective of men, this might appear like a favourable opportunity to 'play sick' (the 'role compatibility' hypothesis once again), whereas, from a woman's perspective, this flexibility reflects the special burden of her sickplace also becoming, hour by hour, a visible testament to a whole series of unfinished and undone household tasks.

How, then, is the world of work gendered? At the level of manual work, physical labouring takes on certain sensual overtones; the toughness, the awkwardness, the fatigue-engendering aspects are positively associated with maleness. This cross-relation of gender with labouring gives to masculinity a particular outward form (Willis, 1977). Once established as a masculine style, it becomes a way of dealing with other aspects of life, perhaps in a 'hard' or 'macho' way. This style is then likely to be adopted in the way such men deal with other areas of life. This includes illness, and its consequences for restrictions in the power of the body to do manual work.

The masculine style is not, of course, restricted to physical work. From her studies of work organizations, Kanter (1975) has proposed that the 'spirit of managerialism' has been suffused with the masculine ethic. This ethic emphasizes the need for successful managers to show tough-mindedness, and to put aside personal emotions in the rational interests of the firm. The masculine ethos is therefore something that becomes infused into the very organizational structure, so that what we call a 'managerial style' is not simply a personal characteristic, but a way of being that draws upon a sphere of activity that is gendered. We shall see, when we look at the role of stress in causing illness (Chapter 8), just how important these issues are in everyday beliefs about how men and women fall prey to particular diseases.

What does this brief consideration of qualitative differences in the social worlds of men and women tell us about health and illness? First, it shows that explanations to do with either numbers or compatibility of roles assume that such roles mean the same for members of either sex. This is a questionable, and arguably a false, assumption to make. Second, it directs attention to what has been called here a 'masculine' or 'feminine' ethos, which has an external form in the way that the social world is organized (i.e. the sphere of work, the domestic sphere). Third, these styles can be conceived as being distinct from people's biological sex identity. Considered as gender-roles, masculinity and femininity are behaviour sets into which members of each sex are socialized. That is, it is possible for individuals of either sex to take on some of the behaviours from the 'opposite' gender-role, becoming andro-gynous in their self-concept and hence being free to engage in either 'masculine' or 'feminine' behaviours (Bem, 1974).

The research considered so far in this chapter was based upon sex (rather than gender) differences, allowing for the possibility of gender role distinction only in the comparison of women who either did, or did not, undertake paid work. A direct attempt to deal with this question was undertaken by Annandale and Hunt (1990), who compared the health of a sample of men and women, taking into account each individual's gender role orientation using the Bem Sex-Role Inventory (Bem, 1974). This is a self-report questionnaire that asks people to endorse a series of statements judged as being typical of either a 'masculine' or a 'feminine' orientation. Therefore, each person can gain a score on masculinity and femininity taken separately. The findings of this research showed first that, compared by sex, females reported poorer physical and mental health, more recent symptoms and visits to the doctor. However, when gender role orientation was taken into account, the effect of sex difference disappeared for scores on number of symptoms and GP visits. Going on to control for each gender role orientation separately, and for sex, the authors found that individuals who scored low on masculinity experienced an average 4.83 symptoms per month. By the same token, those who scored high on masculinity experienced an average 3.58 symptoms per month, these means being significantly different. Similar (but opposite) differences were obtained for the femininity score. High scorers had higher levels of symptom reporting than low scorers. When looking at self-assessed general health by gender role orientation, *those individuals with high masculinity scores had significantly better health* than those with low scores. *This was true for men and for women*, each sex treated separately. There were no such significant differences between individuals in terms of the femininity score.

These are intriguing findings for, as the authors conclude, they point towards an advantageous effect of high 'masculinity' and a disadvantageous effect of 'femininity', *irrespective of the person's sex*. This has consequences for how we think about the health of men and women. On the one hand, it raises questions about the place of 'feminine' qualities in men, and, on the other, it suggests that stepping out of their feminine role expectations (adopting a 'masculine' style) might have health benefits for women.

Does this mean that masculinity in itself carries health benefits, or, alternatively, that being healthy and active in social life tends towards the adoption of a 'masculine' attitude to life? In the final section of this chapter we shall discuss some of the issues arising from this question, and relate them to our earlier analysis of the sick role.

Women, 'masculinity' and the definition of illness

The studies comparing the prevalence of illness among men and women asked questions about 'how many?' or 'how much?' While these are useful, and indeed necessary, questions to ask, they do not bear directly upon the matter of how people make the transition from health to illness. This question involves the meaning that people place upon experience, and implies a need to know about the role of other individuals and social contexts in any change in health status. In short, the comparison of groups by use of the survey method depends upon what we called in Chapter 1 the 'societal perspective'. This is insufficient by itself to provide us with a thorough understanding of the problem.

To illustrate this difference in perspectives, recall that one of the issues in the survey analyses was whether role positions 'caused' health status, or whether health status made it possible for individuals to occupy certain roles. This way of thinking derives from the separation of these two features into distinct variables, a consequence of which is the need to see how they affect one another. Even on the basis of a brief examination of qualitative approaches to this question, it can be argued that good health and role occupation are 'tied up' with each other in the person's experience, making a one-way causal analysis implausible. Following through this criticism will give a different view of the question of illness and gender. It will also make use of ideas that were established earlier on in the book, about what happens when people become sick.

The finding relating illness to gender role orientation, as well as to sex difference, is consistent with the statement made some years before that, 'the ethic of health is masculine' (Phillips and Segal, 1969). I now want to put inverted commas around the word 'masculine' to show that it is not being male that is healthy (the mortality data tell quite a different story), but something about the 'masculine' gender orientation and how it is understood. This something is both subjective, relating to individual experience, and objective, in that it draws upon social structures (e.g. organizations, technical or clinical procedures). In saying this, I am pointing out that 'masculinity' and 'femininity' are not like personality traits, attaching to individual selves. They are orientations, in the strong sense of the word, directions of action that draw upon perspectives and images embodied in societal institutions and ideologies (Berger and Luckmann, 1971; Billig et al., 1988).

How could 'masculinity' be healthy? We can get some help on this question by referring back to the explanation that Herzlich (1973) gave concerning the social representation of health and illness (Chapter 3). Herzlich's argument is that the opposing of health and illness parallels the opposition between active involvement in, and withdrawal from, society. To be active is to be healthy; to be ill is to be withdrawn from society. Stated in this way, there is no essential difference between how men and women should conceive of illness. However, once we add the idea that the 'masculine' ethos defines a sphere in which individuals are concerned with meeting specifiable goals through rational procedures, while the 'feminine' ethos defines a sphere of nurturance, care and maintenance, then some proposals can be made. In particular, those individuals who are involved in the sphere of 'masculine' activity (particularly employment work) have access to a range of benefits. One of these is that merely to be able to fulfil one's duties is to be defined as well. Perhaps we should include here the idea that participation, or involvement, is itself conducive to containing symptoms. This is, in part, because one's attention is directed away from the body and its symptoms to more 'important' things (Alonzo, 1979). Good health may be 'masculine' because of the way that health has come to be defined in terms of paid work, not because it attaches to men as such.

Separating out sex from gender role orientation does not mean that those who participate within the 'masculine' sphere are automatically seen in this way. The problem for women who work, or who claim to orient themselves to the world in a 'masculine' way, is that their claim may not be validated by others. The picture drawn by Ehrenreich and English (1978) of the nineteenth-century middle-class woman with ambition, forced back into domestic passivity by her male doctor, is a telling example of this.

The question then arises: If health is 'masculine', is the ethic of illness 'feminine'? There has been a suggestion that doctors treat women patients differently according to whether they do or do not fit the stereotype of the 'feminine woman', with the implication that doctors prefer women to fit the traditional sex-role stereotype (Fisher and Groce, 1985). However, if one includes in this image of women the characteristics of being 'weak, capricious and . . . morbidly suggestible', then these qualities, applied to hysterical women in the nineteenth century, seem to have drawn negative evaluations from their doctors (Smith-Rosenberg, 1972).

This brings us back to the hypothesis that women are ill more often because it is culturally acceptable for them to be so. Having made the distinction between sex and gender, can we throw some light on this proposition? Are 'feminine' qualities those that are expected of the sick? There would seem to be a contradiction here, because evidence shows that medical staff who operate with a technical-instrumental model do not welcome emotional dependency or personal attachments in their patients (Emerson, 1970; Lorber, 1975). In Chapter 4 it was shown that medical staff have preferences for patients with cultural views that nearly match their own – a dispassionate approach, relying upon the expertise embodied in modern medicine.

One way out of this dilemma is to admit that there are contradictory elements in the way that women (and, perhaps, men) are treated by health professionals. The idea that doctors and nurses have a fixed medico-technical role has already been shown to fall short of the facts. Take, for instance, the example given in Chapter 5 of the doctor who went over stories from the elderly patient's past life in the course of conducting a physical examination. Similarly, Emerson (1970) notes that gynaecologists will talk to their patients in more personal, friendly tones when trying to get them to relax. Not all nurses adhere to the same view of care (Benner, 1984). Among British nurses, it has been shown that those with lower status in terms of technical training give greater importance to patients' emotional care, which, they believe, they are better at providing (Skevington, 1981).

The question then becomes: How and at what points is gender made important in the therapeutic relationship? One way of approaching this problem is by exploring the implications of 'femininity' for the sick role, where physician and patient are of the same or of different sex (Weisman and Teitelbaum, 1985). Studies of the importance of different social characteristics in specific situations suggest that the presence of the opposite sex makes gender more important, as one might expect (Abrams et al., 1990). However, once other aspects of the consultation are added, it raises questions as to when and how gender might be more or less important. Among these other aspects is ethnicity, where the cultural distance between doctor and patient is compounded by race and gender (Anderson, 1987). As well as this, the kind of complaint that is being treated is likely to be important. The naturalization of gender differences in 'women's complaints' almost certainly plays a part in the way that consultations concerning these conditions are conducted.

Rather than see the salience of gender as something that just happens when a particular set of circumstances arises in the consultation, one can argue that the consonance of 'femininity' with the sick role is something that serves particular purposes for specific individuals taking part. More 'feminine' characteristics, be they expressiveness or passivity, can be called out by either doctor or patient as part of the role definition that they wish to construct. Inviting patients into the sick role, in order to facilitate a physical examination, might make use of such qualities. Later on, needing their compliance in following a treatment programme leading to recovery, the doctor might request a more assertive, instrumental approach from the patient.

The explicit juxtaposition of *femininity* with sex role can underline status differences in the doctor–patient relationship, while also serving to mask the reason for the consultation. For example, British middle-aged women often have a deferential attitude to their GPs that is maintained by a strong belief in the doctor's personal goodwill towards them. In their study of women patients and their doctors, Barrett and Roberts (1978) concluded that this attitude led to the women being stereotyped by their physicians. This meant that the problems underlying the reason for their consultation were often not discussed. Being feminine in the consultation puts brackets, as it were, around the problems of the social role of women, and places these outside the boundary of discussion. Within this kind of consultation relationship, such problems can only appear as symptoms of the 'other side' of women's lives, appearing perhaps as headaches indicative of psychosomatic disease.

This stereotyping can also be seen in fictional accounts of medical situations. The importance of these in shaping our beliefs about how we should act in the consultation ought not to be underestimated. In this case, it is not so much the patient's role that is feminized, as the feminine role that is medicalized. In the context of the cinema it has been argued that one kind of 'woman's film' centres upon female madness or hysteria. It utilizes the device of the male doctor to 'eroticize' the medical relationship, thus making gender salient in the treatment of disease (de Lauretis, 1987). A different example of this en-gendering can be given, though this time working in the opposite direction as far as the sexes are concerned. It has been noted that young men who are involved with drugs will occasionally adopt a helpless, passive role in relation to young women from whom they demand care and attention (Auld et al., 1986). This feminizing of their situation by the men places the women in the role of 'nurse' or 'social worker'. As a consequence, sexuality in the form of gender-roles is deployed in the service of constructing an informal 'nurse–patient' relationship, the putative aim of which is to help the young men 'to come off drugs'.

These examples are useful in showing that the question is not best posed as to whether 'femininity' is or is not part of the sick role. Instead, the problem is to understand how and when issues of gender are deployed by doctors and patients in the course of their dealings with each other. One set of questions may concern male doctors and female patients (as well as women doctors and male patients). However, restricting the analysis to sex-role interactions will overlook how gender issues are either introduced or removed in the interests of the individuals and groups concerned.

Chapter summary

● Women and men have different relationships to medicine because of their different reproductive capacities; however, menstruation, pregnancy and childbirth have been fields in which ambiguity and conflict have marked the doctor–patient relationship.

● All the evidence shows that *women have a mortality advantage* over men. This advantage relates to improvements in health care and to the status of women in society. The higher death rate of men is partly explained by lifestyle factors, but owes much to a biological disadvantage compared to women.

● *Women show higher rates of morbidity* than men in terms of self-reported health, physician visits and other use of health services. These differences are affected by socio-cultural factors, but have also been explained in terms of women's roles being either (1) more able to assimilate the sick role, (2) compatible with the sick role, or (3) caused by negative features of their nurturant role.

● Evidence relating to these alternative explanations shows that *employment is health beneficial to women* (and to men). These benefits are particularly important in the case of women who have few other means of increasing their material and symbolic status in society.

● Feminist critiques propose that women's health cannot be understood by means of techniques that make men's and women's experience variations of the same theme. Attention must be paid to the special features of women's lives, within which their experience of health and illness is shaped.

● There is evidence that *the social construction of health and illness is gendered*. The imputation that health is 'masculine' has implications for the ways in which patients present themselves to doctors and how, in their turn, physicians conduct their clinical practice.

Further reading

Annandale, E. and Hunt, K. (1990) Masculinity, femininity and sex: an exploration of their relative contribution to explaining gender differences in health, *Sociology of Health and Illness*, 12, 24–46.

Kane, P. (1991) *Women's Health: From womb to tomb*. Basingstoke: Macmillan.

Miles, A. (1991) *Women, Health and Medicine*. Ballmoor: Open University Press.

Nathanson, C.A. (1975) Illness and the feminine role: a theoretical review, *Social Science and Medicine*, 9, 57–62.

Oakley, A. (1993) *Essays on Women, Medicine and Health*. Edinburgh: Edinburgh University Press.

Rodin, J. and Ickovics, J.R. (1990) Women's health: review and research agenda as we approach the 21st century, *American Psychologist*, 45, 1018–34.

7

Chronic Illness

Many of the examples of disease considered in previous chapters have been of temporary or relatively non-serious conditions, such as colds and influenza. In this chapter we turn to the study of what it means to have more serious, disabling and possibly life-threatening diseases, such as multiple sclerosis, heart disease or cancer. Once again, following the distinction made at the outset, we shall find it useful to differentiate between the disease condition as medically defined pathology, the illness as the experience of the afflicted person, and the sick role that sufferers occupy in relation to the healthy.

Why should we want to separate out chronic conditions from those which, by their temporary nature, are given the label 'acute'? Because these are, by definition, long-lasting illnesses, they raise a different set of questions about how people cope. When acutely ill, the individual moves from being a healthy person to being a patient at the doctor's surgery. However, when chronically ill, s/he changes from being healthy to having to live with illness in the world of health. That is, the chronically ill do not continuously occupy the status of 'sick people', like those who take to their bed with influenza or enter hospital for a minor operation. At least for part of the time, they cope with their condition as individuals who continue to participate in everyday life, but who yet make periodic claims upon doctors for help with a diagnosed disease.

For the most part, chronic diseases are intractable to medical treatment. There is no cure presently available for heart disease, some cancers, multiple sclerosis or rheumatism. Developments in medical technology are often aimed at hindering the course of these conditions (e.g. by-passing blocked coronary arteries), or else, at relieving suffering by use of drug therapy. In part, it is because of the success of modern medicine in combating infectious diseases like smallpox and polio that chronic diseases take up so much of the effort of medical staff today (at least in the West). Having said that, it is important not to assume that chronic disease cannot be infectious, nor that all infection has been eradicated in Western societies. AIDS is an infectious disease, but to contract it is then to live with a chronic illness. Tuberculosis was, until recently, regarded as a chronic disease of the past. However, it is now recurring among the poor of cities like New York and London, where it appears as both an infectious disease and a chronic illness.

Chronic diseases, particularly those like cancer that threaten life, are now central to the modern consciousness of what illness means (Herzlich and

Table 7.1   *Percentage who reported long-standing illness by sex, age and socio-economic group: Great Britain, 1991*

Socio-conomic group	Men (age)					Women (age)				
	0–15	16–44	45–64	65 and over	Total	0–15	16–44	45–64	65 and over	Total
Professionals and white-collar workers	15	21	37	59	28	14	21	36	58	28
Non-professional and manual workers	17	24	45	64	33	13	26	46	60	34
All persons	16	23	42	62	31	13	23	41	60	32

Source: OPCS, 1993

Pierret, 1987; Sontag, 1991). Part of this consciousness comes from medicine's uncertainty about how these diseases are caused and how to cure them. This uncertainty about cause can give rise to a fear of developing a disease like cancer that is perceived to 'just come out of the blue' (Blaxter, 1983). Paradoxically, it can also lead to an apparent lack of concern about diet and the prospect of getting heart disease. This is because there is no certainty that one's habits will affect one's chances of developing the condition (Davison et al., 1991). Nevertheless, the prevalence of chronic diseases has meant that there has been an increased effort to find the risk-factors that lead to onset and, where possible, to persuade people to modify their lives to minimize the risk. Therefore, both in the course of treating people with chronic diseases, and in order to persuade people to change their lifestyles, doctors have found that they must communicate with patients in a different way (Bury and Wood, 1979). As we shall see, because sufferers have to live with, manage and sometimes explain their problems to others, social psychological issues of communication and identity become central to understanding how people cope with chronic illness.

The likelihood of contracting a chronic disease grows with age. This trend is shown in Table 7.1. In an ageing population (such as exists in Western Europe today), more and more resources will need to be targeted at people who suffer in this way. The table also confirms that chronic diseases affect the poorer members of society more than those with better paid jobs. These conditions are especially prevalent among the unemployed in the lower socio-economic groups (Arber, 1987). This is an important point to keep in mind, because later on in this chapter we shall discuss the various ways in which individuals cope with having a chronic illness. Given this differential, the question must be asked whether it means that people must cope with serious illness in different ways.

There are two main features of chronic illness that we should note at the outset, because these will form the basis for much of the discussion in this chapter. One concerns the fact that these conditions are, by definition, chronic or long-lasting. The symptoms might not be there all of the time, but the person's knowledge of the existence of the underlying disease, and the likelihood of symptom recurrence, mean that recovery prospects are often limited at best. The time-scale involved gives chronic illness a particular temporal character, in which present suffering is always perceived against the background of past experience and future possibility (Bury, 1991). Also, because this experience is woven into the person's biography – age, point in the lifecourse, achievement of life-goals, the needs of others – so chronic disease takes its meaning in terms of how it might affect the remainder of the person's life. The future course of the disease, its direction and its speed, give it a significance that is missing in the case of temporary or acute illness.

The second feature to keep in mind is that not all chronic illnesses are the same. Among the most common such diseases in the UK (affecting about one-tenth of the population) are rheumatoid arthritis, cardio-respiratory disorders, multiple sclerosis and stroke (Anderson and Bury, 1988). People may live for many years with these conditions, which, in the short term or in the early stages, might not be regarded as life-threatening. Some, like the skin condition psoriasis, are not usually considered a threat to life, while others, such as cancer and heart disease, are invariably thought to be so.

Conrad (1987) has suggested that being placed in the position of someone likely to contract a disease in the future can also be classed as a 'third type' of chronic illness. Examples of this might include the knowledge that one has excessively high blood pressure, or a very high level of cholesterol in the blood, or is HIV positive. As a result, the person might take special precautions, or even 'mentally prepare' for the prospect of one day contracting the full disease entity (e.g. having a heart attack, developing AIDS). Therefore, the specific disease, the stage of its progress and whether its symptoms can be treated will all be salient features in the minds of people who are afflicted. Note that these are *medical* categories – to do with disease – and so they will matter to the extent that they are seen as providing the authoritative view of one's condition and likely future.

The sick role and the experience of the chronically ill

The idea of the 'chronic patient' is a relatively recent one within medicine, and only partly to do with medicine's success in controlling the infectious diseases. As we shall see in this section, there is more to a 'chronic patient' than being someone whose disease cannot be cured. In effect, for this particular role to be possible, doctors had to be prepared to take account of the effects of the disease upon the person, who in turn became not just a patient but a *sufferer*. In their account of how this came about over the last one hundred years or so, Arney and Bergen (1983) discuss the case of John Merrick, the 'Elephant Man'. He suffered from a genetic condition which meant that he was born with severe abnormalities of his body. They report the initial reaction of Frederick Treves, the London doctor who examined Merrick, who said:

> There was still more of the man than of the beast. The fact – that it was still human – was the most repellent attribute of the creature. There was nothing about it of the pitiableness of the misshapen or the deformed, nothing of the grotesqueness of the freak, but merely the loathing insinuation of a man being changed into an animal. (Arney and Bergen, 1983: 8)

These are the dispassionate comments of a doctor concerned only with disease, coupled with the reactions of horror common to the healthy who had (until he was taken into care) paid to see Merrick in a travelling 'freak show'. Later on, however, Treves was able to house Merrick in the hospital and to create for him a small circle of people who would treat him with respect and compassion. Then Treves saw more and more of 'Merrick-the-person', so that he could eventually write:

> From this day the transformation of Merrick commenced and he began to change, little by little, from a hunted thing into a man. It was a wonderful change to witness and one that never ceased to fascinate me. (Arney and Bergen, 1983: 9)

For Arney and Bergen this shows that the place of the chronic patient was created out of a coming together of the disciplined 'eye' of medicine and the compassionate 'heart' of social obligation. It implies that there has been a shift in the way that doctors see patients, if not all patients and if not all of the time. It also reveals something else that we shall examine in more detail below – that the compassion which the chronic patient elicits is from the world of the healthy. This means that it is the relationship of the sufferer to the world of health that has changed, not just that of the patient to the doctor.

There is an important consequence of taking the view that chronic disease means living with illness in a world of health. To understand the illness condition one must see things in the context of the person's life setting, or from their own point of view. This, the *insider's view* of illness, asks questions about such things as how people first notice that something is wrong, how they react to the diagnosis of the disease, and how they cope with the illness over the course of its progress (Conrad, 1987). The implication here is that the person must take his or her illness and cope with it in his or her own life, removed from the attentions of medical personnel. Where acute illness can be discussed from the perspective of the doctor (that is, from the standpoint of biomedicine), the special problems of living with chronic illness evade these kinds of explanations. Because the doctor cannot prescribe a course of treatment that will lead to a cure, the idea of the sick role, as we have discussed it in earlier chapters, appears less applicable. It has been argued that Parsons' formulation, which depended upon the patient being exempted from normal duties, cannot be applied to the person with a chronic illness precisely because they must continue with normal life as best they can (Segall, 1976). Also, the idea of the temporary legitimation

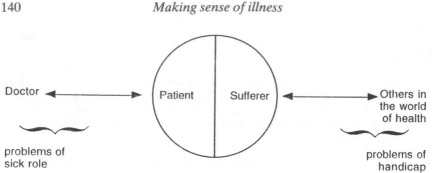

Figure 7.1   *The relationships of sick role and of handicap in chronic illness*

of sickness cannot apply where the person is almost certain to have the disease for the remainder of his or her life.

Another criticism of the sick role's relevance to chronic illness is that it is a formulation from the doctor's perspective (Conrad, 1990). This gives us an *outsider's view* of the condition, which cannot explain the variety of experiences that are so important to an understanding of chronic illness. At the level of specific actions and experiences this is certainly true. We shall see below that individuals have different ways of coping with chronic illness, so that defining them all within one set of role actions would be quite impossible. Also, the influence of the doctor is minimized where people are working out for themselves how to manage, from day to day, with practical difficulties that are outside medical knowledge and skills. Does this mean, however, that the concept of the sick role is of no use in this context?

We can approach this question from another angle, by remembering the effect that Merrick, the 'Elephant Man', initially had on Treves, the doctor. This was an effect that he had on many other 'normal' people of the time. Their reaction of abhorrence at his grotesque appearance was the other side of the compassion that, today, has become established as the accepted social reaction to the handicapped and the afflicted. Both *abhorrence and compassion* belong to the relationship of the sick (and the handicapped) to the healthy (and able-bodied). We need, therefore, to keep this in mind when discussing whether the sick role applies to the chronically ill.

As a way of analysing this further, Figure 7.1 sets out the relationship of the afflicted person to the doctor, on the one hand, and to healthy people, on the other. In this schematic representation, the person is shown as a divided figure. As a *patient*, the individual seeks treatment and may be granted occupancy of the sick role during periods of acute ill-health. As a *sufferer*, the intrusions of chronic disease (e.g. pain, fatigue, motor disability) have implications for the way that the individual relates to other people. Family and friends are likely to be the ones who offer help and compassion where necessary. Quite apart from these individuals will be others who are less well disposed to the afflicted person, who is therefore handicapped in his or her social exchanges with them.

The concept of *handicap* is useful here because it carries the double implication of compassion and abhorrence mentioned above. It should be distinguished from *impairment* (loss or abnormality of physiological or anatomical function), and from *disability* (restrictions in the ability to carry out tasks or to fulfil a role in a normal way) (Wood, 1980). As with the distinction between disease, illness and sickness, these terms do not necessarily fit together perfectly. It is possible (though not likely) to be severely disabled and suffer little handicap, or to be minimally impaired or disabled and yet suffer considerable handicap in relation to others. The point is that the term 'handicap' refers, like that of the sick role, to role expectations, values and identities. It captures, therefore, the disadvantage experienced by people with impairments or disabilities. This means that we can use it alongside the sick role concept to explore the special situation of the chronically ill.

One further point should be made about individuals schematically represented in Figure 7.1. When the chronically ill visit the doctor, they take with them the experiences and problems that derive from their relationships with others. (We have seen that modern medicine sees it as a legitimate part of its practice to 'manage' the chronically ill, e.g. to advise on lifestyle.) Similarly, when living their everyday lives, their diagnosis, treatment and legitimated claims to sickness are relevant to their situation. What the doctor has said to them matters. This is because medical knowledge makes sense of what is happening. It is also the basis of the claims of the chronically ill to special treatment at work or in the home. These individuals make adaptations in their everyday life and still have access to the sick role should their symptoms become severe, or if they need to go into hospital (Bury, 1982). For that reason it is unhelpful, and probably mistaken in many cases, to see the sick role and the handicap state as mutually exclusive terms.

As a conclusion to this section, it would appear that the concept of the sick role, defined in relation to the physician, is insufficient to embrace important aspects of chronic illness. However, this does not mean that it can be dispensed with altogether. Instead, it might be useful to develop the concept of handicap further, in order to see how these two ideas might together explain the experience of chronic illness. We now need to turn to an examination of that experience in order to colour in the rather abstract sketch that has been made so far. In this way it will be possible to say more regarding what is special about chronic illness, and how it compares to having acute conditions that have been the focus of much of the discussion up until now.

The impact of chronic illness: views from the 'inside'

This section is based upon one of the features mentioned in the introduction to the chapter – the temporal nature of chronic illness. This refers to the way in which the disease process and illness experience pass through stages, and to the interaction of these with the person's age and biographical position.

These different aspects give to chronic illness what Bury (1991) has called its *emergent* or *unfolding* character. A picture of what having a chronic illness means can be gained by looking at the stages through which individual sufferers pass. In this section we shall do just this, though it must be remembered that not all people who suffer from a chronic disease undergo the experiences detailed below. Because, on occasion, the initial symptoms may appear obscure, or even trivial, they are likely to be treated within the same terms as less serious and temporary disease. That is, in the early or acute phases of chronic illness, the sick role is seen as appropriate to consultation and treatment. Later on in the illness, questions of handicap are likely to become both more relevant and pressing.

Seeking help for symptoms

Whether people seek medical help for symptoms when they first appear depends upon their severity and how they are perceived. When the symptoms are relatively mild, it is often the case that they will be attributed to something ordinary in the person's life. One disease that is particularly difficult to diagnose in its early stages is multiple sclerosis. In one study, 85 per cent of the individuals questioned had perceived the initial symptoms as being non-serious (Stewart and Sullivan, 1982). Bodily signs were viewed as side-effects of minor ailments, as injuries, or attributed to personal situations (e.g. hard work or pregnancy). Only when these signs became recurrent or more severe did these people go to their doctor. This *temporalizing* is an example of one of Zola's (1973) triggers which indicate the breakdown of the accommodation to bodily change. Bury (1988) has shown how in the case of rheumatoid arthritis other triggers also illuminate the question of when and why individuals seek help. One woman, employed as a cleaner, continued to work with what she believed was just a 'frozen shoulder', but eventually sought medical help when one day she found that she could not comb her hair (Zola's 'interference with tasks').

Similar stories are told by individuals who have had chest pains that were eventually diagnosed as symptoms of coronary disease. There is an attempt to *normalize* the event by explaining the pain as being due to something ordinary and non-threatening, like indigestion (Cowie, 1976). Sometimes knowledge of the condition, say from knowing of others in the family who have suffered from it, will give the signs a significance that others might not recognize. As one man with heart disease reported: 'Oh, I went to the doctor, yes. It was somewhat reminiscent of our father was the old aching arms and angina type of thing' (Radley, 1988: 63).

Family history is one strand in the backcloth of features that are held in mind when people experience such symptoms. By comparison, among heart attack patients, it is not unusual to find some who insist later on that their chest pain was indigestion, and for that reason they resisted going to the doctor. In fact, Zola's argument might lead us to turn this around and say that the need to accommodate illness (i.e. not to give in) produced both the resistance and the misperception of the pain. Even when individuals do recognize the potential importance of what is happening to them, they might not wish to admit this to others, including close relatives. One man who had severe chest pains in the early morning got quietly out of bed without disturbing his wife, crept to the garage, and drove himself to his doctor's house where he promptly collapsed on the doctor's sitting-room floor (Radley, 1988).

Diagnosis: the problem of uncertainty

In the previous section, it was noted that multiple sclerosis sufferers first saw the early signs of this disease as being non-serious (Stewart and Sullivan, 1982). Later on, when the symptoms persisted or became more painful, they sought medical help for what they believed to be a short-term illness. In several cases the doctors could not make a reliable diagnosis, so that the patients were left feeling ill but without a clear medical judgement upon their condition. The effect of this difference in opinion was to place these individuals in an ambiguous position. This was one in which they viewed themselves as sick but were not medically defined as such. Here is a case of *illness*, once its signs have appeared, having to wait on the diagnosis of *disease*. Only then does this legitimate the adoption of the *sick role* by the person concerned.

Similar accounts have been given by individuals suffering from the symptoms of repetitive strain injury (RSI), for whom the failure to convince both doctors and employers of their illness is experienced by them as an assault on their character (Reid et al., 1991). In the case of employees who seek either changes in their working practice or compensation for their injury, there is the added dilemma of searching for relief, while at the same time having to dramatize symptoms to underline the continuation of the condition. When the doctor makes a definite diagnosis that satisfies both the need for treatment and the claim to occupy the sick role, this comes as a considerable relief for many sufferers. Now they have a name for their illness, they receive greater support from others who now see the illness as 'real', and they can place their future within some kind of stable perspective.

The gradual appearance of disease is quite different from, say, that of a heart attack that heralds the presence of pathology in a sudden and dramatic way. In a sense, *illness*, adopting *the sick role*, and the diagnosis of *disease* all come together in one short period of time. In cases where the attack is severe, requiring immediate admission to hospital, most patients are likely to accept the diagnosis and the need for a period of recovery. However, where the person has experienced only moderate chest pain, and the diagnosis has been made on the basis of a subsequent ECG, then there is scope to doubt the doctor's decision. In particular, doubts will be expressed where the diagnosis does not conform with expectations of who should be affected, and at what age. Individuals in their thirties, and those who have never smoked, drunk alcohol to excess or become unfit are among those who find a diagnosis of heart disease particularly difficult to accept (Radley, 1988).

Confirming the presence of chronic disease usually comes after the person has felt unwell and sought medical advice, although this is not always the case. It is possible for disease to be detected before the individual feels any of its signs, and therefore before there is any question of adopting the status of sick person. This happens as a result of check-ups and investigations where, for example, extremely high blood pressure or the presence of a tumour will mean that diagnosis sets a context within which future illness and sickness can be anticipated. This is a different experience from the previous two situations, and one in which doctors' knowledge will be the primary guide in the first instance. The hope will be, of course, that medical intervention at this pre-symptomatic stage will prevent the person from feeling ill, and eventually becoming chronically sick. An exception to this would be the diagnosis of someone as being HIV positive. Here the doubts about when the person became infected, together with the uncertainty about when and how symptoms will appear, generate real difficulties in foreseeing how the condition will evolve in the future (Pierret, 1992).

Here are three different ways in which people can discover that they have a chronic disease. In spite of this variation, one reaction has been found to be important in the experience of all chronic illness – that of *uncertainty*. Two instances of uncertainty have already been discussed, relating first to the meaning of symptoms and second to when a firm diagnosis cannot be made. In addition to this, uncertainty also follows diagnosis and relates to the future course of the disease: What will happen to me? How quickly will it progress? Will it be painful? Will I be able to continue to work?

Of course, not all patients ask these questions; at least, not openly. This was shown in a study of people diagnosed as suffering from Parkinson's disease (Pinder, 1990). There were those who were described as 'seekers', who actively sought for what was likely to happen. Their anxiety was so overwhelming that they were driven to find out as much as possible, though what they found sometimes led to further problems for them. Then there were 'weavers', whose need to know fluctuated. They selectively interpreted information that would suit them at the time. Finally there were 'avoiders' whose unacknowledged fears about what would happen led them to choose ignorance and to stay happy while they could. This strategy is of course one that many people choose in relation to regular check-ups that might reveal the presence of disease. Anxiety relates to knowing of threats both to our mortality and to our social identity. For example, studies have shown that 25–30 per cent of gay men avoid being tested for HIV mainly because a positive result would imply being discriminated against by others (Pierret, 1992).

One feature of 'not knowing' relates to the cause of one's illness. Attribution theory, a cognitive psychological approach, suggests that uncertainty should result in patients being particularly concerned to know what caused their disease. Studies that have used this approach with chronically ill people have found only modest support for this proposal (Lowery and Jacobsen, 1985; Taylor et al., 1984). Only a minority of patients may be concerned to see a causal attribute as important, and there is no simple relationship between the kind of attributions made and how well the patient is doing. Perhaps this shows the limitations of trying to apply general principles, drawn from experimental studies with healthy young adults, to the disruptive experience of sick people. That is to say, the form that uncertainty takes will vary both with the situation of the sufferer and with the temporal course of the illness (Molleman et al., 1986).

We shall see in the course of this chapter that uncertainty is endemic to the situation of the chronically ill, and is not limited to one period of time or to one situation. This arises from the fact that knowledge of the disease progression is but one aspect of the problem. Uncertainty remains as to how others will react when the person is incapacitated, and, in consequence, how the sufferer himself or herself will cope with this situation.

After diagnosis: the problem of disruption

Psychological assessment of patients admitted to hospital at the beginning of a chronic illness has shown them to be more anxious, depressed and angry than a control group of non-patients (Westbrook and Viney, 1982). This is perhaps not surprising, given that these reactions to the diagnosis of chronic disease follow it being perceived as a critical incident in the person's life. Bury (1982) has proposed the concept of *biographical disruption* as a way of defining this sense of the individual's lifecourse being undermined. For example, learning that one has Parkinson's disease or rheumatoid arthritis can lead to a sense of 'premature ageing'; suffering a heart attack at the age of 35 can have a significant impact upon the concept of oneself as a 'basically fit' person. It can be thought of, figuratively, as a tear in the fabric of one's life that can suddenly bring into question all of the assumptions upon which it was based.

Three dimensions have been proposed to be linked to this concept of threatened biography – biographical time, conception of self and bodily capacities (Corbin and Strauss, 1987). Because our bodies are the medium through which we engage the world and other people, when they are affected there are consequences at two different levels. On the level of *performance*, there are implications about what one must do to achieve things more slowly, or which activities might have to be given up altogether. In relation to *identity*, there are important consequences for how the illness will reflect upon the sufferer as a social individual. This quotation from a woman suffering from Parkinson's disease makes this pointedly clear:

> That's the worst thing, the lack of grace. I used to have a friend who said to me that I was deft. I've lost that deftness and I don't like it. I come out of the bank with money, a purse, a handbag and umbrella, and I don't know how to put them away. I've got to think which hand to move first. I resent being ungraceful and clumsy. (Pinder, 1990: 85)

Biographical disruption through chronic illness is often expressed in the question, 'How have I come to be like this, because it isn't me?' Williams (1984) has argued that the way we sustain our sense of the life-course is through narrative, the story that weaves together the variety of events and experiences that make up our life. He proposes that the tear in biography raises questions such as the one above, which the person answers through what he calls *narrative reconstruction*. This is an attempt to link up and to reinterpret events surrounding the onset of illness so that it makes sense in terms of the person's life story. For example, after a heart attack, patients will reconstruct the incident to make it sensible, so that it no longer seems to have come 'out of the blue'. Instead, the heart attack can be seen as the 'obvious outcome' of past events or what one has done previously (Cowie, 1976). The importance of bringing the disease into one's life experience is that, once this is done, it is possible to use it to reflect upon other aspects of one's biography. Williams (1984) cites the case of a man suffering from rheumatoid arthritis who used his illness experience as a way of reinterpreting the work conditions that he believed contributed to his poor state of health.

Initially, therefore, such reconstructions serve as repairs to the disruptions which result from individuals being told that they have, for example, cancer or multiple sclerosis. This is not just a matter of re-establishing personal meaning and re-attaining a positive perspective, important as these might be. It is also working out a future way of living with others as an ill (or potentially ill) person. Bury (1988) has used the term 'meanings at risk' to indicate that such individuals can never be sure that their own perceptions of their illness are shared by others. 'Calls for help may turn out to produce unwanted dependence and calls for sympathy run the risk of rejection' (Bury, 1991: 454). In a later section of this chapter we shall examine this question of risk in more detail, and relate it once more to the issue of uncertainty that was discussed above.

Problems of living with chronic illness

The problems of living with chronic illness are, as was said earlier, those of living with illness in a world of health, to do with disability and handicap. In this section we shall note some of the main problems that have been described, with a view to relating these to the question of how people cope. It has been pointed out that serious illness provides a unique area for studying experience, because people are often highly aware of previously taken-for-granted aspects of self that are now lost (Charmaz, 1983, 1991). In reconstructing a new time-line, the chronically ill person also reconfigures his or her old self, the one that 'used to be'. This self may remain in small or large part, but for many their physical suffering is mediated through a sense of its loss. Charmaz (1983) argues that this is exacerbated by four social psychological conditions – living a restricted life, existing in social isolation, experiencing discredited definitions of self, and becoming a burden. These are linked together by a cultural attitude (the 'American way of illness') that treats such conditions within a medical system designed for acute illnesses. This often leaves sufferers to be looked after by carers in isolated situations. Here is a brief survey of these four conditions.

Chronic illness can lead to a *restricted life* where the person becomes effectively homebound, an example of disability. One way this can happen is through the directly limiting effects of an impairment (e.g. not being able to walk easily). Many restrictions have a symbolic value as well as a practical cost. To be unable to drive any more, perhaps because of failing eyesight, is a reduction in the general scope of one's life. Some treatments restrict the sick person, either directly or indirectly. For example, needing kidney dialysis means a dependence on the dialysis machine, with a consequent loss of mobility and flexibility. The important consequence of living a restricted life is that it fosters an all-consuming retreat into illness.

The person may become *socially isolated*. This might be the result of forced restriction, but it can also come from the person's fears about how others will treat them. For example, hair loss following chemotherapy can mean that the person is unwilling to venture out. Experiences of being ignored, or stared at, or misunderstood can lead the person to withdraw from social life. Sometimes there is a feeling that others have lost patience with the individual, or that carers can no longer bear the strain. These are all examples of handicap.

Certain treatments mean that social engagements must be broken, so that relationships with others are disrupted. Isolation is the consequence of people feeling, or being made to feel, that they have diminished in social worth. It can also be exacerbated where, as with the case of immigrant women, not speaking the language of the country and holding only a menial job means that to divulge one's illness would be to risk one's livelihood (Anderson et al., 1991).

Discrediting definitions of self occur when others show curiosity, hostility or discomfort in relation to the sick person's condition. This handicap is particularly acute for those whose symptoms are visible and open to misinterpretation. For example, having poor motor control and an unsteady gait might lead strangers to think that the individual is drunk. These definitions do not only come from major or traumatic episodes; they also occur in the home. When the sick person can no longer do things that were once taken for granted, then these too can be the source of an increase in negative self-sentiment. The man with heart disease who can no longer play football with his son, or the woman who can no longer take care of her young children are examples of this (Reisine et al., 1987). Some sufferers will be aware of the threat of discrediting definitions from an early stage in their illness, others less so. Examples of the former are HIV positive homosexuals and haemophiliacs, who know that disclosure of their status is almost certain to lead to rejection by other people (Pierret, 1992).

The fourth condition leading to a loss of self is *becoming a burden on others*. Although this usually happens only to those whose illness becomes incapacitating, it can have profound effects on the person's social identity. Now unable to fulfil past obligations, the person can no longer claim with authority the identities that are based upon doing these things. Worse still, s/he may come to feel useless to self and to others, with the consequent increase in strain upon the caregiver.

Note that the problems associated with impact crop up at apparently different levels, sometimes sequentially and sometimes together. At one level are those to do with *impairment*, concerning the control of one's body or one's symptoms. At another are problems of *disability*, where a task must not just be carried out but done so in a 'normal' manner. And finally, there are difficulties of *handicap*, the assumptions that others make about the sick, and their reactions to them. Of course, such problems are not simply divided between these three levels. For example, while restricted mobility is narrowly defined as an 'impairment', its meaning for the individual concerned quickly becomes an issue of 'handicap'.

The problems of chronic illness are to do with retention and loss, not just of 'self' but of a way of life. Later on in this chapter, we shall make use of this distinction between retention and loss of participation in social life. It will form part of a scheme for describing different ways in which people adjust to chronic illness.

At this point, however, we need to shift attention away from the impact of chronic disease to an examination of how people actively cope as individuals. After all, questions of handicap are to do with the meanings that self and others place upon illness, and the scope that is provided for those concerned to live as 'normal' a life as possible. Having outlined some common problems of the chronically sick, the next section highlights the relative success of individuals in dealing with these difficulties, and how they go about achieving this.

Ways of living with chronic illness

If chronic illness can have such damaging effects upon people's lives, how do they go on, how do they cope? That some certainly do cope is clear from everyday experience, just as is the observation that others cannot manage very well. This raises the question whether there are some individuals who, because of their psychological make-up, might cope better than others. However, this 'dispositional approach' (i.e. focusing upon stable personality differences) has generally been abandoned in psychology for work that looks at the different coping behaviours which individuals might use. Health psychology has adopted the view that people employ different *coping mechanisms* to deal with external stressful incidents. These mechanisms may be cognitive, (i.e. a way of thinking), or behavioural, in the form of a course of action (Lazarus and Folkman, 1984). By examining different kinds of coping mechanism it is possible to see which ones might lead to better or worse adaptation to illness. Apart from the distinction between action and cognitive strategies, another main difference has been that between a preference for emotion-based coping and for problem-based coping. *Problem-based coping* implies trying to do something about the difficulties, while *emotion-based coping* describes the attempt to minimize their emotional impact through adopting a particular attitude (Lazarus, 1985).

One study asked a number of chronically ill adults to indicate which methods of coping they were most likely to use (Viney and Westbrook, 1982). It was found that a preference for action strategies was related to social background and illness role, while a preference for control was associated with illness-related factors. Both of these ways of coping were found to be more effective and helpful in dealing with illness than *fatalism*, which was regarded as counter-productive. Which particular coping style individuals used related to social class membership. This supports the view that how people cope is a matter both of the problems that they face and of the resources which they have to meet them.

The idea that some ways of coping are good and some are bad has been seen as being too simple. In the case of problem-based and emotion-based coping, research has shown that in complex, stressful encounters people use a mixture of both (Lazarus, 1985). Also, there are some occasions when a strategy might give positive results, and others when it might be counter-productive. There is yet a third proviso that one needs to keep in mind: just how much difference can people's coping styles make to the problems which they face?

In a study of a range of different problem areas in everyday life (marriage, parenting, household economics and work) Pearlin and Schooler (1978) found that individual coping was *more effective* in areas of *interpersonal problems* (e.g. marriage), and *less* so in situations that are *impersonally organized*, such as work. In the latter cases, which individuals cannot influence to a great degree, making a change in one's emotional attitude is potentially a more effective strategy.

How does this particular finding generalize to the problem of coping with a chronic illness? Do individuals with diseases that are more controllable, like hypertension (subject to a dietary and medical regime), use different ways of coping from individuals with less controllable and potentially fatal diseases, like certain cancers? This has been found not to be the case. In one study of people suffering from different chronic diseases, diagnosis made no difference to choice of coping style (Felton et al., 1984). In fact, the researchers concluded that the effects of individual coping styles on emotional distress are rather modest. This would follow if chronic illness is considered to be (in Pearlin and Schooler's terms) a stressful experience of an *impersonal* kind, in which 'having the right attitude' is the only productive approach to take. However, in this study Felton et al. did find that patients who saw their illness as an occasion for personal growth (a cognitive-based strategy) were happier than patients who reacted to it with blame and avoidance (an emotion-based strategy).

The question remains: is chronic illness an impersonal situation like work? In the sense that severe and worsening disease is uncontrollable, yes;

we should not expect the patient to do alone what doctors cannot do for him or her together. However, living with such illnesses involves considerable adjustments in just those areas that Pearlin and Schooler found coping to be effective – in the family and in interpersonal relationships. Being ill, in the long term, is not a sphere of experience separate from the remainder of life. It often has considerable effects upon other things that people do and think. Therefore, the idea that coping can be defined as a response to an *external* life-strain becomes questionable in the context of chronic illness. Sometimes such an illness appears as an external threat, sometimes it is part of oneself, and sometimes it appears as a problem concerning other people. Indeed, the sick person's way of responding can itself become part of the problem that he or she then has to deal with.

This calls into question the idea of coping as bringing to bear a specifiable psychological mechanism upon a definite external difficulty. This view assumes that these mechanisms have a stable form, like tools in a toolbox. It also assumes that problems appear the same to all individuals, when it is arguably true that a given hindrance might be a challenge to one person, and a major problem for another. It seems more useful, as we have done throughout this book, to look beyond the individual to what researchers into chronic disease have repeatedly observed: that it is the entire lifestyle of the person – physical, social and medical – which is brought into play in the adaptation to long-standing illness (Brooks and Matson, 1982).

However, before looking at lifestyle differences in adjustment, we need to examine some of the strategies that are used by the chronically ill to manage their lives. A *strategy*, as the term is used here, indicates a purposeful activity that is directed towards some end. Examples include the plans made by people with emphysema (acute shortness of breath) to manage the walk to the shop by using 'puffing stations', where they can rest while looking as if their stopping were normal (Strauss, 1975); or the forced marching step of the lady with Parkinson's disease, avoiding the shuffle of an impaired gait (Pinder, 1990); and the arthritis sufferer who uses pain-free days to do as much as possible to make up for days of forced inactivity (Wiener, 1975). The concept of strategy emphasizes that, in contrast to coping styles, this is what people *do*, in the face of illness, to 'mobilise resources and maximise favourable outcomes' (Bury, 1991). They are the means by which individuals engage with other people and with situations, in the light of the raised consciousness of their (potentially) changed situation.

In her study of patients with rheumatoid arthritis, Wiener noted strategies on the levels of action and of outlook. Both were directed at managing the uncertainty that is characteristic of the disease. Earlier, we spoke about uncertainty as a problem concerning the future of the disease. In the case of arthritis sufferers, uncertainty is something that characterizes the days and the hours of the present. It is the unpredictability of when pain might appear, where it will occur, and how long it will last that leads individuals to monitor themselves closely and to pace their activities.

One other strategy mentioned by Wiener is 'covering-up'. For example, this might be quite a small thing, like not wincing when one gets up from a chair. What we have called the negative reaction to chronic illness (the 'abhorrence' expressed by the healthy toward the sick) is indicative of the stigma potential that characterizes the handicap relationship. For individuals with motor disabilities, this is not only embarrassing (e.g. because people might think you are drunk), but it is also discrediting of one's personal identity (Goffman, 1990). Being in control of one's body is a basic assumption of healthy adult life, so that if there is a risk that one cannot maintain this condition, then there is good reason to hide one's illness from others. Examples of people in this situation include those who might fall, or feel they might smell because of having had a colostomy (Kelly, 1992; MacDonald, 1988), or who might lose consciousness as a result of an epileptic fit (Schneider and Conrad, 1980).

The strategies that are likely to help in these situations do not always have to be rediscovered by each individual patient in isolation. Children are taught about their illness by their parents, not only in terms of what to do with symptoms but also how to speak about it to others, so as to minimize stigma. Adults who contract long-term diseases are introduced to patient groups that not only offer advice, but also allow them to tell about their experiences to others who will understand. Paradoxically, one effect of building up such strategies, kept secret from others, is that it makes the chronically sick even more different from the healthy (Schneider and Conrad, 1980). This is an example of what was said earlier, that the means of coping can itself become part of the problem of living with a chronic illness.

Strategies, therefore, deal in value judgements as well as in functional advantages. That is why even the most specific action, or particular experience, can be imbued with significance for the ill person. For example, one report tells of a woman suffering from multiple sclerosis who, after each six-monthly visit to her neurologist, bought 10 pairs of shoes or boots on her way home (Duval, 1984). The reason she gave was that this was not only a statement about her retained mobility, but it was also a metaphor for independence, for her continued existence as a citizen of the world of health.

In the course of dealing with life-problems, symptoms and strategies can become connected, so that various aspects of everyday life are coloured by the illness experience. This is another indication that problems do not retain a fixed form throughout, but are transformed in the course of actions taken to deal with them. The tiredness that first appears in multiple sclerosis as a specific problem that 'one has' can change; later on, through effort, it becomes a general sense of fatigue that 'has you'. Tiredness is no longer a particular symptom that is there among other things, but has become expressive of one's condition, a symbolic background against which new strategies must be created (Monks, 1989). In this way a strategy can be functional – it achieves a specified aim – but it can also be expressive of a way of dealing with illness.

This illustrates how living with a chronic disease can become an orientation that permeates all the levels of a person's life, even if it does not

;nd into all of its corners. In the next section, we shall examine the
cept of *style* as it has been used to account for differences in the way that
ple adjust to illness. This adjustment refers not just to individuals, but
also to relationships with others in the world of health, where the chronically
ill continue to play their part.

Illness as adjustment: resolving the demands of body and society

The previous section drew out two significant relationships for the chronically ill. The first is to do with the relationship of the individual to society,
where the issue is the extent to which people can retain their roles and duties
in everyday life. The second concerns the way in which efforts at coping with
disease become part of the person's way of life; illness becomes, in
Herzlich's (1973) terms, 'incorporated into the self'.

With respect to social duties, the chronically sick are unlike the acutely ill
in this regard. Their 'return to society' (if they ever left it) is now qualified by
the presence of a disease that, probably, will remain with them for the rest of
their life. In Chapter 4 we saw how sickness can be understood as a loss of
social participation, a withdrawal from society that defines the individual,
not just cognitively, but in his or her being (Herzlich, 1973). Taking to one's
bed defines one's sickness completely, but only for a time, until one can
return to activity and to good health. In large part, it is the return to normal
activities that demonstrates one's healthiness, not just the verbal claim that
one 'feels better'. For the chronically ill, return to work or continuation with
one's duties are just such demonstrations. This is the case even though the
person might feel unwell, perhaps because of symptoms that others cannot
see or know about.

Therefore, the problem for people in this situation is how to strike a
balance between containing or attending to bodily symptoms, on the one
hand, and fulfilling the duties that allow them to carry on in the home, or at
work, on the other. We can think of this as *the need to resolve the competing
demands of bodily symptoms and those of society*. With regard to the latter,
the requirements of society are not abstract forces, but expectations
embodied in role-relationships involving sufferers and other people. The
need to balance these competing demands has been well expressed in this
account of the dilemma of the arthritis sufferer:

> . . . two imperatives press their claim upon the arthritic: the physiological, which
> must be monitored for the pain and disability reading of the day, or even the hour;
> and the activity imperative, which must be acknowledged if one is going to
> maintain what is perceived as a normal life. Like two runners in a nightmare race,
> these two imperatives gain, each on the other, only to be overtaken again in a
> constant competition. (Wiener, 1975:98)

The second important dimension in adjustment to chronic illness concerns
the person's attitude to the condition itself, what Herzlich (1973) referred to
as 'incorporation'. Taken literally, this means finding one's identity to be
comprised of both 'healthy' and 'sick' aspects. Certainly, many chronically

Figure 7.2   *Modes of adjustment to chronic illness (Radley and Green, 1985)*

ill people report good and bad days, in which they are either more or less like their 'normal' or even their 'old' self. We can, therefore, imagine a distinction to be drawn between different relationships of the self to illness: on the one hand an acceptance of the illness condition and on the other a rejection of it.

Figure 7.2 shows a conceptual framework, put forward by Radley and Green (1985, 1987), that is based upon these two dimensions. The horizontal dimension refers to the *loss or retention of participation in social life*. The vertical dimension refers to the *relationship of self to illness*, which is either one of opposition or else one of complementarity. In the latter case, this means either that illness is 'fitted into self', or alternatively that 'self is fitted into illness'. By putting the dimensions together in this way, four different modes of adjusting to illness are defined. These modes describe different attempts to resolve the demands of symptoms, on the one hand, and of society, on the other. Let us look briefly at what they involve.

Opposition to illness means fighting to overcome and to defeat it. This is enhanced where the person can use the resources of involvement in everyday life to counter the effects of disease. The bottom left-hand quartile (*active-denial*) defines an approach which is aimed at resisting illness through maximizing one's participation in normal life as far as possible, while simultaneously minimizing the implications of the disease. This modality is seen primarily in individuals who 'go on regardless', don't like to talk about their illness, dislike being looked after, and who treat the disease as if it were of little importance. For example, one study distinguished between different styles of living among men with a low back injury (Murphy and Fischer, 1983). One of these ('absolutely upright') was expressed through the man's stiff, measured way of moving, coupled with a belief that nothing had changed in his life, and that he was blameless with regard to his condition. This illustrates that styles of adjustment to illness are embodied, physical orientations to the world, as well as being social and psychological ones (Radley, 1993).

Reduced participation in social life, owing to symptom severity, can mean loss of one's job, leisure activities and even quality of family life. The bottom right-hand quartile defines the modality where the person stands in relation to the illness as vanquished to victor. Illness is destructive, in having permeated so much of the individual's life. Loss of valued and self-defining roles is signalled by the *resignation* of the individual in the face of its effects. Like the active-denial modality, the resignation mode involves opposing illness, so that even where the person feels undermined by it, the aim is still 'to beat it' if at all possible.

The complementary relation of self to illness can mean that the person first accepts the illness, and then tries to work round it, including its constraints within the terms of his or her life (i.e. the self 'encloses' the illness). It is, therefore, an *accommodation* to the condition. This modality involves a retention of social life, involving a struggle to find ways around one's limitations. In this way the person is trying to get well, to remain in the world of the healthy.

Finally, the upper right-hand quartile shows a modality in which the illness is allowed to become the limits of the person's life (i.e. it 'encloses' the self). *Secondary gain* refers to the positive qualities that can be derived from being ill, so that withdrawal from the burdens of life is seen positively. Herzlich referred to this as 'illness as a liberator', meaning the way in which the condition provides an avenue towards fulfilments outside of the world of work and its rewards.

As a theoretical framework, the scheme shown in Figure 7.2 points two ways: 'internally' to the experience of the individual, and 'externally' to the social relationships in which he or she lives. Whether a person will adopt one or other of the modalities, or, as is more usual, employ several in varying balance, depends upon a number of things. These include what other people expect of the sick, and what they will accept of the sufferer's claims to be healthy or ill. Whatever modalities are used by the person to resolve the dual demands of symptoms and society, we can speak here of him or her having a particular *style of adjustment to illness*.

This does not mean that styles of adjustment are equivalent to individual qualities or personality traits. How a sufferer will deal with illness depends, as it has been said, on significant others and upon the resources of his or her context. How much pain low back injury sufferers report has been shown to relate to spouse concern (Block and Boyer (1984), while adaptation to home dialysis among people with renal failure has been shown to depend upon their relationship with the spouse-helper (Chowanec and Binik, 1982). In relation to circumstances, to be a farmer who is diagnosed as having heart disease is to have to work with the constraints of the seasons and the weather, as well as with the demands of one's social world (Jacobsen and Eichhorn, 1964).

These contextual features were revealed in a long-term study of male heart patients and their wives, where it was shown that adjustment style related both to marriage roles and to the social network of the couples (Radley, 1988). For example, *accommodations* were made more readily by middle-class men and their wives. Because of their economic security, number of social contacts and their educational advantage, they could discuss ways of changing their life to adapt to the effects of illness. By comparison, patients who were manual workers had been forced to give up or to curtail work, so that their wives worked to support the family. These men were either more *resigned* to their situation and/or resolved to defeat their disease by fighting it (active-denial).

The 'way of life' that makes its appearance in the patient as a 'style of adjustment' is also being endorsed, or even resisted, among other people in the person's social circle. However, this does not mean that a person's social situation wholly determines the way that he or she will cope with disease. It emphasizes, instead, that becoming chronically ill (compared with being acutely sick) does not remove one from society but, 'if anything, it amplifies one's position within it, so that what people adjust *with* is as important a matter as what people attempt to adjust *to*' (Radley, 1989:243, emphasis in original). What this theoretical perspective proposes is that adjustment to chronic illness is an activity that goes on between the sufferer and significant others; it is not just a rearrangement of ideas in the mind of the patient considered in isolation.

This view is consistent with the theoretical approach in medical sociology that has been termed the *negotiation model*. This proposes that adjustment to long-term disease is a matter of the person actively responding to the challenge of illness, managing one's situation as best one can. The alternative model, deriving from labelling theory in sociology, sees the chronically ill, like the disabled, as relatively passive people whose identities are changed for them by the healthy, who allocate them a marginal position in society. This has been called the *crisis model* (Gerhardt, 1989).

Although there are wider theoretical differences between these two positions, all we need to note here is that they suggest different ways of responding to chronic illness. On the one hand is active negotiation of how to participate in the world of health in spite of one's illness. On the other, there is an acceptance that one's life is changed by a condition that will always hold a key position in everything one does, and in the way that others treat you. The scheme in Figure 7.2 allows for both of these possibilities as potential outcomes, depending upon the person's scope of influence and the degree to which the illness erodes normal life. For example, patients who have received surgery for bowel cancer (ileostomy) are particularly prone to interiorizing negative cultural beliefs when they think about potential sexual encounters (Kelly, 1992). At these times, the illness attains what has been called a *master status* in relation to other aspects of the person's identity. On occasions when the body is less important, say at work, sufferers can renegotiate a 'normal self' along lines that establish their ordinariness as persons.

In terms of the conceptual framework shown above, this distinction is not just to do with different occasions, but also concerns different resources and roles (retention of participation in society). Illness becomes a crisis when it removes the basis upon which people establish their identity. This also happens when they have reduced access to the means of formulating, and communicating, their fears and anxieties about what might happen to them. For this reason, what is a crisis for one person might well be seen as a challenge by another.

Stigma, legitimation, and making a 'good adjustment'

To speak of adjusting to chronic illness suggests that, one way or another, people come to terms with their pain or their limitations. In some cases this adjustment appears to be satisfactorily achieved, in the sense that sufferers do not complain or find alternative ways of doing things. In terms of the theoretical framework presented in the previous section, it was mentioned that accommodation as a style involves just this 'working around things'. It is equivalent to the approach that Herzlich (1973) called 'illness as an occupation', one aim of which is to 'be a good patient'. This raises the question of just what kinds of expectations the healthy have of the chronically ill. If we speak of adjustment as an attempt to resolve the dual demands of symptoms and society, then we need to say more about how those demands are made. Although there are specific expectations about how an individual might carry out his or her work, or participate in the home, it is the demands that the world of health makes upon all of the chronically ill that we need to examine.

To do this we need to return to the point made earlier, that the relationship of the chronically sick to the healthy is one of handicap, with its two constituent sentiments, *abhorrence* and *compassion*. Abhorrence is the reaction of the healthy to the stigmata that the chronically ill may bear. Of course, afflicted people will vary as to whether they bear any visible mark of the disease, and as to how that disease is viewed in general. For example, heart disease carries little in the way of stigma compared with, say, rectal cancer. The latter is felt to be, as Sontag put it, 'obscene – ill-omened, repugnant to the senses' (1991: 9). Nevertheless, to be labelled chronically ill is to be made exceptional, and, like all marginalized people, to be burdened with the task of continually having to make oneself 'acceptable' (Goffman, 1990). What makes stigmatized groups different from outgroups or minority groups is that they are devalued by the broader society or culture (Crocker and Major, 1989). Arguably, this is the fate of the chronically sick in cultures that place high value upon personal independence, task performance and physical attractiveness (Douglas, 1978).

The question of whether the symptoms of disease are visible to others is an important one, because having visible disabilities means that the individual is already discredited in the eyes of the healthy. In the case of diseases where symptoms are opaque, the problem for the individual is the prospect of being found out, of being *discreditable* rather than *discredited* (Goffman, 1990). However, the problem is not just one of keeping these facts hidden from others, but also of whom to tell and when to tell, in order that close relationships can be maintained.

The question of adjustment can, therefore, be seen to do with the kinds of value judgements made by the healthy about the sick. While negotiations might be made with one's family and friends about how one wishes to be treated, there remains the difficulty of determining when, and with whom, such negotiations are appropriate. For example, one man who had received surgical treatment for coronary disease said, about going dancing:

> You feel different. You can't do these things and people that don't really know somebody will come along and explain to them why you are not [dancing] and that makes you feel even more different really. I often think, 'I wish you'd hold your noise'. Just leave it be and not explain to anybody else why I'm sitting still. (Radley, 1988: 171)

The problem of being discreditable is the threat of having all of one's identity overshadowed by the value judgements made about one's illness. In the above example, this hinged upon the loss of a capacity for which the man would not (in the main) be held to account. In other cases, the stigma attaching to chronic illness extends to things for which people *are* normally held accountable, and which matter precisely because to fail these standards is to risk being judged as 'less of a person'. This can be illustrated using the case of a woman in her sixties, diagnosed as having rheumatoid arthritis (Williams, 1993). Her physical limitations meant that it was an effort to find ways to remain independent of others. Equally important was her concern to be able to keep her home clean, a state that expressed a standard beyond mere housekeeping:

> The other week, the district nurse came running in saying, 'Do you mind if I use your toilet?' Now the first thought in my mind was 'She's a nurse, they're particular, she wouldn't ask to go to my toilet if I was dirty'. . . . That was something important. She can't think I'm careless, and she's not frightened of touching anything in the house. (Williams, 1993: 98)

This illustrates that the chronically ill feel themselves to be subject to the same normative judgements as the healthy, and that they feel *more so*. The idea of 'living with illness in a world of health' takes on added significance when we see it for what it often is – a position where balances must continually be struck between doing too little and doing too much. If sufferers ignore symptoms and press on as normal, they risk being perceived as 'reckless'. If they take great care of themselves, they run the risk of being seen as 'invalids' or as 'malingerers'. The key point here is that this dilemma does not exist in a vacuum; it arises out of the demands that the world of health makes upon the sick.

Two further examples can help to make this point clear. One concerns the case of officials in an English seaside town who acted upon requests from a man's neighbours that he should close his curtains while dialysing at home. The reason for this was that while the neighbours sympathized with his plight, they felt that they should not have to be witness to this 'unpleasant' procedure. Another example is reported by Goffman (1990), who told of a man, paralysed in his legs, who left his wheelchair and tried to climb the stairs of an outdoor restaurant by pulling himself up bodily by the handrail. He was stopped by the waiter, who declared that they could not have him acting in a way that would be disturbing to the restaurant's other customers.

What this shows, to use the terms introduced earlier, is that the price of the healthy person's compassion is the concealment of things by the afflicted, things that could be considered abhorrent. The chronically ill must bear their illness in ways that do not imply either that this burden is too heavy for them, or that bearing it makes them markedly different from the healthy (Goffman, 1990:147). On the other hand, should they, like the man dialysing in view of his neighbours, act as if they are 'really normal', then sanctions will be applied to remind them of their 'true' status. This means that the 'good adjustment' of the handicapped is actually a quality granted to them by others. Then people say about them things like, 'he's very brave', or 'she's always so cheerful'.

Therefore, good adjustment does not spring ready-made from the individual sufferer. The dilemmas that the chronically ill often experience are grounded in the contradictory expectations of the healthy. An example that makes this explicit is given in the account of a family of a child polio sufferer (Davis, 1963). Although this is taken from the field of physical handicap, which cannot stand for all chronic disease, it is useful in drawing out issues that apply to any stigmatization due to illness.

> Seven year old Polly Manning, for example, decided to enter a contest sponsored by a magazine issued for handicapped children by a local welfare society. The contest asked the children to submit a name for the magazine. When Polly told her mother her first choice – 'The Crippled Children's Book' – Mrs Manning replied, 'Well, that's right long. They said they wanted a short happy name, and that doesn't sound too happy.' Polly then suggested 'Cheer'. With her mother's approval, this was the name she submitted. (Davis, 1963: 140)

This quotation shows that sufferers (and families) who belong to stigmatized groups 'need' to present themselves as people who are bearing up under their burden. It is a matter of maintaining an impression of oneself as ordinary ('just like other people'), against the background of evidence that one is clearly not so. Minimizing the seriousness of the condition in communications with others is part of this presentation. This would explain the finding of one study that showed that parents of children with one particular disease (either epilepsy, diabetes or asthma) rated the seriousness of that disease lower than did parents of children with either of the other two diagnoses (Marteau and Johnston, 1986).

Part of this impression management is to do with the containment of symptoms. In another study of families with handicapped children, Voysey (1975) gives the example of a mother who claimed that her child with Down's syndrome was 'coming on as fast as his brother'. This claim was discredited when the child failed to be able to hold a cup offered to him by the paediatrician. Here, the child who exemplifies sickness in a spontaneous way 'lets down' the mother who is attempting to lay claim to the normality of their family life.

In this example, the division of spontaneous sickness and deliberate claim to health is separated between two people. However, if we consider these two aspects as being within one person, then it is possible to see how this analysis can be applied to the individual sufferer. In certain chronic disease conditions (e.g. rheumatoid arthritis, multiple sclerosis) the person has, as we have said, a 'healthy' self and a 'sick' self. This means that it is possible for the claims made on behalf of the former to be discredited by the appearance of symptoms of the latter. For example, a person might attempt to carry off the role of party-goer, but fall in the course of dancing in a way that is untypical of people who have full control of their bodily movements.

Therefore, it is not plain prejudice with which most chronically ill people are faced. The majority are met by a conditional acceptance, one that requires their cooperation in making adjustments, such as the one Polly Manning made to her magazine title. As with many other stigmatized groups, not all chronically ill people suffer from lowered self-esteem. Where they can selectively devalue those things that they are not good at, and value those attributes on which they excel, then it is possible for their self-esteem to be raised, at least for a time (Crocker and Major, 1989; Susman, 1994). This is made possible because they are encouraged by the world of health to redefine their misfortune in positive ways, so as to minimize their difference from the norm (Voysey, 1972). This has the effect of avoiding the threat of embarrassment (and situations of abhorrence) for 'normals', while at the same time showing how the chronically ill should regard themselves. It legitimates their position, making them appear as creditable and worthy persons. This applies particularly where disease or impairment is of a kind that cannot be denied, where, in effect, the potential for embarrassment (abhorrence) is at its greatest. Where individuals struggle against severe pain or considerable difficulties, these attempts to 'normalize' are then seen (by healthy and sick alike) as 'strength of character'; they are rewarded with compassion. However, this attribution of strength can never be taken for granted by the chronically ill. They have to earn it again and again through their efforts to 'go on as well as possible'.

There is one exception to this argument that should be mentioned here. Plain prejudice is, indeed, faced by AIDS sufferers, for whom the mass cultural response is not compassion (even at a price) but abhorrence in the form of media comment. Only the arts have explored the situation of AIDS sufferers from their point of view. The media have, more often, been concerned to distance themselves and the majority from a group which, they argue, are undeserving of the compassion normally accorded to the chronically ill (Goldstein, 1991).

Conclusion

This analysis has shown that living with illness in a world of health is more than meeting the demands of specific tasks or fulfilling particular duties. Being a chronically ill patient can be like being acutely sick, on those occasions when one is defined in relation to medicine (e.g. when symptoms are severe, or at the terminal stages of disease). Having been treated in the past, currently being on a medical regime or anticipating the need for future treatment each provide the basis of claims regarding the individual's status as a sick person. However, when managing symptoms in the everyday sphere, the salient relationship is to the healthy, where issues of handicap apply. That is why the Parsonian model of the sick role is insufficient by itself to embrace the experience of chronic illness. Instead, we have to look beyond medicine to culture; to relationships (e.g. friends, acquaintances) and institutions (e.g. the family, work), which provide both the criteria for 'good adjustment' and the means whereby it can be achieved.

In the next chapter we shall look again at these relationships and institutions, in the context of how they act as sources either of support or of strain. For the chronically ill, issues of support are central, and these will be addressed in that chapter. Finally, towards the end of the book, we shall take up, once again, the question of what it means for the world of health to establish a framework of values about illness, in both its acute and its chronic form.

Chapter summary

- Acute diseases are often treatable, so that sickness is *temporary*. By comparison, having a chronic disease often means *continuing to live with one's illness in the world of health*.
- Because the chronically sick must manage and explain their condition to others, issues of *communication* and *identity* are central to explanations of their experience and how they cope.
- Chronic illness is not adequately explained by the concept of the *sick role*; this is because, in addition to the role of patient, being chronically ill involves relationships with the healthy who express *compassion* and *abhorrence* towards the sick.
- It is useful to distinguish between the *impairment* of chronic disease, the *disability* of chronic illness and the *handicap* defined by the social status of the chronically sick.
- The main problems of chronic illness have been described as those of restriction, social isolation, discrediting definitions of self and becoming a burden on others. These problems can reflect wider *disruptions* to biography and *uncertainty* about the future course of the disease.
- Living with chronic disease has been defined in terms of attempts to *reconstruct* one's life, involving specific *strategies* for handling symptoms, *ways of coping* with the perceived consequences of disease and *styles of adjustment* to illness in social relationships.
- The different styles of adjustment that are adopted by chronically ill people are to be understood in the context of their *social situation*. The resources that people have available (material, social, educational) will be

important, as will the *biographical context* in which illness arises and takes its course.

● The way that chronically ill people make, or try to make 'good adjustments' are attempts to *make themselves acceptable to the healthy in the world of 'normality'*. This means that the experience of chronic illness may best be regarded as one of *handicap*, involving obligations of appearance and manner, rather than as sickness, where people are excused duties of task performance.

Further reading

Anderson, R. and Bury, M. (eds) (1988) *Living with Chronic Illness: The experience of patients and their families*. London: Unwin Hyman.

Bury, M. (1991) The sociology of chronic illness: a review of research and prospects, *Sociology of Health and Illness*, 13, 451–68.

Charmaz, K. (1983) Loss of self: a fundamental form of suffering in the chronically ill, *Sociology of Health and Illness*, 5, 168–95.

Corbin, J. and Strauss, A.L. (1987) 'Accompaniments of chronic illness: changes in body, self, biography, and biographical time', in J.A. Roth and P. Conrad (eds) *Research in the Sociology of Health Care, Volume 6: The Experience and Management of Chronic Illness*. Greenwich, Conn.: JAI Press.

Radley, A. (1989) Style, discourse and constraint in adjustment to chronic illness, *Sociology of Health and Illness*, 11, 230–52.

Voysey, M. (1975) *A Constant Burden: The reconstitution of family life*. London: Routledge and Kegan Paul.

Williams, G.H. (1993) 'Chronic illness and the pursuit of virtue in everyday life', in A. Radley (ed.) *Worlds of Illness: Biographical and cultural perspectives on health and disease*. London: Routledge.

8

Stress, Illness and Social Support

The idea that stress contributes to illness is commonplace in industrialized societies. By examining the concept of stress, this chapter approaches health and illness from a different perspective from the one we have adopted so far. In previous chapters the issue has been how people act in the course of becoming ill; here the question concerns what have been called 'the social causes of illness' (Totman, 1987). From seeing social life as the medium through which people give meaning to their symptoms, we move to seeing it as the possible cause or reason for them being ill in the first place.

The words 'cause' and 'reason' in the last sentence imply quite different things. The former denotes a particular determining relationship, in which something in the person's life or setting 'made' them ill. The latter implies that stress could be a way in which people understand their illness, or act in ways they believe will preserve their state of health. The literature on stress (which is considerable) reflects both of these points of view, sometimes separately and sometimes combined. One of the aims of this chapter is to unravel these perspectives, and then to relate them to analyses of health and illness made in earlier chapters.

Similar to the idea that stress causes illness, it has been argued that lack of social support has a detrimental effect on people's health. For this reason, it makes sense to discuss both of these topics together in this chapter. Also, both topics are underpinned by some common assumptions. These include the proposition that the two problems can be studied using the methods of behavioural science. The line taken in this chapter is to question this assumption, with the aim of showing how it is at odds with the idea of illness as involving meaning and social action.

As a way of approaching this topic, it is useful to remind ourselves how people experience illness and adapt to its demands. We need to do this if we are not to be swept along by the prevailing scientific and popular view that 'stress is one of the main causes of illness today'. The other reason for looking back over previous ideas is that, once one plunges into the literature on this topic, some guidelines are needed if one is not to become confused.

There are four points which need to be underlined:

First, there are different social science perspectives in relation to biomedicine, so that what one thinks stress 'is' depends upon the assumptions made about the relationship of the body to the social world. If, for example, one takes a *behavioural view*, then questions about causal relationships of specific stressors to particular effects in the organism are basic to research. If, on the other hand, one takes a *societal perspective*, then the issue of stress becomes tied up with questions of social inequality, and of which people are more likely to become ill. (We have seen an example of this in Chapter 6, where one hypothesis concerning women's relatively high morbidity was that a woman's nurturant role is inherently more stressful.)

Second, people have their own ideas about health and illness, and stress is one of these. Notions of susceptibility and strength of constitution relate the individual's health to the dangers of the environment. More precisely, however, people use this concept in their everyday thinking, and account for conditions such as 'heart attacks' and 'nervous breakdowns' in these terms (Pollock, 1988). They will also often explain illness by using the word 'stress' to link disease to the pace of social change.

Third, people fall ill in the context of their way of life. What has been called *illness behaviour* draws attention to the differing ways in which individuals respond to the onset of symptoms and try to cope with them. For example, the kind of explanations that they have for their symptoms will depend upon their social situation. Those people who use more 'psychologic' as opposed to 'physicalistic' explanations might be more aware of stress, or more likely to act to reduce what they believe to be its effects.

Finally, illness, particularly when chronic or life-threatening, is quite a 'stressful' thing in itself. One must accept that being ill can itself become part of the very process assumed to be its cause.

Keeping these points in mind helps to counter the apparently logical deduction that if 'stress causes illness', then we must seek out the connections between the 'stressful causes' in the environment and the (by implication) 'stressful effects' in the body. Instead, it is necessary to review the history of the concept, and see how a biological proposition became a widespread psycho-social approach to the origin of disease.

Stress: definition and interpretations

A review of the history of the stress concept shows that it had a popular meaning even as far back as the seventeenth century, indicating 'hardship, adversity or affliction' (Hinkle, 1973). Later on it acquired the connotation of its use as a term in physics, meaning 'force, pressure or strong effort'. By the early twentieth century, physicians were using the term 'stress' in this quasi-scientific sense. It is this that has been carried over into the modern usage of the term, implying that people fall ill owing to some kind of pressure under which life places them. It was only later on that biologists, following Selye (1956), defined it in terms of a specific physiological condition, the *general adaptation syndrome*. This syndrome, or set of physiological changes, is not caused directly by outside stimuli, but is the result of the organism's own adaptive response to this stimulation. This means that although the syndrome itself is specific (i.e. particular changes to certain organs of the body), the condition of stress it signifies is a *generalized state of the organism*, not a specific flaw brought about in a part of it.

Many of the problems and uncertainties to do with the concept of stress today derive, not from this biological view directly, but from its use as a kind of metaphor for how people fall ill. In order to draw out the different approaches to be taken in this chapter, we can examine this basic notion of stress for its internal tensions and contradictions.

First, note that stress has a double aspect: the noxious stimuli presumed to be the origin, on the one hand, and the reaction of the organism to that stimulation, on the other. If we choose to focus upon the stimuli, we make an analysis of different 'stressors' and their effects. If, on the other hand, we focus upon the organism, we make an analysis of its contribution and the resulting effects. (Note here that it might be difficult, if not impossible, to separate the body's [psycho-]physiological adaptive reaction from the [psycho-]physiological effects we are labelling as 'stress'.) Here, then, is the question of whether to investigate stress primarily in terms of its outer stimuli ('stressors'), or in terms of its inner contribution ('coping mechanisms'). This gives us our first dimension of difference, relating to an *inner versus outer* view.

In the biological model the stress syndrome is a specific collection of signs, although the state of stress, in general, affects the whole body. Furthermore, the stimuli that bring this about are presumed to be non-specific, meaning that it is not particular things that are stressful, but their pattern, timing or context. This raises the question of whether one should be looking at specific reactions of the person under stress (e.g. particular disease entities, particular psychological reactions), or whether one ought to examine more general reactions. Similarly, the biological model raises questions about whether specific events can be labelled 'stressful' in themselves, in spite of our feeling that some seem more so than others. This gives us the second dimension of difference, relating to a *general versus specific* form of analysis.

Before putting these dimensions together, there are two further points we can take from the biological model (Hinkle, 1973). The first is that stress 'acts through the central nervous system'. This implies that the relationship of stressor to internal state is based upon communication and symbolic interchange, not a change in energy (i.e. it is not a physical force). This suggests that the *meaning of events* will be important to the individuals concerned. It also suggests that to speak of psycho-social problems as physical stress (e.g. being 'under pressure' or 'under strain') is to use a *metaphor* without being aware of doing so.

The second point concerns the suggestion that stress involves change to which the organism must adapt. As Hinkle (1973) and others subsequently have pointed out, change is an essential aspect of life, so that it is hard to conceive of a state of stress which is qualitatively different from any other state of being alive.

Now we are in a position to set out some alternative ways in which psycho-social stress has been studied, using the two dimensions of difference outlined above. These dimensions can be considered as the lines along which behavioural and social scientists have extrapolated the concepts put forward by Selye and others. In that sense, these are all approaches which have

Table 8.1   *Some alternative approaches to the study of stress*

	General	Specific
Outer	'Social structure'	'Life-events'
Inner	'Social type'	'Causal chains, coping'

addressed stress as if it is a 'real cause' of disease. They form a set of four possibilities, as defined in Table 8.1.

The four approaches to stress research are defined by their position with regard to the issues of focus – inner versus outer, and general versus specific. They will form the basis of the discussion to follow, and because we know their relationship to each other on the question of basic differences, we shall be in a better position to form a critical impression of the topic as a whole.

The focus upon *social type* looks at the health status (physical and mental) of groups of people who are believed to be at risk due to their life situation. Becoming unemployed, or being bereaved, are examples of this kind. These situations are 'general' in the sense that they are taken as a whole, while the focus upon the 'inner' aspect points to a concern with the responses and resources of the persons concerned. One variant of this approach is to focus upon a particular 'inner' outcome (e.g. heart disease), and try to discover the general conditions that brought it about. This, of course, is to use the diagnostic classification system in a way that parallels its use in medicine, as if social events were like germs targeting specific organs of the body. The logic of this position has been heavily criticized, on the grounds that bodily stress is a general state (Cassel, 1976). This underlines, once more, that picking out some diagnoses as 'stress diseases' while leaving others aside is arbitrary and unwarranted.

The second contingency, *life-events*, takes an 'outer perspective', but does so by looking at 'specific' events in the life of individuals (Dohrenwend and Dohrenwend, 1974). We shall examine this approach in more detail below, but note for now that it tends towards finding stress in the events themselves, or in their number or rate. This perspective has been criticized by researchers holding a 'general' view. They insist that the 'life-event' approach misses the fact that it is not specific occurrences that matter, but the long-term strains that go with certain kinds of social situations (Pearlin, 1989). This, the *social structure* position, emphasizes the problems and conflicts within certain role sets, such as difficulties in marriage, job or parenthood. (Being a 'nurturant woman' comes in this category, as does the stress hypothesis of Gove and Hughes, 1979.) The point here is that these chronic strains are 'general' relative to particular life-events, in being 'naturalistic' groupings of difficulties assumed to provoke stress.

Finally, the *causal chains, coping* approach is one that assumes a perspective that is both 'inner' and 'specific'. Emphasis is placed upon the adaptive capacities of the person, not upon the events that provoke threat. Researchers using this perspective believe that it is the person's response to the event that is the key to the stress process (Leventhal and Tomarken, 1987). Here we find reference to the point made earlier on, that stimuli are not inherently stressful but are *interpreted* to be so, and that the individual's own ability to cope is something that is part of this appraisal (Lazarus and Cohen, 1977). As a consequence of breaking down the process into its specific parts, this approach has a tradition of using experimental designs and analyses. These are aimed at establishing what are presumed to be the vital links between event, response and outcome (Leventhal and Tomarken, 1987).

Having outlined the four possible approaches, it is possible to see how, if not why, there is some uncertainty in this field about what stress 'is' and how it should be studied. The four kinds of approach are possibilities that arise from the inner/outer and the general/specific tensions that we have examined. For that reason they are *ideal types*, in that many of the actual theories and research efforts overlap the table entries. Nevertheless, together they make a sufficiently good fit for us to use the scheme as a basis for reviewing some of the main findings about stress.

Stress in society: vulnerable groups and times of crisis

The idea that there are particular times in life when individuals will suffer increased stress appears obvious. Examples of these times include the death of a close relative or friend, being made unemployed, or being forced to move from one's home. This section will look at some of the arguments that have been made for a connection between these events and the increased likelihood of becoming physically ill. In particular, it will focus upon the groups of people who occupy these transitional positions. This research has tended to study 'the bereaved' or 'the unemployed' in ways that try to capture their general situation, rather than the specific events that might provoke their illness. As well as looking at individuals who are suffering unwanted change, it is possible to consider those whose position in the social order places them at a continuing disadvantage throughout their lives. The ones with least in the way of economic and other resources – the poor, members of ethnic minority groups, migrants – are among those who come into this category. Referring to our table of possible approaches to stress, these are studies that make a general analysis rather than a specific one.

There is one other group that should be mentioned here, and that is women. Chapter 6 raised the question of whether there is something endemic in the nurturant role that women occupy that causes them to be ill more often than men. This 'stress hypothesis' was criticized on the grounds that it did not embrace the evidence about multiple roles, and the way in which women might present or withhold their symptoms. These reservations might well be kept in mind as we discuss the possibility that certain other groups become ill more often through the 'stressfulness' of their position.

It has been found repeatedly, and in several different countries, that people in the lower social classes have more illness and a lower life expectancy than those in the upper classes (Antonovsky, 1967; Morris, 1979; Wilkinson, 1992). A review of health differentials in Britain showed that occupational class is associated with a diverse number of health measures, in which people in the lower echelons of society are disadvantaged in terms of both chronic and acute illness (Macintyre, 1986). Whether this is due to 'stress' or to other causes has been, and continues to be, a matter for debate. Living in run-down housing (or on the streets) will have direct effects upon one's physical condition. Exposure to cold, to physical injury, to infection and to a poor diet will each play its part in increasing the likelihood of becoming ill. These material conditions are not to be forgotten in the concentration upon the symbolic effects of change in social status or self-esteem (Wright and Weber, 1987).

Having recognized the presence of physical disadvantage, researchers in this field have continued to believe that the higher rates of disease in the manual classes owe something to the stressfulness of disadvantage. There have been calls for research that can disentangle the substantive from the symbolic causes of illness, while still focusing upon the general rather than the specific risk factors involved (Syme and Berkman, 1976). This call from researchers who use an epidemiological approach has its limitations, because physical events do not appear independently of their meaning. If this were so, it would be expected that all individuals, in broadly similar situations, exposed to similar stressors, would be likely to fall ill to the same extent. However, early studies using particular groups of people (e.g. telephone operators) showed that some individuals who were frequently ill did not express dissatisfaction with their lives, while others who were healthy had histories full of deprivation and difficulty (Hinkle, 1974).

The emphasis upon groups of people in similar social circumstances is supported by the argument that life situations are long-term. These make for different contexts in which difficulties not only arise, but also become elaborated on the basis of their being organized together (Pearlin, 1989). This is another reason given for focusing upon the general situation rather than specific events taken out of context. Pearlin suggests that we should distinguish between primary stressors – the precipitating event – and secondary stressors – those that result from the initial disruption. Referring this back to the question of social class differences, this could mean that one source of stress might be the 'knock-on' effects of events, which are somehow halted or dispersed by the way that life can be reorganized by the middle-classes. (Certainly this can be true of serious illness as an event; for example, manual workers who suffer from heart disease are more likely to have their earning power markedly reduced, with all the consequences that this implies.)

Linked to social class is the phenomenon of social change. Running through the stress literature is the assumption that change is unhealthy, and particularly so when it involves a discontinuity or a contradiction in social status (Cassel, 1976). In one study it was shown that there was a marked increase in deaths from coronary heart disease in the course of a rural area becoming urbanized (Tyroler and Cassel, 1964). The explanation put forward for this was that the deaths resulted from an 'incongruity' between the rural culture and the faster pace of urban life that was imposed upon the people concerned. Evidence for this specific hypothesis has been patchy, although a relationship between modernization and some physiological indices, such as raised blood pressure, has been demonstrated (Dressler et al., 1987).

One of the most influential studies in this area was carried out by Marmot and Syme (1976; briefly mentioned in Chapter 1). They focused upon Japanese men who had immigrated to California, establishing the degree to which they had retained their links with traditional Japanese culture. Those men who had lost their traditional culture, and embraced a modern American lifestyle, had a three- to five-fold excess likelihood of suffering from coronary disease. The important feature of this design was that the researchers statistically controlled for the substantive risk factors like smoking, diet and blood cholesterol. That is, they demonstrated that there was something about the men's way of life that affected their chances of contracting coronary disease.

These studies of social position, or of social change, all utilize the *societal* perspective defined in Chapter 1. They also take a general, and largely 'outer', view of the social causes of illness, in seeking to identify what it is about some people's life setting that predisposes them to higher rates of disease. As with the Marmot and Syme study, much of the research focuses upon a specific disease outcome. In spite of this, the lesson often taken from these studies is that it is a predisposition to disease in general that is at issue here, not a link between particular circumstances and specific types of pathology.

Two examples of groups believed to be liable to stress will be briefly mentioned in this section – the unemployed and the bereaved. The effects of unemployment on health have been studied using large-scale statistical data, sometimes pertaining to whole countries, thus linking economic cycles to mortality rates (Colledge, 1982). These analyses suggest a link between unemployment and health, although they differ as to when in the cycle (recession or recovery) the effect is meant to occur. In any event, such macro-analyses are of limited help in this book, because they have nothing to say about how stress 'works', if this is the nature of the link proposed. It is known that even hearing that one is to lose one's job has measurable effects, in terms of an increase in the number of days reported as feeling ill (Kasl et al., 1972). Once unemployed, both men and women report psychological distress and increased physical symptoms (Payne et al., 1984; Starrin and Larsson, 1987).

One of the problems with research in this area is that of disentangling the effects of unemployment from those of other events. Inevitably, there will be people who are ill prior to losing their job, for some of whom this reduction in their state of health will have been the reason for them leaving work. One study of a group of unemployed men and their families examined the relationship between their health prior to and after the men's job loss (Fagin and Little, 1984). It found that health issues were prevalent among the majority of the sample, but that any links between these issues and unemployment were complex, to say the least. For example, some of the men appeared to use illness to express their state of despair, in a way that made the whole experience more bearable. To try to explain this, Fagin and Little adapted Parsons' sick role model to show the way in which sickness can legitimize the situation of the unemployed. This does not mean that these people were not 'really' ill. Rather (using ideas from Chapter 4), we have to remember that symptoms justify our withdrawal from activity when we are in work. Fagin and Little argue that for some unemployed men, who have no access to other ways of maintaining their status, the sick role provides a way of bearing that experience that makes it lighter.

Two kinds of explanation are running in tandem in this account. On the one hand, the 'stress' model provides its explanation in terms of direct cause. On the other, the 'cultural acceptability' hypothesis points up the stigma potential of unemployment as compared with the acceptability of legitimated illness. To accept the latter hypothesis, even in relation to a minority of people, is to undermine the suggestion that unemployment is a discrete event, a 'thing' that has a unitary and direct cause upon health. Also, to admit that people act in the light of their judgement about the valuation of unemployment is to recognize its stigma potential. This suggests that there are important differences between individuals in how they think others see them in their new, lesser, status.

One can think of unemployment as an example of a transition, or fundamental change, that involves a loss of something important in life (Parkes, 1971). Another example would be bereavement, which has been argued to have consequences for both mental and physical health. One study, of over four thousand widowers, found that they had a 40 per cent excess mortality rate over a similar group of married men in the first year after bereavement (Parkes et al., 1969). The implication of this, and similar studies, is that such deaths are directly attributable to stress from loss of the partner. However, it has also been shown that widowers suffer higher mortality rates than widows, so that any stress theory must account for this difference. This makes it difficult, without presuming higher levels of endemic grief for men, to account for the observed connection between bereavement and disease in terms of the stress hypothesis (Stroebe and Stroebe, 1983).

To conclude this section, the isolation of particular experiences as being 'stressful' in relation to certain groups underlines the idea that illness might have a social cause. What this approach has been accused of failing to do is to show the exact links between the antecedent 'stressors' and the outcomes, expressed in terms of symptoms of disease.

One line of research that retained the 'outer' perspective, looking at social causes, extended the notion of stressful event so as to survey a wide range of possible stressors. In the next section we shall see that this had the effect of particularizing events and disconnecting them from each other. This, in turn, had the effect of removing them from the groups of people with whom, by virtue of their social position or their life situation, these events could be identified.

The study of stressful life-events

The idea that a large number of demanding experiences predisposes people to disease is the focus of research into *stressful life-events* (Dohrenwend and Dohrenwend, 1974). It emphasizes the events themselves, and the need to specify more precisely which ones (separately or in combination), give rise to disease. This means that it best fits the 'outer/specific' category defined in Table 8.1 above. To remind ourselves, the scheme defined four different approaches to the question of how stress might cause illness. Therefore, the difference between the life-event perspective, and those that take a more global or 'inner' view, is partly to do with the methodological approach taken. Where the 'social type' approach focused on groups, life-event research shifted the emphasis to happenings that could occur in the life of anybody.

The original assumption underlying this approach is that what happens in life requires individuals to make adaptations. These adaptations, if they are serious enough, involve significant changes to the pattern of people's everyday existence. This means that a 'desirable' continuity or steady state of existence is disrupted by events that can be considered 'undesirable' or 'stressful'. To gauge the extent to which people are exposed to such events, we first need a way of estimating their stressfulness. While this cannot be done absolutely, it is possible to compare events in terms of the amount of *relative* readjustment that each calls for.

The problem remains as to how one might compare events in this way. A solution was provided by Holmes and Rahe (1967), who selected 43 items that (they believed) reflect change in the average American life-course. They asked nearly four hundred people to estimate, regardless of the desirability of the event, how much readjustment each one would require. This was done comparatively, so that each event was given a number relative to 'marriage', which was accorded a value of 500. By averaging the judgements, and by the use of scaling procedures, a series of weighted events was produced, which is shown in Table 8.2. This list, the 'Social Readjustment Rating Scale' (SRRS), can be presented to any individual, who checks off which events apply in his or her recent past. A score is obtained by summing the relevant weighted values. Three ranges of score (or life-change units – LCU) have been used to define different levels of change: a mild life crisis (150–99 LCU); a moderate crisis (200–99 LCU) and a major life crisis (300+ LCU) (Holmes and Masuda, 1974; Holmes and Rahe, 1967).

Table 8.2   *Social Readjustment Rating Scale*

Rank	Life-event	Mean value
1	Death of spouse	100
2	Divorce	73
3	Marital separation	65
4	Jail term	63
5	Death of close family member	63
6	Personal injury or illness	53
7	Marriage	50
8	Fired at work	47
9	Marital reconciliation	45
10	Retirement	45
11	Change in health of family member	44
12	Pregnancy	40
13	Sex difficulties	39
14	Gain of new family member	39
15	Business readjustment	39
16	Change in financial state	38
17	Death of close friend	37
18	Change to different line of work	36
19	Change in number of arguments with spouse	35
20	Mortgage over $10,000	31
21	Foreclosure of mortgage or loan	30
22	Change in responsibilities at work	29
23	Son or daughter leaving home	29
24	Trouble with in-laws	29
25	Outstanding personal achievement	28
26	Wife begin or stop work	26
27	Begin or end school	26
28	Change in living conditions	25
29	Revision of personal habits	24
30	Trouble with boss	23
31	Change in work hours or conditions	20
32	Change in residence	20
33	Change in schools	20
34	Change in recreation	19
35	Change in church activities	19
36	Change in social activities	18
37	Mortgage or loan less than $10,000	17
38	Change in sleeping habits	16
39	Change in number of family get-togethers	15
40	Change in eating habits	15
41	Vacation	13
42	Christmas	12
43	Minor violations of the law	11

Source: Holmes and Rahe, 1967

The originators of the SRRS reported a number of findings relating high scores to the presence of deterioration in general health. For example, in one study the percentage of life crises associated with health changes over time were shown to relate to the overall LCU score. Individuals with mild scores had 37 per cent of their life crises associated with times of poor health; those with moderate scores 51 per cent; and those with major scores 79 per cent (Holmes and Masuda, 1974). One of the problems with this kind of research is that it depends upon retrospective judgements, so that one cannot be sure that the occurrence of the illness has not influenced the person's recollection of events. This problem can partly be eased by the use of a control group. For example, it was found that a group of patients who had had a heart attack reported a greater reduction in socializing, and in 'goal-directed activities', than a group of matched healthy controls (Totman, 1979). (For a review of early work on life-events and illness, see Totman, 1987.)

The question of people's views of past events being confounded by their experience of illness has led to studies that use a prospective design. Information about recent events is gathered at one interview point, and a health record is then kept over the weeks or months that follow. In their original pilot study, the authors of the SRRS followed up 84 physician-subjects and found, nine months later, that of the high risk (300+) group, 49 per cent reported illness; 25 per cent of the medium risk (200–99) group reported illness; and 9 per cent of the low risk (150–99) did so. They later confirmed this finding in a larger study using American sailors. Here it was found that the highest association between life-events and illness was for older, married sailors, suggesting that the SRRS assumes an individual's potential exposure to the full range of items (Rahe, 1972). Younger sailors who did not have a wife to divorce, whose parents were not aged and therefore likely to die, and had no mortgaged property were restricted in the events that could apply to them.

In recent years, other scales aimed at measuring desirable and undesirable life-events have been developed. This has been to overcome problems with the SRRS, which has been the focus of considerable criticism (Harris and Brown, 1989). However, the emphasis upon the need for prospective designs has remained. A typical example of this kind of research is a study of the onset of colds in the context of life changes (Evans et al., 1988). Using a scale measuring the desirability of experiences, these authors found that, relative to matched control days, there was a significant decline in desirable events during the four days immediately prior to symptom onset. This implies that one is more likely to develop a cold in the absence of 'uplifts', rather than as a consequence of the presence of 'hassles'.

In spite of the many studies that have used the SRRS, there have been a number of important criticisms of its ability to measure the relationship between stressful life-events and ill-health. Inspection of the items in Table 8.2 shows that a high LCU score can be achieved in a number of ways. For example, checking several items at the bottom of the list will gain a higher score than indicating only that one's spouse or partner has died. This seems peculiar, given what people generally believe about the importance of bereavement. In fact, the procedure of adding together event units to provide a composite score has been fundamentally questioned, and subjected to an empirical test that we shall discuss below (Brown and Harris, 1978). This is part of the wider question of whether it is legitimate to take events in isolation, and to ask people to judge them as if they are self-contained units rather than part of the enduring thread of life (Pearlin, 1989).

Substantial criticisms have been made of the assumption that the items in the SRRS have a common meaning for respondents (Brown, 1989). 'Divorce' does not mean the same thing to someone whose spouse initiates separation as it does to a couple who have been fighting in the matrimonial home for years. In the latter case, it might even be said that divorce was a relief compared to the strain of remaining in the marriage. A similar criticism can be made of other items in the inventory. One group of investigators asked subjects to elaborate upon what happened in each event, and subsequently discovered considerable differences in the amounts of change involved (Dohrenwend et al., 1987). That is, people have different things in mind when rating these events. This matters because the life-event perspective seeks to establish, from an 'outer' viewpoint, which particular events are potentially stressful. This criticism is especially serious because it throws the whole checklist approach (not just the SRRS) into doubt as a way of studying health following social change.

From another point of view this criticism can be turned to advantage. Instead of trying to determine which events are 'stressful', in their inherent capacity to provoke excessive adaptation, we can ask which events are indicated, by which groups of people, in relation to health changes. There is evidence, using the SRRS, that people in urban situations view events such as marriage, arguments with spouse, and taking out a large mortgage differently from those who live in rural settings (Miller et al., 1974). One recent study found that husbands and wives report exposure to different kinds of event (men, financial; women, social relationships), and also react to these events with different symptoms (Conger et al., 1993). This is consistent with the idea that, while the checklist and its scaled weighting of items makes the measurement of life-events appear objective, the appraisal of the event, and even whether it is reported at all, will depend upon the biographical and social situation of the people concerned.

This problem is not restricted to the reporting of life-events alone. We know from Chapter 4 that individuals in different situations will vary as to the symptoms of illness that they consider worth reporting. This means that whether a symptom is reported or not is likely to be influenced by the events and circumstances that people have experienced, and how they wish to present themselves. This is similar to what Mechanic (1974), in this context, has referred to as individuals 'manipulating illness definitions for the benefits they deliver'.

The problem of trying to locate stress in the accumulation of specific external events has highlighted another need: to pay attention to how people make sense of what happens in their lives. After all, events are only distressing, threatening or encouraging insofar as individuals think and feel them to be so. The adjustment that must be made in the face of change involves a consciousness of what has happened, or even what could happen. One of the drawbacks with the SRRS-based research is that it says nothing about events that do *not* occur; this was acknowledged by the originators (Rahe, 1972). On reflection, one can see how those things that are anticipated with special pleasure can provide, in their failure to happen, a keen feeling of disappointment. For example, a couple finally realize that they will not be able to have children; or a person becomes resigned to making no further progress in his or her career. There might be no outward change in these people's behaviour, but these feelings of lack still count as significant matters in their lives.

In their study of women who were diagnosed as suffering from depression, Brown and Harris (1978) tried to deal with this issue of meaning by allowing their patients (and 'normal' respondents) to talk at length about each event mentioned. This project, carried out in London, has become a landmark in the field of life-event research. Therefore, it is worth our while seeing just what these authors were trying to achieve. A sample of women who had been diagnosed as suffering from depression were interviewed about past events, and compared with a control sample of 'normal' women. The difference from the checklist approach was that the interview was semi-structured. Although there was a list of topics to be covered, the respondents were asked to talk about their thoughts and feelings before, during and after each event considered. Once transcribed, the interviews were then rated on a number of scales to assess their implications. The reason for doing this was to avoid confounding the importance of the event with the women's feelings in telling it. In this way, Brown and Harris could make measures of the respondent's evaluations at the time of interview. They could also assess the contextual, or wider threat of the event, as judged by a third party listening to the complete tape.

The results showed that it was *severe events only* that distinguished the depressed from the non-depressed women. It was also found that the assumption 'the more events, the worse the health outcome' (i.e. adding events as in the SRRS), received only limited support. In fact, the procedure of treating all events as separate did not make sense. To illustrate this, Brown and Harris gave the example of a woman who learns that her husband has cancer, tells of his entering hospital and then of his subsequent death. These are not unrelated events in her experience, so the rationale for treating them as such is flawed. This is an important point, for it is at the base of the finding that the depressed women were more likely to have suffered two or more *unrelated* severe events before the onset of their illness.

The question of how different events work together to undermine good health is at the centre of the question of stress. Brown and Harris concluded that change in itself (i.e. adding up events) is of no importance. Rather, everything turns on the meaningfulness of what happens. It is the meaningful implications that events and difficulties have for each other which is crucial. That is why apparently small events can provoke a major crisis. They reflect, or symbolize, a wider difficulty that the person has been living with for some time. For example, it was found that pregnancy and birth were associated with a greater risk of depression for women in the sample, but only in the context of ongoing conditions like bad housing or a poor marriage.

This point is well illustrated in the study's findings about social class differences. Working-class women in the sample had more difficulties than middle-class women, but these did not account for their higher rates of psychiatric diagnosis. An increase in the likelihood of becoming depressed occurred when these provoking events occurred to women who had what Brown and Harris termed *vulnerability factors*. These were related to social class, and included such things as the lack of an intimate other or confidant, having three or more young children at home, and the woman having lost her mother before the age of 11.

In spite of its focus upon mental illness, what can this work tell us about the role of life-events in the onset of disease? First, the idea that events are in themselves stressful is shown to be too simplistic. This is because there may be long-term difficulties in people's lives which they do not recognize as 'stressful'. In addition, other provoking agents might be given enormous weight in their calculation of undesirable happenings in their lives. This is not to say that people do not know what might contribute to their ill-health, but rather that there are focal and background features that are given significance in the course of making sense of events as they happen or fail to happen. The focal features are what individuals elaborate upon; the background features may be those that they share with others in their social setting. Many important difficulties are long-term, endemic to certain social positions, so that they form the basis of how those individuals will understand and will cope with problems that arise. Hence, meaning is important, not because it makes cognitive factors central, but because it highlights the way that people appraise and cope with the situation in which they find themselves.

Second, life-events are not discrete phenomena which are potentially applicable to each and every individual. Along these lines, Rahe (1972) has imagined the stress of life-events as being like separate rays of light, some stronger and penetrating, others mild and more easily filtered out by people's coping mechanisms. However, this credits each event with an intrinsic degree of potential stressfulness, with each one isolated from the other except in their supposed additive effect upon the individual. Brown and Harris' analysis moves us away from this perspective, which focuses upon outer causes and individual disease, to one emphasizing social context and a biographical accommodation to events. This is more consistent with the line of argument presented in Chapter 4, when we discussed symptom reporting following a breakdown of accommodation to bodily signs (Zola, 1973); and that discussed in Chapter 7, concerning the attempt to reconstruct one's life in the light of chronic illness (Bury, 1982; Williams, 1984).

What can we make of the work on life-events on the basis of this brief overview? Does it show a link between 'stressful occurrences' and the onset of disease? If by this is meant a direct causative effect, the answer must be 'no'. If we mean 'is there a link between people's likelihood of becoming ill and their experience of social life?', then the answer is that some relationships have been found. However, whether the concept of 'stress' adds anything to our understanding of these findings is questionable. Certainly, the focus upon pathogenic events misses out those things in life that might be health protective. This includes prior instances of successful coping with undesirable events, for the simple reason that these could not issue in a 'stressful' outcome in the person's experience (Pollock, 1988).

One feature of vulnerability that Brown and Harris pinpointed as important in the genesis of depression was lack of close social relationships. Other people may play a large part in helping individuals to cope with undesirable occurrences, just as they may be the very source of the unwanted events in the first place. One major criticism of life-event research is that it has detracted from an exploration of the role of social relationships, and the negotiation of meaning in the process of falling ill. These are central to the concerns of this book, so that we need to examine this literature if we are to understand more about why some people in society become ill more readily than others. We need to turn to this work in order to see what relationship there is, if any, between people's social contacts and their propensity to maintain or to lose their good health.

Social support and health status

One of the factors believed to be involved in the likelihood of people becoming ill – either physically, mentally or both – is lack of support from other people. The way this has been conceived is in terms of the web of social relationships that 'tie in' a person to his or her community. The concept of *social network* summarizes this web of social relationships. It is often measured in terms of the number of relationships that a person has, indicated by frequency of contact or by membership of different groups or institutions. In the *Health and Lifestyles Survey*, for example, people were asked about the number of times they visited family, had gone out with friends, or made contact with these people by phone or letter. Taken together with their family circumstances (i.e. whether they lived alone, had a spouse/partner, or had children), these gave an indication of their degree of 'social integration'. They were also asked about their feelings about these other people – did they make them feel loved, could they be relied upon to help, did they give support and encouragement when times were difficult? Answers to these questions gave a somewhat different measure, concerning 'perceived social support'. It can be seen that these two measures, though similar, are not the same. One attempts to describe the extent of an individual's social contacts; the other tries to gauge the person's own feelings about their importance.

By analysing the health status of people in the survey in terms of both of these measures, it was found that reported illness, psycho-social health and the presence of diagnosed disease/disability were all greater where either social integration or support were diminished (Blaxter, 1990). This finding is consistent with a number of studies that have shown the health of individuals with fewer social ties to be poorer. Among these are large-scale prospective studies that have assessed the social ties of people, and then followed them up over a number of years attempting to predict mortality. Berkman and Syme (1979), for example, constructed an index based upon number and importance of social contacts, as well as membership of groups and church attendance. Using a sample of nearly seven thousand people, they found that the extra risk of death for the most isolated was between two and three times greater than for those individuals with most social contacts. Other prospective studies have made similar findings, suggesting a link between social support and mortality risk (for reviews, see Berkman, 1984; Cohen, 1988; House et al., 1988).

This kind of research fits squarely into the *societal* perspective defined in Chapter 1. It examines the health outcomes of large groups of people, indicating relationships between health and social circumstance, without, however, being able to say how the process of social support actually works. We have already said that this is unsatisfactory because it leaves un-addressed (let alone unanswered) a number of important questions. These concern how social contacts are made, and how they are experienced and made use of by individuals when either healthy or ill. For this reason, we need to examine more closely the relationship between health status and different kinds of support, as well as looking at the role of social relationships when people become sick.

Before doing this, it is worth stopping to consider some of the assumptions that underlie this line of inquiry. Like the stress concept, to which it is often linked, there is a common-sense validity to the notion that social support equates with good health. One assumption, stemming from the literature in sociology, concerns the hypothesized poorer mental health of marginal individuals. These are people who have been displaced from their traditional groups either through mobility or through the loss of traditional family ties (Pilisuk and Froland, 1978). There is a shift in emphasis here towards a concern with the individual-at-risk, whose loss of close social relationships leaves him or her without the 'buffer' of close family, and perhaps of friends.

This approach assumes that merely having social contacts is to be assured of support. However, it has been pointed out that not all social networks have to be supportive. Some might not be so, and therefore it is a mistake to merge the two concepts together (Berkman, 1984). Confirming this possibility, one study of widowed women found that a lower level of well-being was significantly related to the number of different problematic social relationships reported, but not to the amount of social support (Rook, 1984). The possibility that some relationships are actually detrimental to health is lost by equating the concept of 'social network' with that of 'social support'. If this happens, it results in a similar, but opposite, situation to that which typifies the literature on stress. In that context, all change has been seen as pathological and hence 'stressful'; in the context of social support, all contacts have been seen as positive and hence 'supportive'.

A related question concerns the relative importance of what have been termed the 'core' and the 'extended' aspects of the person's social network (Hammer, 1983). In part, this is a matter of methodological concern. It has arisen because some researchers have asked only about contacts with significant others (e.g. family and friends), while others have assessed the full range of social contacts made in people's daily lives. This (perhaps unintentionally) supports the proposition that different people play different parts in either avoiding 'stress' altogether, or else in helping during 'stressful' episodes. In the case of emotional well-being, it has been found that for college students companionship (meaning shared leisure relationships) is more important than social support (where this is understood as extent of social transactions) (Rook, 1987). The idea that lack of an intimate friend with whom one can share one's feelings is associated with poorer health has been seen in the case of depressed women (Brown and Harris, 1978). This result has been confirmed for patients attending their general practitioner, relating to the presence of both mental and physical symptoms (Ingham and Miller, 1986). In this latter study, however, the lack of many casual, less intimate friends was also associated with higher symptom levels. This might be because, as seen already, the larger the network that people have, the less likely they are to delay in using health services (Salloway and Dillon, 1973).

One reason for examining the wider social network, rather than just a person's immediate relationships, is provided by the finding that low social network scores have been found for more than half of the individuals in the lowest social stratum, but for only a quarter of those in the highest social class (Hammer, 1983). If having many social contacts is important for good health, then might this be more important for some people rather than others in society? An answer to this is given in Blaxter's (1990) analysis of the results summarized at the beginning of this section. On the basis of these data she asked the question: which is more damaging, socio-economic disadvantage or deprivation in social relationships?

The *Health and Lifestyles Survey* showed that both income level and perceived social support were independently related to health status. Examining the sample by age showed that for men and women over 40 *support made more difference if income was low*; having little social support if income was high did not make a significant difference to reported illness. Therefore, for the over-forties, income (as an indicator of social class) was more important for health than social support. On the other hand, for men under 40, *income made no difference* to health status, *as long as there was no lack of support*. Among the younger women, social support had a greater effect than income.

This suggests that the single term 'support' is too global to capture the variety of ways in which people seek and receive help or advice from others (Belle, 1991). This is so in relation both to gender and to age, given that these are basic features of the course that any individual will steer through life. Against the background of Blaxter's (1990) finding that income was more important than support for the over-forties, it should be considered that this is likely to be so particularly during the years when people are employed. When they retire, these income differences, though certainly remaining, might no longer symbolize such different ways of life. In one study of persons over 65 years of age, the best prospective predictor of mortality was *perceived* social support (Blazer, 1982). Whether this was due to changes in the importance of social contacts during the latter years of life, or whether more physical illness had led to a recognition of need for help from others, is not certain. What is not in dispute is that the relationship between social support and health is two-way: not only is low social integration and support associated with poorer health, but being disabled or having a chronic ailment will affect one's relationships with others. (We saw this 'isolation effect' when discussing chronic illness in the previous chapter.)

Finally, in considering how social support might work differently for different sections of the population, comparisons of men and women have repeatedly thrown up marked variations. In general, women mobilize more varied social supports in times of stress than do men; they maintain more emotionally intimate relationships than do men; and they provide more frequent and effective social support than their male counterparts (Belle, 1991). This means that they draw benefit from their contacts with friends and relatives in terms of both diminished relative mortality (Berkman and Syme, 1979) and lower morbidity (Flaherty and Richman, 1989). However, the unequal burden they carry in providing care for others (e.g. children, elderly parents) also takes its toll (Finch, 1984). In the context of the marriage relationship (and by implication anywhere a man and a woman forge a household together), the sharing of this burden equally has been found to improve the health of the wives *and of the husbands* (Pratt, 1972). The key feature here would appear to be the high degree of companionship that such an equal sharing makes possible, with its consequent health benefits for both partners.

If social integration and support function differently in various life-contexts, then their relationship to health and to illness might also be different in these situations. This makes the search for a single answer to the question 'how does social support protect health?' appear less relevant to how people move from the world of health to that of illness.

One issue in the literature worth noting, however, is whether social support works directly, providing protection through positive feeling, or whether it works indirectly, acting as a kind of buffer against events provoking stress (for discussions of this argument, see Cohen, 1988; Cohen and Wills, 1985; Payne and Jones, 1987; Wills, 1991). So far, the evidence suggests more support for a direct, or main, effect than for the 'buffering hypothesis'. In part, this is because it is difficult to separate the effects of events upon social relationships from the influence that these relationships have, in turn, upon the person's exposure to future happenings (Thoits, 1982).

The social support literature shares this problem of confounded variables with the stress approach, with which it is conceptually linked. Both have tried to use predictive, causal explanations to address the question of the movement from health to illness. Unfortunately, this is a matter that does not yield to such an approach. In part, this is because the problem of the mutual influence of relationships and events is not a difficulty to be overcome, but is actually a vital part of the human condition of being more or less healthy, 'poorly but not sick', not wholly one or the other. Falling ill is not a discrete movement from absolute health to absolute illness, because it involves the social world in our understanding of bodily signs. Similarly, having a chronic illness often does not mean total isolation, but rather the reconstruction of life through an alteration in social relationships.

Social support in times of illness

Important things can be learned about social support by studying people who have already become ill, and the consequences of this for their relationships with others. Retaining social contacts matters when one is sick, as was shown in a prospective study of men who had suffered a heart attack. It was found that those who were classified as being socially isolated, and having high levels of 'life stress', had more than four times the risk of dying as compared with men low on both of these measures (Ruberman et al., 1984). Relative social isolation is also an indicator of poor outcome for patients either waiting for surgery, or in the period after hospital treatment. Men who were to receive heart surgery, and who, with their wives, reported most strain at this time, not only had fewer contacts, but also expressed a wish not to speak to others about their condition, or about problems arising from it (Radley, 1988). Followed up 12 months after surgery, these couples revealed different expectations about recovery, reflected in the pattern of their social relationships. Those couples who saw the man returning 'back to normal', with all this entailed, were those who reported least change in relationships over the period. Where these expectations proved unworkable – as when the men had a return of disabling chest pain – then the couple's social contacts tended to decline markedly. It was among couples who were more prepared to entertain a modification of their lifestyle that social contacts were sometimes increased, and for whom their own relationship moved towards an equalitarian pattern and increased companionship.

There are two further points that we can pick up from this discussion of the part that relationships play during illness. One concerns the role of lay helpers, who are usually members of the sick person's immediate family. It has been shown that men had a more favourable outcome after a heart attack when their wives had a wider support network. Among working-class families, it is the adult children who sometimes play important roles in providing direct help, being 'lay consultants' and giving advice and information where this cannot be gained from other sources (Finlayson, 1976).

The second point relates to a paradoxical feature of social support which deserves mention here. Sometimes support achieves its aim by its relative absence. In one study of a single family, where the father was awaiting heart surgery, as the man's admission to hospital drew near so the family's communications were reduced to concise exchanges. This meant that anxieties and fears could be contained by the collective resolve not to air differences: 'the family stayed together in the same field by getting out of each other's way' (Bermann, 1973: 82). Similarly, among men interviewed after heart surgery were those who wanted to get back to normal; they avoided discussions and situations in which their illness (their 'difference') would be made apparent. In the later stages of recovery, what was also valued by these men was when people did *not* offer help (Radley, 1988).

This reflects the fact that competent adults are defined by their ability to function autonomously. We generally seek to avoid receiving help that might define us as 'not coping', while often professing ourselves quite willing to give assistance to others. Giving and receiving help have social significance in all cultures, so that measuring amount of support does not capture this important element of meaning.

Rather than see social support as 'causing' or even allowing certain kinds of adjustment to take place, it is perhaps better to interpret the patient's social relationships as the medium through which adjustments are made possible. Support does not so much have an independent effect upon coping, where these are understood to be two separate phenomena (Bloom, 1982), as reflect an outlook about recovery that patient and carer(s) forge together. Nor should it be thought of as a single entity that remains unchanged from one situation (or one group) to another. For example, the support that patients need just after being discharged from hospital is not necessarily the same support that they need when they eventually return to work.

The ill person expects or invites different things from family, friends and colleagues; in their turn they expect and offer different things at these various times. If this is true at times of sickness, then it is also true in times of relative health. Pregnancy, childbirth and old age will call out certain kinds of support, though not perhaps from the same (other) people. What can, ought and may be done to support others depends upon social expectations and identities. These are simply absent, as measures, from attempts to assess social support as a global index. It is this absence that limits much of the literature (which adopts a causal, 'societal' approach) to demonstrating, repeatedly, that social life has health implications. However, making this connection alone does not tell us how, in experience, this is brought about.

'Stress' as discourse and mythology: a critique of the concept

The final section of this chapter examines some criticisms made of the concept of stress as a focus for research. By reviewing these criticisms, it is possible to place the topic of stress within the broader framework of our discussion of health and illness. This section also anticipates some issues to be discussed in the final chapter, which relate to the question of individual responsibility in health care.

One of the limitations of the stress and social support literatures is that they rest upon a view of society and individuals as unchanging. They take what is called an *ahistorical view* of social events. For example, the notion that some events simply are more stressful than others makes this into one of their essential qualities. Also, the ways that people cope with these events are presumed to be psychological processes that lie somehow 'inside' the individual, owing more to the person's biology than to their social history (Young, 1980). This is a paradoxical conclusion to draw in the light of the frequent mention in the stress literature that it is change (especially unwanted change) that is harmful to health. This conclusion can be clarified by showing that the changes that are cited within stress research are those that apply to the *individual*, e.g. divorce, bereavement, redundancy. These changes are to be understood as deflections of the person from a way of life that is comprehensible within a set pattern of social existence - an expected or 'usual' life-course. Hence, the view that change (deflection of the individual) leads to illness is entirely consistent with the assumption that good health comes from stability and from social integration.

This assumption has been criticized, not least because it overlooks the effects of modernization upon societies and the health of their citizens. Economic changes not only make for differences in social structure, but they also create different potentials for individuals to aspire to attain its rewards (Dressler, 1985). This means that people's ideas about change, and about the desirability of social movement, form part of the background of their thinking concerning what happens in their lives. The idea that stress is peculiarly modern, applying only to late capitalist society, comes from the assumption that traditional societies are protected from psychosomatic diseases owing to their integrated social system. In some way, it is assumed, their illnesses are 'natural' while many of ours are 'psycho-social'. In fact, we do not know whether this is true, so it is unwarranted to draw conclusions regarding the lack of (di)stress suffered by people in traditional societies either of today or of the past.

The argument that social integration is, by definition, healthy is also worth questioning. This suggests that being 'tied in' to society is health protective, but this notion is so abstract that it fails to capture the demands that society can make of individuals (Mestrovic and Glassner, 1983). In his classic study of suicide, Durkheim (1951) pointed out that the aspirations which society inculcates in individuals, and the demands it makes upon them to achieve, can be pathological in their degree. He gave the example of the (male) scholar who dies from excessive devotion to study being someone who can reasonably be regarded as having killed himself by his labour. Today, there is a notion of the businessman having a heart attack as a result of excessive levels of work, though work of a particular kind. He is someone who is hard-driving, ambitious, might put his firm before his family and be seen by colleagues as ruthless in his dealings with others. This kind of 'workaholic' approach has been summed up in terms of the 'Type A Behaviour Pattern' (Friedman and Rosenman, 1974). Its constituent characteristics have been recognized to have an oddly double nature. On the one hand they are the very qualities that arise from being highly socialized into modern (business) society; on the other, they make up what is seen as a stressful risk-factor for developing coronary heart disease (Helman, 1987). To paraphrase Durkheim, apparently self-imposed stress can be a close kin to genuine virtues (e.g. ambition, devotion, discipline), which it simply exaggerates.

What does this criticism mean for our understanding of stress? Does it imply that stress works in a different way from how we had originally thought; that it ought to be measured more precisely, or that we need to pay attention to different groups in society? In fact, it has a wider implication, to do with how we invoke the concept in the first place. Before tackling this directly, let us remind ourselves of the approach that we have taken in earlier chapters of the book. There, it was emphasized that people have, in the past, used various representations of health and illness, and have at different times conceived of disease and its causes in different ways. These social representations of health and disease not only enabled people to treat their conditions as best they could, but they also made their condition sensible to them in the context of their lives.

The concept of 'stress' can be thought of in precisely this way, as a modern social representation that people use to make sense of the illnesses that beset them. Far from being just a scientific concept, or even a specific 'thing', stress is a general term that is often used in everyday life to make the extraordinary sensible. It can provide a personally meaningful explanation of illness in answer to questions concerning the particularity of one's misfortune: 'Why me? Why now?' It does this by providing a *working mythology* where people lack clear understanding of why they are ill, or what they can do to make themselves well again (Pollock, 1988).

It has also been shown (Chapter 4) that individuals will often try to accommodate signs of pathology, only going to the doctor when these adaptations no longer contain them. These signs are then interpreted as symptoms, having implications for those aspects of life that they affect (e.g. the painful wrist that stops one playing tennis). This way of thinking is consistent with an approach that sees illness as arising in the context of a social world, in which individuals take an active part. Diseases may happen to one's body, but falling ill is never a matter of cause alone. The meaning of the illness is not a cause because it is not an antecedent. The 'trigger' that provides the reason for going to the doctor is grasped retrospectively, in the light of the failure to accommodate the initial bodily sign. Then, for example, we say to the doctor that we have come about 'a sprained wrist' that needs attention because we 'are playing in a tennis match tomorrow'. It is the effect on the potential level of our game that provides the reason for the consultation, and transforms the bodily sign into a symptom requiring attention.

I go over this example once more to illustrate the perspective that a focus upon stress always threatens to erode. We can draw a parallel between the symptom and the outcome of stress as this appears in the experience of the individual. It can be argued that the bodily sign, and the stressful event to which it is attached, stand in a similar relationship to one another. *We only know the event to have been stressful retrospectively*, in the light of the symptoms that, in their turn, take their meaning from it. For example, a headache that stops one from working on an essay becomes a symptom in the light of this perception. The event that is believed to have triggered the headache ('working too hard') is then understood to be a 'stressful situation', or one that 'causes stress'. If we then succumb to these symptoms, perhaps taking an aspirin or else lying down for a rest, it is possible to say that we are engaging in illness behaviour. Then, within the logic of our thought and action, there is a link between the stressful essay and the headache. However, this link is a *symbolic one* in relation to *illness*, not a causal one in the sense of something causing us to have become *diseased*.

In this case, the meaning attaching to the event and to the symptom are the product of *simultaneous interpretations*. This is only made mysterious if we imagine that the stress came first, and that it caused the headache to appear later. Once convinced of this state of affairs, we are but a short step away from believing that stresses in the environment cause disease. Indeed, this is the basis of much of the thinking that underlies the research effort into the role of stress in health and illness.

Putting forward a critique of this kind of scientific practice, Young (1980) has suggested that stress is part of a wider *discourse*. It is a way of talking and thinking about the world. Social scientists and medical researchers use the term ('stress') because it allows them to address problems of illness within a scientific perspective, premised upon ideas of cause and effect. This has two aspects, both vital to the appearance of stress as being a useful and significant idea in the investigation of disease.

Although the word 'stress' is difficult to define, it is in fact this very imprecision that allows researchers to keep discarding and proposing 'relationships' and 'variables' to try to make firm predictions. This involves the use of an approach modelled on natural science, so that the aim is to establish causal links between outer 'stressors' and 'inner' diseases or 'psychological strains'. For example, stressful events in the SRRS have been referred to as 'objective events', as if these are shorn of subjective appraisal. Even in the work of Brown and Harris (1978), the idea of having third parties judge the interview tapes was intended to remove the bias of the women's feelings about the events they reported, in order to establish a more reliable causal link between event and illness.

The appeal to stress, with its echoes from the world of physical things, helps to make events which have social meanings (e.g. divorce) resemble natural objects that can be objectified and dissected. Organizing these objects together in a research design then legitimates the exercise as one that is scientific, aiming at a dispassionate and value-free truth.

There is a second aspect to the stress discourse that Young (1980) puts forward. This relates to the questionable assumption that these variables, whether life-event or coping style, are distributed through the population in a potentially even manner. This is to focus upon individuals (as opposed to groups), who are considered in abstraction from the social relations (material and symbolic) in which they live their lives. Young calls this the 'decomposability of society', where all social processes are reduced either to attributes of individuals (e.g. coping styles), or else to discrete moments in lives (e.g. events) that are, for analytic purposes, indistinguishable from one another.

Taken together, these two aspects of the stress discourse have a significant effect upon both expert and layperson. They make the concept of stress appear more solid and definite, on the one hand, and more personally significant, on the other. As far as social scientists are concerned, these criticisms show stress to be an ideological concept, not a neutral factor or causal agent. By focusing upon individuals, about whom all kinds of tacit assumptions are made (e.g. that they don't like change), and by linking stress to the models of biomedicine, social scientists are able to produce results that have the appearance of hard facts.

For us, as students of health and illness, these results appear convincing because we, too, share in the cultural assumptions that make the stress discourse viable. It is in that sense that Pollock (1988) called stress a mythology, because it works to make life sensible. It brings together the paradoxical aspects of life in ways that do not challenge the social processes and ideologies on which we rely. These are matters that we shall take up in the final chapter, making use of some of the ideas that we have addressed above.

Conclusion

This chapter has shown that we have to consider the concept of stress very carefully. Three broad uses of this term have been examined, and found to be different from each other. They are not interchangeable, and at key points are directly contradictory. The biomedical definition places stress firmly in the state of the organism's physiology. The behavioural/societal perspective treats it as a negative feature of external events, some applying only to certain sections of the population, others to everybody. These external 'stressors' are presumed to 'cause' disease. The third use corresponds to the cultural perspective introduced in Chapter 1. Here, 'stress' appears as part of a cultural discourse, helping people to explain their illness situation. As a *social representation*, it serves to organize people's illness experience, and to relate this to the world of which they are a part. Stress research, in its natural scientific form, helps in this sense-making for researchers and laypeople alike.

The approach of this book has been to emphasize that falling ill not only concerns the interpretations of individuals, but also involves social meanings and cultural practices. That is why research that seeks to link external causes (stressors) to internal effects (disease) makes little sense in these terms. One of the main aims of this chapter has been to draw the reader's attention to the limitations of this 'cause and effect' approach. This does not mean that there is no relationship between social context and people's state of health. The differences between social groups, in the amounts and kinds of illness reported, suggest that social context does matter. Whatever the material connection, the relationship between social context and health status is a matter of symbolic interpretation. We still lack research of a kind that poses its problems in these terms. How individuals think about events and life situations, as well as how they respond to difficulties and opportunities, are key to understanding the influence of social conditions upon health status.

Chapter summary

- The concept of stress is ill-defined because researchers disagree as to whether it refers to *general* or *specific* reactions, and to whether it should be understood in terms of its *inner* (coping) or its *outer* (stressor) conditions.

- There is evidence that higher rates of illness attach to groups that are either *disadvantaged* and/or subject to *rapid social change*, though how much this is due to material (e.g. income) or to symbolic (stress) conditions is often difficult to ascertain.

- Researchers using schedules such as the *SRRS* have tried to relate exposure to *accumulated life-events* to risk of illness or death. This approach has been criticized for the shortcomings in its methodology, and for making unwarranted assumptions about the meaning of the events chosen for consideration.

- More sophisticated studies have shown that life-events are not additive in their effect upon health; instead, their relationship to health appears to be in terms of their *potential to symbolize experience*, i.e. their meaning. In particular, events can act as *provoking agents* against the background of *vulnerability* factors that often attach to disadvantaged groups.

- There is evidence that better health is enjoyed by people with *strong or extensive social networks*, though how this works is not yet understood. *Social support* is believed to come both directly from participation in society and indirectly as a buffer against stressful events. Overarching concern with how to measure social support has meant that it is sometimes poorly conceptualized, and its relevance for questions of health and illness is thereby considerably reduced.

- Stress has been argued to be a product of *discourse* about illness and the social world. Rather than being exclusively a scientific concept, it can be regarded as a *social representation* that organizes everyday and scientific knowledge to make illness sensible in the social world. 'Stress' makes sense because it supports the idea of individuals having to make their own way in a world of contradictory demands.

Further reading

Brown, G.H. and Harris, T. (1978) *Social Origins of Depression: A study of psychiatric disorder in women*. London: Tavistock.

Cohen, S. (1988) Psychosocial models of the role of social support in the etiology of physical disease, *Health Psychology*, 7, 269–97.

Dohrenwend, B.S. and Dohrenwend, B.P. (eds) (1974) *Stressful Life Events: Their nature and effects*. New York: John Wiley.

Lazarus, R.S. and Folkman, S. (1984) 'Coping and adaptation', in W. Gentry (ed.) *Handbook of Behavioural Medicine*. London: Guilford.

Pollock, K. (1988) On the nature of social stress: production of a modern mythology, *Social Science and Medicine*, 26, 381–92.

Totman, R. (1987) *Social Causes of Illness*, 2nd edition. London: Souvenir Press.

9

Promoting Health and Preventing Disease

This final chapter is concerned with the interventions that have been made to improve health and to limit disease. At an everyday level, the signs of these interventions are commonplace in developed societies. Immunization, information programmes and exhortations to change one's lifestyle, while often perceived as ways in which people are encouraged to improve their health, are actually attempts to reduce the likelihood of people developing *disease*. This is not quite the same as persuading them to improve their health. We need to make a distinction between what can be called the control of disease, through attempts to reduce its incidence, and the promotion of good health by means of improving the quality of life.

Social psychologists have, for some time, been studying the most effective ways of changing behaviour and attitudes with regard to health (Lewin, 1958). While this early research had much to say about the specific conditions likely to promote compliance, it did not explore the background as to why people adopt or resist the message being delivered. As far as the issue of health is concerned, this is an important omission; it does not tell us how people think about these matters in everyday life. If governments or medical agencies want to affect how people look after themselves, then they have to understand the ways in which people normally think and talk about these issues.

People hold medical and lay beliefs at one time. This suggests that questions of health promotion should not be reduced to matters of technicalities, such as 'how to put the message across effectively'. This view brackets out the wider – and important – questions about the value judgements involved in the control of illness. These judgements are made both on the side of 'the experts' and on the part of lay people concerned. That we should want to tackle issues such as these, is consistent with the approach taken so far in this book. How individuals perceive their health, the health of others, what they regard as symptomatic of disease, and what constitutes a good reason for seeking medical advice are all matters of social judgement. Another way to put this is to speak of people's illness behaviour being shaped by cultural meanings and values, ideologies within which matters of health and illness are 'tied into' the wider beliefs that people share about their world. We have much to learn by recognizing the ideological basis of individual action, and the complexities of shared beliefs that come from their being acted upon in the context of people's lives (Billig et al., 1988).

The very distinction between health and illness is part of such an ideology which forms the basis of attempts to make changes in this area. This means that the definition of these terms will make some interventions more likely, and others less so. It will also make some appear more sensible, and others appear morally correct. In the course of this chapter we shall examine two examples which illustrate this: one is in the area of disease prevention, and the other in the field of health promotion. The aim will be to show how these interventions make use of ideological positions, and how the actions that appear to follow from them reveal the dilemmas faced by people trying to 'look after their health'. In effect, we learn something about the social form of health and illness by examining what some people do to influence others to change their way of life.

This approach brings into question the focus and the aims of both health promotion and disease prevention. This critical view cannot be achieved by studies limited to the technical problem of how to get people to comply, or to believe, or to adopt a different lifestyle. Of course, within the terms of a psychology (or sociology) allied to medicine, these are legitimate objectives aimed at making medical procedures more effective. However, this approach derives from a particular relationship of these disciplines to biomedicine. By accepting, implicitly, its ideological basis, it becomes possible for psychologists and social scientists to contribute to the treatment of specific disorders. However, the self-imposed limitations of these applications mean that they can tell us something about the treatment of disease, or the experience of illness, but little or nothing about the place of health in everyday life. (For some specific applications of psychology in the clinic, see the studies reported in Mathews and Steptoe, 1982, and in Oborne et al., 1979.)

The remainder of this chapter will examine two particular efforts to affect people's health status. One focuses upon disease prevention in the attempt to modify people's risk-factors for coronary heart disease. The other examines sufferers' use of self-help groups to control their illness. Both of these initiatives, as we shall see, raise questions about the rights and wrongs of focusing upon disease rather than health, upon the individual as opposed to the social context, and upon holistic care as an alternative to that provided by traditional medicine.

Disease prevention as context

One of the enduring beliefs in the field of health care is that prevention is better than cure. In Britain this tenet is allied to the idea that the National Health Service treats illness, i.e. that it is primarily a 'sickness service' (Murcott, 1979). The alternative to treating the sick is to try to prevent disease, so that Britain (along with other developed countries) has for some time encouraged this line of action. On the face of it, disease prevention might appear straightforward, but in fact it raises a number of dilemmas when put into practice. Taking a social policy perspective, Lambert and McPherson (1993) identify four such dilemmas:

1 How should one decide the best balance between promotion, prevention and cure? Resources are limited, so should we concentrate upon
   one at the expense of the others?
2 When innovations in treatment are translated into preventive measures
   (such as cholesterol-lowering drugs, or those for hormone replacement
   therapy), how can we be sure that changes in the pattern of disease are
   due to these measures, and in what degree?
3 Should initiatives be undertaken with regard to those groups of people
   most likely to be affected, or with reference to the population as a
   whole? For example, should fluoride be added to all tap-water, or be
   provided as an additive only for those most in need of it (e.g. children)?
4 To what extent are health promotion and disease prevention morally
   justified where they impinge upon people's freedom of action? There is
   a dilemma here about the responsibilities of the state towards the
   population, set against the individual's pursuit of pleasure. What things
   can people rightly be prevented from doing, and how conscious should
   they be made about their health status?

Lambert and McPherson argue that the first dilemma has been ameliorated by redefining all health-care activities as involving some measure of prevention. This provides a now widely shared classification in terms of three levels:

(a) primary prevention – strategies that aim to prevent the onset of disease
    (e.g. dieting, taking exercise);
(b) secondary prevention – strategies that aim to detect a disease at the
    earliest stage possible and to bring about a cure (e.g. screening for
    cervical or breast cancer);
(c) tertiary prevention – strategies that aim to minimize the effects or
    reduce the progress of an already established disease (e.g. coronary
    bypass surgery).

This redefinition is consistent with the point made at the beginning of the book: that there has been a shift in focus from illness to health. The problem is that this is not just a shift from like to like. Health, as an aim, is inseparable from what people perceive the 'good life' to be. It has an essentially moral and ideological character to it, because it is tied up with what people believe is 'good' or 'correct', or 'responsible' (Murcott, 1979).

The third dilemma concerns the focus of action upon special groups, where this is justified because the prevalence of the disease is highest among those populations. Examples of such diseases include higher rates of rickets among Asian babies, or of lung cancer and heart disease among social classes IV and V (manual workers). What happens here is that the behaviours or beliefs of those groups are targeted for change. Asian parents are told to change their diet; working-class people are advised to give up smoking and to eat more 'healthily'. This, however, can give rise to resistance and resentment because (a) the socio-economic situation of such groups is overlooked, and (b) there is no understanding of the role of these 'unhealthy' practices in the everyday lives of the people concerned (Donovan, 1984).

The fourth dilemma is also relevant here, raising as it does the question of the relationship of medical knowledge to everyday life. It was the medical viewpoint, with its objective gaze, that made possible the separation of the person from disease, and so the removal of blame for falling ill. Paradoxically, with the shift in medicine from cure towards prevention, it is that same profession that has been accused of exercising an increasing amount of control over everyday life (Zola, 1972). As more and more of life's aspects, from diet, through exercise to mental attitude, become linked with the onset of disease, so the medical view reattaches moral judgements to activities rather than to groups.

The identification of individuals who act in a certain way means that they come under increasing scrutiny and pressure to change. This is one sense in which Zola has accused medicine of being an institution of social control. Whether this is perceived in these terms by those concerned is another matter. For example, many women patients who are accepting of their GP's advice about smoking and diet are less so about the need for exercise (Pill et al., 1989). There are important issues here about the extent to which people should change their lives for what *others* regard as the good of their health. It is not only medical practitioners who are involved in this. The behavioural sciences have justified their usefulness to medicine in terms of their ability to encourage just this kind of lifestyle change. For example, in the field of exercise, claims have been made as to psychology's promise to increase people's motivation to be active (Biddle and Fox, 1989). In the area of employment, there are now programmes that claim to reduce stress among workers, so that a harmony is obtained between 'healthy people' and the 'healthy businesses' that employ them (Pelletier and Lutz, 1991).

Inevitably, any involvement of health psychology and medical sociology in health care also means confronting the dilemmas listed above. While, as social scientists, we can comment upon these matters, we are not free of the problems that attach to them. It has been pointed out that medical sociologists have, on occasion, criticized medicine with the benefit of hindsight. They have sometimes done this against the background of a naïve and rosy picture of life before medical care (Strong, 1979b). One example is the case of modern obstetric practice, which, whatever its shortcomings, is a great improvement on the horrors of childbirth experienced by poorer women 60 or 70 years ago.

It can be argued that the involvement of social scientists in health promotion has pointed up, more than ever, the dilemmas facing those who direct and execute policy. Unlike biomedicine, social science has the concepts to grasp just those issues that appear to be inherently dilemmatic. In order to illustrate what this means, we can examine one area of disease prevention and health promotion in more detail – that of coronary heart disease.

An illustrative account: the case of coronary proneness

Deaths from coronary heart disease have, for some time, been seen as a problem that ought to be tackled by preventive measures (Holmes, 1993). Among these is the possibility of screening people for the presence of risk-factors which have been implicated in the development of the condition. The primary factors, apart from family history, which cannot be altered, are smoking, lack of exercise, high blood cholesterol and diet. In recent years there has been an accepted view that following a low-fat diet will lower the risk of heart disease, and programmes to encourage this have been pursued in several European countries as well as the USA. In spite of this conviction, there is now evidence that the data connecting diet to heart disease are far from complete, and that findings showing no link between the two have largely been overlooked (Holmes, 1993).

Medical interventions for this condition have been carried out by testing blood cholesterol and blood pressure levels, prescribing medication to reduce these where necessary. The problem arises with the question of whether one should test all of the population or just selected groups. While it might seem beneficial to screen for early prevention, this raises problems in relation to the third dilemma mentioned above. As well as errors that might occur (either false positives implying disease where it does not exist, or false negatives failing to detect it), *mass screening* can itself raise psychological problems (Marteau, 1994). This applies, for example, to people who must live through the period of uncertainty that is involved in waiting for the results of tests and X-rays.

A further illustration of the implications of mass screening concerns those people who are identified as being, if not ill, then at high risk of developing coronary disease. This refers to the actions to be taken either by medical practitioners, on behalf of those individuals, or the actions that they should take themselves. For example, it has been suggested that, if it were only practically possible, it might be desirable to offer coronary arteriography to every adult person in Britain (Petch, 1983). This procedure shows whether a person's coronary arteries are severely narrowed, increasing the risk of a heart attack. Occasionally, routine investigations do reveal that a person with no symptoms has occluded arteries, and s/he is recommended for coronary bypass surgery. Here is an example of the situation of someone having a disease (diagnosed by a doctor) but not feeling ill nor having need to adopt the sick role. Nevertheless, this knowledge can have important consequences for the person's life if they refuse treatment for a condition from which they do not, literally, suffer. There was a case during the 1980s of a British academic administrator who was threatened with dismissal by his college for refusing to have surgery for a heart condition. Although, in this case, the person was already suffering from heart disease, it shows the possible implications of mass screening for proneness to various diseases. Individuals who are not feeling ill might be required to have treatment, or to take measures to avoid developing these diseases in the future.

The problem with *targeting* is that it tends to exclude those factors that affect everybody in the population, though in different ways. This has already been mentioned in relation to disease among mothers and children (Lewis, 1980), and among people in minority groups (Donovan, 1984). The general distinction has been described as one of taking either a *universalistic* view, or of adopting an *exceptionalistic* gaze (Ryan, 1976). The universalistic position begins from the premise that all people are affected in some way by a common problem. To alleviate the problem, one needs to change the situation that encourages its conditions to exist. For example, public health policy that provides clean, safe drinking water for everyone in the population is a provision of this kind. So, too, is the addition of fluoride to the drinking water supply to improve the health of people's teeth.

The exceptionalistic view assumes that the problem arises only for certain individuals, because of special features in their lives. It is only to these people that attention needs to be paid. This defines the approach that targets certain groups who are at risk of developing particular diseases, and limits its efforts at change to these individuals only. It is sometimes justified in terms of resolving the first dilemma noted above: that one can only do so much with scarce resources. However, it also follows as a recommendation in terms of the second dilemma in the list. In the case of coronary disease, both rehabilitation and prevention programmes using psychological techniques have been shown to be of only moderate effectiveness, with even positive change being sometimes short-term (Bennett and Carroll, 1994). Reviewing the research effort, Bennett and Carroll question whether the failure to be effective is the result of not identifying the target groups adequately, or tailoring the intervention appropriately. This means that more effort might go into attending to special interventions using particular individuals. However, this approach, even if effective, diverts attention away from the general conditions that might influence the development of heart disease in the general population.

In a later section we shall see how this distinction between the 'universalistic' and the 'exceptionalistic' is relevant to the focus on the individual in health promotion and disease prevention. First, we need to look at how people in everyday life perceive and respond to recommendations about avoiding heart disease.

In Britain, the attempt to reduce deaths from coronary heart disease has included a programme of screening the population. This has the intention of changing 'negative' features in people's lifestyle, including smoking, poor diet and lack of exercise. However, a recent large-scale study of the effectiveness of such interventions has revealed an overall reduction in risk of coronary disease of just 16 per cent (Family Heart Study Group, 1994). While, at first, this might seem a reasonably large reduction, it was obtained against the background of an intensive intervention programme. This involved nurse advisers who adopted a family-centred approach, meeting with individuals in follow-up sessions. This high level of input led the report's authors to conclude that health promotion by general practitioners, who can provide no follow-up, probably results in little or no benefit.

The question then arises: why do people not follow the advice of health educators, either when given through the media or by their own doctors? One answer is that health education programmes have assumed that specific information will, if given in the right way, lead to a change in people's behaviours. They assume a cause and effect relationship between the expert's advice and the layperson's actions. What this approach fails to recognize is that people conduct their lives – including those things thought to be 'healthy' and 'unhealthy' – according to beliefs that involve a range of other concerns apart from health alone. As has been pointed out many times, it is not at all clear that people change 'at-risk' behaviours for health reasons alone.

In one study that collected qualitative data about why individuals did or did not alter their behaviour, it was found that such changes did not follow a formal health message. Instead, these occurred after a period of time when (for reasons not altogether clear) these behaviours seemed more important to the individuals concerned (Hunt and MacLeod, 1987). These people did not cite health as the main reason for change, but often other matters, to do with such things as finance, change of social scene, family problems or appearance.

The various meanings that people give to health are related to their way of life, so that 'health as fitness' means being able to do what *they* want to do (e.g. run for a bus, walk the dog), not what a health expert defines as optimum fitness (e.g. in terms of levels of activity in an exercise regime). Hunt and MacLeod reported that where desirable behaviour changes did occur, they often followed a period of thought, or of sporadic attempts that had previously resulted in failure. In particular, change occurred when these behaviours became salient against the background events of everyday life. They were then worth changing because of what they reflected about *other* aspects of life, some of which were reported as 'triggers' for change. We can, once again, compare this to two previous examples of a similar process in people's awareness about the onset of illness. These are the triggers that Zola (1973) described as making symptoms worth taking to the doctor, and the triggers that provoked the women in Brown and Harris' (1978) study to become depressed.

These findings suggest that health promoters lack knowledge about the everyday beliefs which people hold about health and illness. These beliefs include, of course, the very messages that health promoters have, over the years, been putting forward. 'Lay' beliefs about health and illness take up certain ideas from medicine. Among these is the idea of which kind of person is a candidate for a heart attack. If asked, people will identify a range of characteristics – from obesity and having a red face, to stress and hard manual labour – that they believe are associated with a predisposition to heart disease (Davison et al., 1991). What is interesting is that this aggregate of qualities is so flexibly held that it allows for the exceptions which inevitably occur. This would include, for example, the person like Winston Churchill, who lives a long life in spite of an appetite for rich food, alcohol and cigars; and the individual with few, if any, of these characteristics, who suddenly drops dead in middle age. Davison et al. argue that the repetition of health messages about coronary proneness serves to heighten these contradictions in the public consciousness. This is because the number of individuals with these qualities who survive their risky behaviours becomes more apparent, while the case of those who have a heart attack 'out of the blue' are made even more inexplicable. Once they become aware of these contradictions, people can easily become distrustful of simple health messages, and particularly of those applied to the population as a whole. Against this background, it is not surprising that some have called into question the whole thrust of health promotion where it appears to be based upon spurious correlations, lack of systematic theory and frequent reversals of advice (Becker, 1986).

Here, then, is a case in which the promotion of a message that has a clear rationale within the logic of health promoters takes a different direction to that intended. It is not that people do not listen, or that they wilfully disregard the advice given to them. Rather, the behaviours that are the subject of the experts' concern cannot be changed in a social vacuum. Ideas about health and illness are far more complicated than the cause and effect relationships upon which advice about behaviour changes are based. These ideas are not just about cause, but touch upon moral questions about what one 'should' or 'should not' do if one is not to be thought 'dull', 'self-obsessed' or just plain 'cranky'. There is a need to replace the traditional model (the 'top down' approach) with one that identifies 'how cultural or sub-cultural processes influence the impact of any intervention, and which modifies initiatives accordingly' (Bennett and Murphy, 1994: 128).

Coronary proneness: changing the Type A individual

Perhaps the most important addition to the traditional risk-factors for coronary heart disease has been the 'Type A Behaviour Pattern' (TABP). This is a particular complex of behaviours that is believed to attach to individuals more likely to develop coronary disease. The TABP includes such qualities as impatience, a sense of time-urgency, always thinking of more than one thing at a time, feeling guilty when not working, and being overly ambitious and challenging (Friedman and Rosenman, 1974). The correction of this risk-factor depends, first, upon identifying which individuals in the population are 'Type A', and which ones (lacking these features) are 'Type B'. Once this is determined, it is then possible to suggest how Type A people can change their behaviour, in order to lower the risk of their developing coronary disease. While there have been attempts to use specific parts of the profile in behavioural programmes (e.g. modifying anger), the originators of the concept have also addressed their work directly to individuals. Once told how to recognize whether one is a Type A person, it becomes possible to take advice upon how to change one's whole approach to life.

As part of this advice are proposals that 'you' take steps to 'eliminate as many events and activities as possible that do not contribute directly to your socioeconomic well being' (Friedman and Rosenman, 1974: 207). One of the key people in this exercise is 'your secretary', who must be made to cooperate in this slow-down. This assumes, of course, that 'you' are included in the list of people whom Friedman and Rosenman cite as the target of their advice – dentists, attorneys, physicians and business executives. The secretary, too, may be Type A (because 'you' hired 'her'), though any benefit 'she' will gain from this exercise seems more second-hand than direct. It is possible, of course, that 'you' might only add to the stresses on 'her' day; but that is not considered in the guidance given.

What are we to make of this? Two points need to be drawn out here, one of which relates to the focus of health promotion upon the individual, as opposed to the social context. Note that the advice given to the Type A person assumes that the problem of time-urgency rests with 'him', or with 'his' immediate work schedule. Perhaps the choice of professional careers in the list, where there is greater scope for such change, makes this seem practical. But what, as we have noted, of the secretary 'herself'? Women also suffer from heart disease, as do people from all walks of life. The problems of one's work schedule, the demands of superiors, the worries of fitting in different obligations and duties, each have their origin in the social contexts of everyday life. The resolute focus upon specific groups of people, who have scope to restructure their working day, detracts from the inability of many others in the population to do just this. Therefore, it is necessary to make two points. First, that emphasis upon the individual misses the role of the social context, in creating the circumstances of Type A. Second, that Type A, as a concept, assumes a certain kind of individual, and a certain kind of society.

This last comment leads on to a further point that should be made about Type A Behaviour as a risk-factor for heart disease. Unlike smoking or diet, it presumes that people have a particular 'social nature', a way of being that has developed as a result of the Western way of life. The previous chapter noted that the very features which define Type A Behaviour as negative are the ones that are encouraged by society and often rewarded. Particularly in the world of business, ambition, hard-driving, a willingness to take on jobs and to complete them within a tight schedule are matters for congratulation or admiration – not criticism. A good example of this duality is to be found in the invited introduction to Friedman and Rosenman's own book. The immunologist Sir Peter Medawar (1974) made the point that, because Type A people 'cut such a poor figure' in the text, he wanted to say something in their favour – 'they are the great *doers* of the world'.

A further example of this apparent contradiction is shown in work reporting that executives high in stress, but reporting less illness, have 'a stronger commitment to self, an attitude of vigouresness toward the environment, a sense of meaningfulness, and an internal locus of control' (Kobasa, 1979: 1). This demonstrates that the very qualities that are regarded in one context as associated with good health are in another context labelled as the precursors of serious illness. What is common to this paradox, however, is that the individual becomes responsible, if not for being that sort of person, then at least for changing his or her lifestyle.

We need to put this paradox in context; it emerges within the individual as a dilemma, and is maintained by society as a contradiction. That is to say, if there is a 'coronary-prone' behaviour pattern, then it is not a personality defect, but the embodiment of a way of acting that is embedded in social relationships (Radley, 1984). That is why it has been suggested that the Type A Behaviour Pattern is a 'Western culture-bound syndrome', meaning that it can only be understood in the context of Western capitalist society, its values and moral concerns (Helman, 1987). The typology does not just denote a neutral entity, a 'risk-factor', but embodies the paradoxes that exist in a society that demands that we both strive in a self-interested way, and yet care for others. This means that attempts to correct Type A Behaviour by influencing individuals to change, for example by being less hurried, flies in the face of the contradictory demands that beset people who must continue to live in the social world. Furthermore, these demands fall unequally on people in different sections of society, upon whom are also placed different limits to their scope for individual action (Freund, 1982).

Summing up this section, we can see that promoting 'healthier lifestyles' to reduce the risk of coronary heart disease must involve an appreciation of the social and psychological contexts in which designated 'risky' behaviours operate. More than this, we need to understand that the definition of what is risky is not value-free, either for health experts or for the individuals concerned. Specific behaviours are woven into everyday patterns of life that reflect cultural values. Lifestyles are subject to scrutiny and evaluation in a society that otherwise depends upon personal 'flexibility' and 'competition' for its functioning. These are the paradoxical features that are largely overlooked by health promotion campaigns, which focus almost exclusively upon the individual. The consequences of this approach for health promotion are the subject of the section to follow.

Individual responsibility for health: obligation and blame

Research into the Type A Behaviour Pattern is indicative of two trends in health promotion. One concerns the individual as the focus for disease prevention, and the other a shift to a concern with chronic rather than acute disease. Chapter 7 noted that the increased interest in chronic diseases, and how people manage to live with them, comes in part from the lack of a medical cure for these conditions. This perceived failure of medicine to

remove these diseases, and the consequent financial demand placed upon
health services to care for the chronically sick, provide the backdrop to the
call for the individual to be responsible for improving the health of the
nation. Using the USA as an example, it has been argued that the control of
communicable disease (e.g. typhoid, scarlet fever) depended upon improvements to the environment, e.g. to such things as housing and water
supplies. By comparison, control of conditions like cancer and heart disease
depends upon 'modification of the individual's behavior and habits of living'
(Knowles, 1977: 61).

This argument is supported by reference to work that finds good health to
be associated with certain basic habits, such as getting regular meals,
moderate exercise, and avoidance of smoking and high alcohol intake. It
holds that, if only each individual were willing to adhere to these basic rules
for healthy living, then there would be a resultant benefit to personal and
national health. If each individual is unwilling to do so, then 'he should stop
complaining about the . . . costs of medical care' (Knowles, 1977: 78).

This position is one that finds favour in many developed countries
burdened with the ever increasing costs of health care. However, the
coupling of communicable disease with environmental change, and of
chronic disease with individual lifestyle, is not an argument that bears close
examination. There is repeated evidence of a strong association between the
prevalence of chronic disease and position in the social structure (Morris,
1979). This has been underlined most recently by evidence concerning the
health of people in northern England over the period 1981–91. Census data
show that mortality differentials have continued to widen between the most
and the least economically advantaged groups (Phillimore et al., 1994).
This, Phillimore et al. conclude, re-emphasizes the link between public
health and material conditions, rather than with individual behaviour.
Indeed, it has been noted that the most effective preventive measures seem
to be those that require the least individual effort, such as the public health
management of water, air and sewage. The most difficult measures to make
effective are those for which the individual is responsible, namely controlling smoking and drug abuse (Saward and Sorensen, 1978). In spite of these
difficulties, the rationale for health promotion campaigns continues to retain
the modification of individual behaviour as its aim. As social scientists, we
need to examine the assumptions and the consequences of this position in
the light of what we know about ideas of health and the social context.

A direct challenge to the individualist position has been made by
Crawford (1977), who argued that its consequences show something of the
ideological assumptions underlying it. The primary result of holding
individuals responsible for their health is that they can be blamed for failure.
We have seen, in Chapter 3, that most people do not hold themselves
responsible for falling ill, but they may blame themselves for not looking
after their health. Notably, the presence of self-blame does not tally with
people's scope to exercise control over their health, i.e. those who are
disadvantaged may not recognize their relative deprivation. This means that

individuals who are least able to adopt healthy lifestyles (e.g. eat fresh foods, exercise regularly) are sanctioned for their failure to remain healthy. Should they fall ill, the question then arises as to whether they should receive the same level of treatment as other, more 'responsible' individuals. In the context of the surgical treatment for coronary disease, one recent case in Britain involved a surgeon who questioned whether it was worthwhile operating on a man because he continued to smoke. The patient's lifestyle was said to contravene the prospect of a good therapeutic result.

Imputing blame to individuals for illness also has other implications, some unanticipated by health promoters. Groups who previously might have drawn sympathy for their plight, such as victims of heart disease, may now be regarded critically and as unworthy of special help. Specialist organizations that give information about how individuals can reduce the risk of heart disease (with the implication of avoiding it) paradoxically reinforce the notion that sufferers have brought it upon themselves. This knowledge can result in charitable donations to those organizations being withheld by members of the public (Radley and Kennedy, 1992). The stigma that once derived from the view that certain groups of the sick are 'different' is compounded by their also being held responsible for living a life that directly led to their condition (Wang, 1992).

The dilemmas that were mentioned earlier on in this chapter become apparent once again. On the one hand, the focus on the individual obscures the structural differences in society that affect health. It does this by assuming that all individuals have an equal opportunity to live the kind of life that experts recommend. On the other, to dismiss all talk of individual responsibility for health runs the risk of seeing people as helpless victims of social circumstances. Experts then underestimate the changes that people could bring about, if only they had sufficient knowledge and support (Allison, 1982).

Health promotion and consumer culture

In recent years, health issues have become caught up in a wider consumer interest in the body (Featherstone, 1982). This is apparent in the number of articles about health and illness that appear in newspapers, magazines and on television. Health is a topic that is now run together with other, equally important concerns, particularly about the need to 'feel good' and to 'look young'. The leisure industry promotes its products (everything from jogging suits to exercise bikes) on the basis that to be fit is to be healthy. Similarly, the beauty and personal hygiene industries promote their products through notions of 'good health', while advertising about food is peppered with information about its 'health-giving' qualities.

The establishment of a society in which individuals must constantly monitor the healthiness of their lifestyles has implications for everyone, but particularly for the ageing. Older people can no longer take refuge in their grey hairs as a symbol of wisdom or authority. A culture that values the individual over the group, and the negotiation of values over tradition, is one where harsh judgements about personal achievement (and failure) are likely to be made. Little is to be gained from taking up the sick role, and it is better to keep fit lest 'the judgement "He doesn't look after himself" or "She doesn't worry about her looks" is said in a rebuking tone . . . to the person concerned' (Douglas, 1978: 31).

In developed societies, health promotion takes its place within a culture of consumerism that is already well-established. A key aspect of this culture is the use of advertising to create a sense of emotional vulnerability. As part of this, people are urged constantly to monitor themselves for bodily imperfections, which are no longer to be regarded as natural (Featherstone, 1982). Weight gain, hair loss (or growth, in the 'wrong' places) and increased perspiration are familiar targets in this area. Modern advertising has gained its power, in part, by undermining traditional values of authority. Individuals are told that they can now choose for themselves. When applied to health, this means a movement away from the authority of medicine toward the individual, who becomes a 'client' or 'consumer' where previously s/he was a patient (Fox, 1977). However, far from leading to a de-medicalization of society, this move has amplified health as a modern concern. The difference is that in the recent past health and illness have been issues to do with medical control (effectively a single institution). Now they are subject to a form of control that potentially depends upon the self-discipline of each and every citizen. With the emphasis upon 'looking after yourself', health matters have gained in social and personal significance. This means that, whatever changes have occurred in the relationship of medicine to society, there is no evidence that any *cultural* de-medicalization has taken place in the USA or in other developed societies (Fox, 1977).

To provide a better perspective on this issue, the next section examines one development resulting from changes in people's views about health, and how it should be managed. Along with the concern about individual responsibility for health, there is also interest in the role that individuals can play in the treatment of their own illnesses – in effect, in helping each other.

Self-help groups and the management of illness

The modern philosophy of self-help has its origin in the changing place of medicine in society. Therapeutic and economic limitations to medicine's power have led people to question whether they should rely only upon doctors to prevent and to cure disease. As a response to this, there has emerged a belief in the need for people to take control of their own health, and to do this together. The formation of self-help groups, particularly by and for those suffering from particular diseases, is now widespread. These groups have been formed by people suffering from chronic diseases (e.g. cancer, arthritis), from disabilities of various kinds, from the effects of drug and alcohol abuse, and from various forms of mental illness.

The key features which self-help share are widely acknowledged as being contradictory. On the one hand, individuals take personal responsibility for their situation rather than depending upon someone else; on the other, they help each other in a process of mutual aid (Borkman, 1991). This latter aspect underlines the way such groups are said to function as alternative social networks or communities of interest. This provides the alternative label sometimes applied to them – *support groups*.

Linking individual responsibility to mutual aid has been used to show that the former need not result in 'victim blaming', as described in the previous section. This argument proposes that to see people only as victims is to caste them in a passive, dependent role. This is one that is neither necessary nor desirable (Allison, 1982). By speaking, instead, of 'self-reliance' and pointing to the possibilities that might flow from people becoming 'critically conscious' of their situation, they might be able to change it. This hope owes something to the advances that have been made by other kinds of group, similar to those belonging to the women's movement. Such groups have managed to achieve personal (if not social) change for their members (Zola, 1991). How true this is in the health context can be assessed by examining what self-help groups have achieved so far, and the reactions of others to their aims and programmes.

At this point it is worth spelling out why we should pay attention to such groups in this book, given that they form, as yet, a small part of most people's experience of health care. First, self-help groups reflect a particular, and increasing, response by individuals to their perception that their illness is not best left to experts. Second, this perception has implications for the way that people think about their health in general. In Chapters 2 and 3 we saw that health beliefs are woven into other social attitudes, as well as drawing upon the relationship of medicine to society at any particular time. If this relationship is felt to be changing, then we should expect people's beliefs about health in general to change as well. Third, the issues of stress and social support have been discussed in relation to ideas about the causes of illness. Once these phenomena (whatever their scientific status) become part of the public consciousness about the origins of disease, then it seems likely that they will figure increasingly in people's views about what they should do to recover good health, and to keep it. To summarize, including this topic here is an acknowledgement that health and illness are not finished objects, but are part of ongoing social change. This change, as we have seen, need not be smooth and continuous. It often involves struggles with issues that are problematic, if only because they seem to pose dilemmas for those concerned.

What are the characteristics of self-help groups; how do they work? Two main themes have been pointed up: 'sharing' and 'project work' (Robinson, 1980). The first involves the sharing of information and common experience. This often occurs through informal discussion at face-to-face meetings, and the use of a networked publication, such as a newsletter. One of the purposes of shared information is to explore the common experiences of members that drew them together (e.g. the nature of symptoms, everyday difficulties). For example, groups of cancer sufferers discuss matters to do with fear and helplessness. However, they also pool information about services available locally, and any new medical advances concerning their disease (Brown and Griffiths, 1986). Members also discuss how others see people like themselves. This has the important function of de-stigmatizing the group, raising the feelings of self-worth for individual members, and creating a positive identity for those concerned.

The 'projects' that groups engage in will depend upon both the nature of the condition and the local membership. It might involve running programmes to help members acquire specific skills, or to set up a wider network of contacts. It might involve meetings with medical professionals, or raising funds to support research related to the disease which defines the membership. Whatever the case, these 'projects' serve to build up and to sustain personal relationships within the group, as well as to elaborate its identity (Robinson, 1980).

Research into the functioning of self-help groups has shown that many of the tensions surrounding the issue of 'individualism versus mutuality' remain and, if anything, are sharpened (Vincent, 1992). While some manage to establish a structure allowing full membership participation, others develop an organizational structure that focuses upon service provision, either through voluntary aid or through fund-raising. This raises the question: should the group look after the needs of its present membership, or should it work towards a future cure for others? This is one dilemma faced by these collectives. Another is whether the group should attempt to be an alternative to traditional medical care, or else work with doctors in a complementary way, trying to achieve a cure within the framework of biomedical treatment.

These questions are reflected in the findings of one study looking into the workings of a self-help group set up for sufferers of a form of chronic arthritis, ankylosing spondylitis (Williams, 1989). Analysing the minutes of the group's meetings, it was found that its early resolve to deal with issues of education and welfare were met with reservations by a rheumatologist. He was worried that patients might be given the 'wrong' sort of information, which would 'do more harm than good'. Expressions of determination to be a 'pressure group' ('even on doctors') were diffused by a medical practitioner who told the group that its role was to teach medical professionals 'what their problems really are'. Analysis of the newsletter showed that there was coverage of personal stories of difficulties experienced by members. However, these accounts were sometimes redefined away from roles and family, and represented as better or worse responses by individuals to their disease. That is to say, they became portrayals of 'good adjustment' in the face of adversity, the ideology that praises individual fortitude in the face of events whose social history remains unexamined (Cross, 1981; Voysey, 1975).

The pertinence of this finding is not its message of limited self-help, but its revelation that how we think about health in modern society is characterized by tensions. To underline what has been said before, health and illness do not exist in a social vacuum. They embody something of the individual's relationship to society, or rather what people *believe* this relationship *should* be. The belief in the worthiness of self-reliance, on the one hand, and in mutual aid, on the other, appear in the ideology of these groups as twin virtues which are brought together in harmony (Allison, 1982). However, research into both the general and the specific forms taken by self-help groups tells another story: that self-help is really not so simple, based as it is upon social contradictions and personal dilemmas (Vincent, 1992; Williams, 1989). This suggests that, as well as *what* we think about health and illness, *how* we think about these matters may be changing.

The self-help movement has been criticized for its failure to address either the wider social issues surrounding ill-health or the dominance of medical knowledge. In part this is because it is perceived to depend upon a psychology not only of the individual, but also of what has been termed the 'fantasy of the whole person' (Coward, 1989). This idea assumes that being 'whole' or 'balanced' is healthy for the individual's 'personality'. Within this perspective, the possibility of accepting, let alone confronting, conflicts and contradictions is inadmissible. While it is incorrect to assume that all self-help organizations are the same, there is a clear suggestion that few such groups confront the social problems which affect the health of their members. Perhaps this is not surprising, given that holistic medicine draws heavily upon the counterculture of the 1960s. This outlook rejected one set of bourgeois values only to embrace a narcissistic view of the 'self', with the consequent loss of a critical social consciousness (Freund, 1982).

This situation has led, in some quarters, to impatience with 'alternative' approaches to treatment, which are seen as no alternative to the failings of orthodox medicine (Wilkinson and Kitzinger, 1993). Only when self-help is linked to broader social divisions is there a clear sense of members opposing those structures and beliefs which (they hold) contribute either to ill-health, or to deficiencies in treatment. This is true for women (Zola, 1991), and it appears to be so for blacks as well (Vincent, 1992).

The study of self-help is, by comparison with other areas of health-related research, still in its infancy (Borkman, 1991). The reason for discussing it here has been to place it in the context of health promotion and illness prevention. In that sense, self-help can be seen as part of the movement towards a greater sense of personal responsibility for health care. And yet it also shows, in these initial attempts by people to find an alternative to orthodox medicine, something of the tensions that are central to considerations about health and illness in general. For that reason, the study of self-help should not be thought of as merely an examination of an alternative therapeutic technique. It offers, instead, the opportunity to see how ideologies of health and illness reflect society's conflicting interests concerning disease prevention and the care of the sick.

Mind, health and society

In the course of this chapter we have seen that health promotion and disease prevention are based upon assumptions about the relationship of the individual to society. These claims also rest upon assumptions about the nature of 'mind'. It is not just *what* people think about health and illness that is at issue here, but *how* this way of thinking embodies ideas about our relationships to each other, and to society as a whole. Much of this book has been to do with the illness experience of individuals, because we, in the West, locate this experience within the afflicted body of the person concerned. The biomedical perspective, with its emphasis upon objectivity and the general laws governing the body, cannot encompass issues to do with subjective judgement and moral values. However, this chapter has shown that to reinforce medical interventions with similarly based psychological ones is to raise problems which did not appear before.

The shift in focus to self-help, or towards holistic treatment, does not escape the ideological basis to our understanding of health and illness. Drawing upon what is, in large measure, an individualistic psychology, such movements seek to locate health in the individual, someone who is passive with respect to interventions within his or her body, but exhorted to be active in adjustment to his or her situation. In that sense, we are divided individuals, and present intractable problems for researchers who try to find causal relationships between societal context, subjective ideas and physiological responses. Such approaches retain, often tacitly, the cultural idealism of the individual who has a fixed relationship to society (Sampson, 1977). The idea of the free individual who resists collective action is a theoretical axiom, not an absolute truth. It might be just as inappropriate for our purposes as the concept of the man or woman of the Middle Ages who was bounded by guild and family.

A similar point can be made about emancipated individualism, which forms the ideal of modern society. The disenchantment that often accompanies extreme individualism has been taken as a symptom of ill-health, suggesting that society is 'the only medicine capable of giving life to the individual who has lost the taste for living' (Moscovici, 1990: 82). This plea sets up community as a 'healthy' alternative to individualism, although, in doing this, Moscovici appears to be trying to make the kind of idealist definition of health that Murcott (1979) has argued is never possible.

These criticisms are aimed at approaches that displace questions of health and illness from the physical and social body to the individual considered in isolation. They are not, in themselves, calls to understand health as simply 'social integration', along the lines of some of the social support literature. Rather they point to the fact that, if we wish to study health and illness from a social scientific point of view, we cannot begin by assuming individuals who share ready-made capacities.

Instead, the lesson of this book's survey is that people's ideas of health and illness have always reflected the kind of society in which they live. Also, that the way that individuals talk about these matters is expressive of a more general way of thinking about life – and, we should add – death.

Health and illness are not just another set of topics for study in psychology or sociology, to which existing theories can easily be applied. As with other important matters, how people think about them, and what they do about these questions, are reflections of key cultural concerns. They are parts of the social order that reflect something of the whole. We have seen throughout how, when people speak of their health, they often do so by invoking other everyday, but often important, issues. These might be to do with work, or with family or with religion. The common theme in this is that health and illness do not have a ready-made form, but take their meaning from the social fabric through which they are portrayed. We are not merely healthy or ill, but appear so. We try to be well, strive to avoid falling sick, or ultimately consent to bear illness with what grace and fortitude we can muster.

Chapter summary

- The perceived limitations of modern medicine, and the scarcity of economic resources, have provided the conditions for an emphasis upon disease prevention and education for good health; however, health as an aim is inseparable from what people conceive the 'good life' to be – *health is ideological.*
- Health promotion faces certain *key dilemmas* to do with issues of resource allocation, evaluation of effectiveness of interventions, whether to target at-risk groups, and the degree to which it is proper to limit people's freedom of choice.
- One major programme of health education has aimed to reduce deaths from coronary heart disease. Attempts to alter people's behaviour both in the population and in the clinic have met with only modest success. One reason might be that people have different views about the causes of disease, and which individuals are likely to develop it. Research shows, however, that individuals change health-related behaviours for *non-health-related reasons.*
- The recent emphasis upon identifying individuals in terms of the Type A Behaviour Pattern has been shown to ignore its basis in everyday ideology. Instead of being a stable personality characteristic, the Type A Behaviour Pattern has been shown to reflect dilemmas about behaviour in Western society; it is an example of a *culture-bound syndrome.*
- *Self-help groups* have emerged in recent years as a way for sufferers to cope with illness alongside, or outside, of the medical sphere. These groups operate in terms of self-reliance and mutual aid, which express a tension, and sometimes a contradiction, in their modes of operation. Critics of the self-help movement see it as another example of *individualism* in health care; this results in the individual being held responsible for his or her illness, and in being victimized for failures to recover or to maintain health.

- Health promotion and disease prevention have tended to rest upon a philosophy of individual responsibility which is explicit, and upon assumptions about society which have remained tacit; examining these interventions shows that ideas about *health and illness reflect ideological issues* that are part of everyday thinking.

Further reading

Crawford, R. (1977) You are dangerous to your health: the ideology and politics of victim blaming, *International Journal of Health Services*, 7, 663–80.

Holmes, R. (1993) 'Coronary heart disease: a cautionary tale', in B. Davey and J. Popay (eds) *Dilemmas in Health Care*. Ballmoor: Open University Press.

Hunt, S.J. and MacLeod, M. (1987) Health and behavioural change: some lay perspectives, *Community Medicine*, 9, 68–76.

Lambert, H. and McPherson, K. (1993) 'Disease prevention and health promotion', in B. Davey and J. Popay (eds) *Dilemmas in Health Care*. Ballmoor: Open University Press.

Vincent, J. (1992) 'Self-help groups and health care in contemporary Britain', in M. Saks (ed.) *Alternative Medicine in Britain*. Oxford: Oxford University Press.

References

Abercrombie, M.L.J. (1960) *The Anatomy of Judgment: An investigation into the processes of perception and reasoning*. London: Hutchinson.

Abrams, D., Thomas, J. and Hogg, M.A. (1990) Numerical distinctiveness, social identity and gender salience, *British Journal of Social Psychology*, 29, 87–92.

Allison, K. (1982) Health education: self-responsibility vs blaming the victim, *Health Education*, 20, 11–13 and 24.

Alonzo, A.A. (1979) Everyday illness behavior: a situational approach to health status deviations, *Social Science and Medicine*, 13A, 397–404.

Alonzo, A.A. (1984) An illness behavior paradigm: a conceptual exploration of a situational-adaptation perspective, *Social Science and Medicine*, 19, 499–510.

Anderson, D.B. and Pennebaker, J.W. (1980) Pain and pleasure: alternative interpretations of identical stimulation, *European Journal of Social Psychology*, 10, 207–12.

Anderson, J. (1987) Migration and health: perspectives on immigrant women, *Sociology of Health and Illness*, 9, 410–38.

Anderson, J., Blue, C. and Lau, A. (1991) Women's perspectives on chronic illness: ethnicity, ideology and restructuring of life, *Social Science and Medicine*, 33, 101–13.

Anderson, R. and Bury, M. (eds) (1988) *Living with Chronic Illness: The experience of patients and their families*. London: Unwin Hyman.

Angel, R. and Thoits, P. (1987) The impact of culture on the cognitive structure of illness, *Culture, Medicine and Psychiatry*, 11, 465–94.

Annandale, E. and Hunt, K. (1990) Masculinity, femininity and sex: an exploration of their relative contribution to explaining gender differences in health, *Sociology of Health and Illness*, 12, 24–46.

Antonovsky, A. (1967) Social class, life expectancy and overall mortality, *Milbank Memorial Fund Quarterly*, 45, 31–73.

Appels, A. (1986) Culture and disease, *Social Science and Medicine*, 23, 477–83.

Apple, D. (1960) How laymen define illness, *Journal of Health and Human Behavior*, 1, 219–25.

Arber, S. (1987) Social class, non-employment, and chronic illness: continuing the inequalities in health debate, *British Medical Journal*, 294, 1069–73.

Arber, S. (1991) Class, paid employment and family roles: making sense of structural disadvantage, gender and health status, *Social Science and Medicine*, 32, 425–36.

Arber, S., Gilbert, N. and Dale, A. (1985) Paid employment and women's health: a benefit or a source of role strain?, *Sociology of Health and Illness*, 7, 375–400.

Armitage, K.J, Schneiderman, L.J. and Bass, M.A. (1979) Response of physicians to medical complaints in men and women, *Journal of the American Medical Association*, 241, 2186–7.

Armstrong, D. (1983) *Political Anatomy of the Body: Medical knowledge in Britain in the twentieth century*. Cambridge: Cambridge University Press.

Armstrong, D. (1984) The patient's view, *Social Science and Medicine*, 18, 737–44.

Armstrong, D. (1987) 'Bodies of knowledge: Foucault and the problem of human anatomy', in G. Scambler (ed.) *Sociological Theory and Medical Sociology*. London: Tavistock.

Arney, W.R. and Bergen, B.J. (1983) The anomaly, the chronic patient and the play of medical power, *Sociology of Health and Illness*, 5, 1–24.

Askham, J. (1982) Professionals' criteria for accepting people as patients, *Social Science and Medicine*, 16, 2083–9.

Auld, J., Dorn, N. and South, N. (1986) 'Irregular work, irregular pleasures: heroin in the 1980s', in K. Matthews and J. Young (eds) *Confronting Crime*. London: Sage.

Bales, R.F. (1950) *Interaction Process Analysis: A method for the study of small groups*. Cambridge, Mass.: Addison-Wesley.

Balint, M. (1964) *The Doctor, His Patient and the Illness*, 2nd edition. London: Pitman Medical.

Barrett, M. and Roberts, H. (1978) 'Doctors and their patients: the social control of women in general practice', in C. Smart and B. Smart (eds) *Women, Sexuality and Social Control*. London: Routledge and Kegan Paul.

Bartley, M. (1985) Coronary heart disease and the public health 1850–1983, *Sociology of Health and Illness*, 7, 289–313.

Bartley, M., Popay, J. and Plewis, I. (1992) Domestic conditions, paid employment and women's experience of ill-health, *Sociology of Health and Illness*, 14, 313–43.

Baumann, B. (1961) Diversities in conceptions of health and fitness, *Journal of Health and Human Behavior*, 2, 39–46.

Beardsworth, A. and Keil, T. (1991) Health-related beliefs and dietary practices among vegetarians and vegans: a qualitative study, *Health Education Journal*, 50, 38–42.

Becker, M.H. (1986) The tyranny of health promotion, *Public Health Review*, 14, 15–23.

Bellaby, P. (1990) What is genuine sickness? The relation between work-discipline and the sick role in a pottery factory, *Sociology of Health and Illness*, 12, 47–68.

Belle, D. (1991) 'Gender differences in the social moderators of stress', in A. Monat and R.S. Lazarus (eds) *Stress and Coping: An anthology*. New York: Columbia University Press.

Bem, S. (1974) The measurement of psychological androgeny, *Journal of Consulting and Clinical Psychology*, 42, 155–62.

Benner, P. (1984) *From Novice to Expert: Excellence and power in clinical nursing practice*. Menlo Park, Calif.: Addison-Wesley.

Bennett, A., Knox, J.D.E. and Morrison, A.T. (1978) Difficulties in consultations reported by doctors in general practice, *Journal of the Royal College of General Practitioners*. 28, 646–51.

Bennett, P. and Carroll, D. (1994) Cognitive-behavioural interventions in cardiac rehabilitation, *Journal of Psychosomatic Research*, 38, 169–82.

Bennett, P. and Murphy, S. (1994) Psychology and health promotion, *The Psychologist*, 7, 126–8.

Berger, J. and Mohr, J. (1967) *A Fortunate Man: The story of a country doctor*. London: Allen Lane.

Berger, P. and Luckmann, T. (1971) *The Social Construction of Reality*. Harmondsworth: Penguin.

Berkman, L.F. (1984) Assessing the physical health effects of social networks and social support, *Annual Review of Public Health*, 5, 413–32.

Berkman, L.F. and Syme, S.L. (1979) Social networks, host resistance, and mortality: a nine-year follow-up study of Alameda County residents, *American Journal of Epidemiology*, 109, 186–204.

Bermann, E. (1973) Regrouping for survival: approaching dread and three phases of family interaction, *Journal of Comparative and Family Studies*, 4, 63–87.

Bernstein, B. (1971) *Class, Codes and Control: Theoretical studies towards a sociology of language. Volume 1*. London: Routledge and Kegan Paul.

Bernstein, B. and Kane, R. (1981) Physicians' attitudes toward female patients, *Medical Care*, 19, 600–8.

Biddle, S.J.H. and Fox, K.R. (1989) Exercise and health psychology: emerging relationships, *British Journal of Medical Psychology*, 62, 205–16.

Billig, M. (1988) Social representation, objectification and anchoring: a rhetorical analysis, *Social Behaviour*, 3, 1–16.

Billig, M., Condor, S., Edwards, D., Gane, M., Middleton, D. and Radley, A. (1988) *Ideological Dilemmas: A social psychology of everyday thinking*. London: Sage.

Bishop, G.D. and Converse, S.A. (1986) Illness representations: a prototype approach, *Health Psychology*, 5, 95–114.

Blair, A. (1993) 'Social class and the contextualization of illness experience', in A. Radley (ed.) *Worlds of Illness: Biographical and cultural perspectives on health and disease*. London: Routledge.

Blaxter, M. (1983) The causes of disease: women talking, *Social Science and Medicine*, 17, 59–69.

Blaxter, M. (1985) Self-definition of health status and consulting rates in primary care, *Quarterly Journal of Social Affairs*, 1, 131–71.

Blaxter, M. (1990) *Health and Lifestyles*. London: Tavistock/Routledge.

Blaxter, M. (1993) 'Why do the victims blame themselves?', in A. Radley (ed.) *Worlds of Illness: biographical and cultural perspectives on health and disease*. London: Routledge.

Blazer, D. (1982) Social support and mortality in an elderly community population, *American Journal of Epidemiology*, 115, 684–94.

Bloch, C. (1987) Everyday life, sensuality and body culture, *Women's Studies International Forum*, 10, 433–42.

Block, A.R. and Boyer, S.L. (1984) The spouse's adjustment to chronic pain: cognitive and emotional factors, *Social Science and Medicine*, 19, 1313–17.

Bloom, J.R. (1982) Social support, accommodation to stress and adjustment to breast cancer, *Social Science and Medicine*, 16, 1329–38.

Bloor, M.J. and Horobin, G.W. (1975) 'Conflict and conflict resolution in doctor/patient interactions', in C. Cox and A. Mead (eds) *A Sociology of Medical Practice*, London: Collier-Macmillan.

Borkman, T.J. (1991) 'Introduction' to Special Issue on Self-Help Groups, *American Journal of Community Psychology*, 19, Whole No. 5, 643–50

Briscoe, M.E. (1987) Why do people go to the doctor? Sex differences in the correlates of GP consultation, *Social Science and Medicine*, 25, 507–13.

Brooks, N.A. and Matson, R.R. (1982) Social-psychological adjustment to multiple sclerosis, *Social Science and Medicine*, 16, 2129–35.

Brotherston, J. (1976) 'Inequality: is it inevitable?' in C. Carter and J. Peel (eds) *Equalities and Inequalities in Health*. London: Academic Press.

Brown, G.W. (1989) 'Life events and measurement', in G.W. Brown and T.O. Harris (eds) *Life Events and Illness*. London: Unwin Hyman.

Brown, G.W. and Harris, T.O. (1978) *Social Origins of Depression: A study of psychiatric disorder in women*. London: Tavistock.

Brown, J.S. and Rawlinson, M.E. (1977) Sex differences in sick role rejection and in work performance following cardiac surgery, *Journal of Health and Social Behavior*, 18, 276–92.

Brown, T. and Griffiths, P. (1986) Cancer self-help groups: an inside view, *British Medical Journal*, 292, 1503–4.

Brown, V.A. (1981) From sickness to health: an altered focus for health-care research, *Social Science and Medicine*, 15A: 195–201.

Burke, P.J. (1973) 'The development of task and social-emotional role differentiation', in R.J. Ofshe (ed.) *Interpersonal Behavior in Small Groups*. New York: Prentice-Hall.

Bury, M. (1982) Chronic illnes as biographical disruption, *Sociology of Health and Illness*, 4, 167–82.

Bury, M. (1986) Social constructionism and the development of medical sociology, *Sociology of Health and Illness*. 8, 137–69.

Bury, M. (1988) 'Meanings at risk: the experience of arthritis', in R. Anderson and M. Bury (eds) *Living with Chronic Illness: The experience of patients and their families*. London: Unwin Hyman.

Bury, M. (1991) The sociology of chronic illness: a review of research and prospects, *Sociology of Health and Illness*, 13, 451–68.

Bury, M. and Wood, P.H.N. (1979) Problems of communication in chronic illness, *International Rehabilitation Medicine*, 1, 130–4.

Butler, J.R. (1970) Illness and the sick role: an evaluation in three communities, *British Journal of Sociology*, 21, 241–61.

Byrne, P.S. and Long, B.E.L. (1976) *Doctors Talking to Patients*. London: HMSO.

Calnan, M. (1983a) Managing 'minor' disorders: pathways to a hospital accident and emergency department, *Sociology of Health and Illness*, 5, 149–67.

Calnan, M. (1983b) Social networks and patterns of help-seeking behaviour, *Social Science and Medicine*, 17, 25–8.

Calnan, M. (1984) The Health Belief Model and participation in programmes for the early detection of breast cancer: a comparative analysis, *Social Science and Medicine*, 19, 823–30.

Calnan, M. (1987) *Health and Illness: The lay perspective*. London: Tavistock.

Calnan, M. and Williams, S. (1991) Style of life and the salience of health: an exploratory study of health related practices in households from differing socio-economic circumstances, *Sociology of Health and Illness*, 13, 506–29.

Campbell, J.D. (1975) Illness is a point of view: the development of children's concepts of illness, *Child Development*, 46, 92–100.

Cassel, J. (1976) The contribution of the social environment to host resistance, *American Journal of Epidemiology*, 104, 107–23.

Cassell, E.J. (1976) Disease as an 'it': concepts of disease revealed by patients' presentation of symptoms, *Social Science and Medicine*, 10, 143–6.

Charmaz, K. (1983) Loss of self: a fundamental form of suffering in the chronically ill, *Sociology of Health and Illness*, 5, 168–95.

Charmaz, K. (1991) *Good Days, Bad Days: The self in chronic illness and time*. New Brunswick: Rutgers University Press.

Chesebro, J.W. (1982) Illness as a rhetorical act: a cross-cultural perspective, *Communication Quarterly*, 30, 321–31.

Chowanec, G.D. and Binik, Y.M. (1982) End stage renal disease (ESRD) and the marital dyad, *Social Science and Medicine*, 16, 1551–8.

Chrisman, N.J. (1977) The health-seeking process: an approach to the natural history of illness, *Culture, Medicine and Psychiatry*, 1, 351–77.

Clarke, J.N. (1983) Sexism, feminism and medicalism: a decade review of literature on gender and illness, *Sociology of Health and Illness*, 5, 62–82.

Cleary, P.D., Mechanic, D. and Greenley, J.R. (1982) Sex differences in medical care utilization: an empirical investigation, *Journal of Health and Social Behavior*, 23, 106–19.

Cohen, S. (1988) Psychosocial models of the role of social support in the etiology of physical disease, *Health Psychology*, 7, 269–97.

Cohen, S. and Wills, T.A. (1985) Stress, social support, and the buffering hypothesis, *Psychological Bulletin*, 98, 310–57.

Colledge, M. (1982) Economic cycles and health: towards a sociological understanding of the impact of the recession on health and illness, *Social Science and Medicine*, 16, 1919–27.

Conger, R.D., Lorenz, F.O., Elder, G.H., Simons, R.L. and Ge, X. (1993) Husband and wife differences in response to undesirable life events, *Journal of Health and Social Behavior*, 34, 71–88.

Conrad, P. (1987) 'The experience of illness: recent and new directions', in J.A. Roth and P. Conrad (eds) *Research in the Sociology of Health Care, Volume 6, The Experience and Management of Chronic Illness*. Greenwich, Conn.: JAI Press.

Conrad, P. (1990) Qualitative research on chronic illness: a commentary on method and conceptual development, *Social Science and Medicine*, 30, 1257–63.

Corbin, J. and Strauss, A.L. (1987) 'Accompaniments of chronic illness: changes in body, self, biography, and biographical time' in J.A. Roth and P. Conrad (eds) *Research in the Sociology of Health Care, Volume 6, The Experience and Management of Chronic Illness*. Greenwich, Conn.: JAI Press.

Cornwell, J. (1984) *Hard-Earned Lives: Accounts of health and illness from East London*. London: Tavistock.

Cousins, N. (1976) Anatomy of an illness (as perceived by the patient), *New England Journal of Medicine*, 295, 1458–63.

Coward, R. (1989) *The Whole Truth: The myth of alternative health*. London: Faber and Faber.

Cowie, B. (1976) The cardiac patient's perception of his heart attack, *Social Science and Medicine*, 10, 87–96.

Crawford, R. (1977) You are dangerous to your health: the ideology and politics of victim blaming, *International Journal of Health Services*, 7, 663–80.

Crocker, J. and Major, B. (1989) Social stigma and self-esteem: the self-protective properties of stigma, *Psychological Review*, 96, 608–30.

Cross, M.J. (1981) The psychology of physical disability – helpful or harmful?, *Bulletin of the British Psychological Society*, 34, 456–8.

Davis, F. (1963) *Passage Through Crisis: Polio victims and their families*. Indianapolis: Bobbs-Merrill.

Davison, C., Davey Smith, G. and Frankel, S. (1991) Lay epidemiology and the prevention paradox: the implications of coronary candidacy for health education, *Sociology of Health and Illness*, 13, 1–19.

de Lauretis, T. (1987) The female body and heterosexual presumption, *Semiotica*, 67, 259–79.

d'Houtaud, A. and Field, M.G. (1984) The image of health: variations in perception by social class in a French population, *Sociology of Health and Illness*, 6, 30–60.

Diekstra, R.F.W. (1990) Psychology, health and health care, *Psychology and Health*, 4: 51–63.

Dingwall, R. (1976) *Aspects of Illness*. London: Martin Robertson.

Dingwall, R. and Murray, T. (1983) Categorization in accident departments: 'good' patients, 'bad' patients and 'children', *Sociology of Health and Illness*, 5, 127–48.

Dohrenwend, B.S. and Dohrenwend, B.P. (eds) (1974) *Stressful Life Events: Their nature and effects*. New York: John Wiley.

Dohrenwend, B.P., Link, B.G., Kern, R., Shrout, P.E. and Markowitz, J. (1987) 'Measuring life events: the problem of variability within event categories', in B. Cooper (ed.) *Psychiatric epidemiology: Progress and prospects*. London: Croom Helm.

Donovan, J.L. (1984) Ethnicity and health: a research review, *Social Science and Medicine*, 19, 663–70.

Douglas, M. (1973) *Natural Symbols: Explorations in cosmology*. Harmondsworth: Penguin.

Douglas, M. (1978) *Cultural Bias* (Occasional Paper No. 35). London: Royal Anthropological Institute of Great Britain and Ireland.

Doyal, L. (1979) *The Political Economy of Health*. London: Pluto.

Dressler, W.W. (1985) Psychosomatic symptoms, stress, and modernization: a model, *Culture, Medicine and Psychiatry*, 9, 257–86.

Dressler, W.W., Mata, A., Chavez, A. and Viteri, F.E. (1987) Arterial blood pressure and individual modernization in a Mexican community, *Social Science and Medicine*, 24, 679–87.

Duden, B. (1985) Historical concepts of the body, *Resurgence*, 112, 24–6.

Duesberg, P. (1988) HIV is not the cause of AIDS, *Science*, 241, 514–17.

Durkheim, É. (1951) *Suicide*, trans. J.A. Spaulding and G. Simpson. New York: Free Press.

Duval, M.L. (1984) Psychosocial metaphors of physical distress among MS patients, *Social Science and Medicine*, 19, 635–8.

Ehrenreich, B. and English, D. (1978) *For Her Own Good: 150 years of the experts' advice to women*. New York: Anchor Press/Doubleday.

Eisenberg, L. (1977) Disease and illness: distinctions between professional and popular ideas of sickness, *Culture, Medicine and Psychiatry*, 1: 9–23.

Eiser, C., Patterson, D. and Eiser, J.R. (1983) Children's knowledge of health and illness: implications for health education, *Child: Care, Health and Development*, 9, 285–92.

Eiser, J.R. (1986) *Social Psychology: Attitudes, cognition and social behaviour*. Cambridge: Cambridge University Press.

Emerson, J. P. (1970) 'Behavior in private places: sustaining definitions of reality in gynecological examinations', in H.P. Dreitzel (ed.) *Recent Sociology*. New York: Macmillan.

Engel, G.L. (1977) The need for a new medical model: a challenge for biomedicine, *Science*, 196, 129–36.

Evans, P.D., Pitts, M.K. and Smith, K. (1988) Minor infection, minor life events and the four day desirability dip, *Journal of Psychosomatic Research*, 32, 533–9.

Eyer, J. (1977) Does unemployment cause the death rate peak in each business cycle? A multifactorial model of death rate change, *International Journal of Health Services*, 7, 625–62.

Fabrega, H. (1975) The need for an ethnomedical science, *Science*, 189, 969–75.

Fagin, L. and Little, M. (1984) *The Forsaken Families*. Harmondsworth: Penguin.

Family Heart Study Group (1994) Randomised controlled trial evaluating cardiovascular screening and intervention in general practice: principal results of British family heart study, *British Medical Journal*, 308, 313–20.

Featherstone, M. (1982) The body in consumer culture, *Theory, Culture and Society*, 1, 18–33.

Felton, B.J., Revenson, T.A. and Henrichsen, G.A. (1984) Stress and coping in the explanation of psychological adjustment among chronically ill adults, *Social Science and Medicine*, 18, 889–98.

Festinger, L. (1954) A theory of social comparison processes, *Human Relations*, 1, 117–40.

Finch, J. (1984) Community care: developing non-sexist alternatives, *Critical Social Policy*, 3, 6–18.

Finlayson, A. (1976) Social networks as coping resources: lay help and consultation patterns used by women in husbands' post-infarction career, *Social Science and Medicine*, 10, 97–103.

Fishbein, M. and Ajzen, I. (1975) *Belief, Attitude, Intention and Behavior*. Reading, Mass.: Addison-Wesley.

Fisher, S. and Groce, S.B. (1985) Doctor–patient negotiation of cultural assumptions, *Sociology of Health and Illness*, 7, 343–74.

Fitzpatrick, R.M. and Hopkins, A. (1981) Patients' satisfaction with communication in neurological outpatient clinics, *Journal of Psychosomatic Research*, 25, 329–34.

Fitzpatrick, R.M., Hopkins, A. and Harvard-Watts, O. (1983) Social dimensions of healing: a longitudinal study of outcomes of medical management of headaches, *Social Science and Medicine*, 17, 501–10.

Flaherty, J. and Richman, J. (1989) Gender differences in the perception and utilization of social support: theoretical perspectives and an empirical test, *Social Science and Medicine*, 28, 1221–8.

Foucault, M. (1973) *The Birth of the Clinic: An archaeology of medical perception*. trans. A.M. Sheridan Smith. London: Tavistock

Fox, R. (1977) 'The medicalization and demedicalization of American Society', in J.H. Knowles (ed.) *Doing Better and Feeling Worse: Health in the United States*. New York: Norton.

Frankenberg, R. (1980) Medical anthropology and development: a theoretical perspective, *Social Science and Medicine*, 14B, 197–207.

Frankenberg, R. (1986) Sickness as cultural performance: drama, trajectory, and pilgrimage, root metaphors and the making social of disease, *International Journal of Health Services*, 16, 603–26.

Freidson, E. (1962) 'Dilemmas in the doctor-patient relationship', in A.M. Rose, (ed.) *Human Behaviour and Social Processes: An interactionist approach*. London: Routledge and Kegan Paul.

Freidson, E. (1970) *Profession of Medicine*. New York: Dodd, Mead.

Freund, P.E.S. (1982) *The Civilized Body: Social domination, control and health*. Philadelphia: Temple University Press.

Friedman, M. and Rosenman, R.H. (1974) *Type A Behavior and Your Heart*. London: Wildwood House.

Geertsen, H.R. and Gray, R.M. (1970) Familistic orientation and inclination toward adopting the sick role, *Journal of Marriage and the Family*, 32, 638–46.

Gentry, W.D. (1982) 'What is behavioral medicine?', in J.R. Eiser (ed.) *Social Psychology and Behavioral Medicine*. Chichester: Wiley.

Gergen, K.J. (1973) Social psychology as history, *Journal of Personality and Social Psychology*, 26, 309–20.

Gerhardt, U. (1989) *Ideas about Illness: An intellectual and political history of medical sociology*. Basingstoke: Macmillan.

Gochman, D.S. (1971) Some correlates of children's health beliefs and potential health behaviour, *Journal of Health and Social Behavior*, 12, 148–54.

Goffman, E. (1961) *Encounters: Two studies in the sociology of interaction.* Indianapolis: Bobbs-Merrill.

Goffman, E. (1971) *The Presentation of Self in Everyday Life.* Harmondsworth: Penguin.

Goffman, E. (1972) *Interaction Ritual: Essays on face-to-face behaviour.* Harmondsworth: Penguin.

Goffman, E. (1990) *Stigma: Notes on the measurement of spoiled identity.* Harmondsworth: Penguin.

Goldstein, R. (1991) 'The implicated and the immune: responses to AIDS in the arts and popular culture', in D. Nelkin, D.P. Willis and S.V. Parris (eds) *A Disease of Society: Cultural and institutional responses to AIDS.* Cambridge: Cambridge University Press.

Gove, W. and Hughes, M. (1979) Possible causes of the apparent sex differences in physical health: an empirical investigation, *American Sociological Review*, 44, 126–46.

Graham, H. and Oakley, A. (1986) 'Competing ideologies of reproduction: medical and material perspectives on pregnancy', in C. Currer and M. Stacey (eds) *Concepts of Health, Illness and Disease: A comparative perspective.* Leamington Spa: Berg.

Greenberg, J.H. (1966) *Language Universals.* The Hague: Mouton.

Gross, E. and Stone, G.P. (1964) Embarrassment and the analysis of role requirements, *American Journal of Sociology*, 70, 1–15.

Haavio-Mannila, E. (1986) Inequalities in health and gender, *Social Science and Medicine*, 22, 141–9.

Hammer, M. (1983) 'Core' and 'extended' social networks in relation to health and illness, *Social Science and Medicine*, 17, 405–11.

Hannay, D.R. (1980) The 'iceberg' of illness and 'trivial' consultations, *Journal of the Royal College of General Practitioners*, 30, 551–4.

Harré, R. (ed.) (1986) *The Social Construction of Emotions.* Oxford: Blackwell.

Harris, D.M. and Guten, S. (1979) Health-protective behaviour: an exploratory study, *Journal of Health and Social Behavior*, 20, 17–29.

Harris, T.O. and Brown, G.W. (1989) 'The LEDS findings in the context of other research: an overview', in G.W. Brown and T.O. Harris (eds) *Life Events and Illness.* London: Unwin Hyman.

Heath, C. (1986) *Body Movement and Speech in Medical Interaction.* Cambridge: Cambridge University Press.

Helman, C.G. (1978) 'Feed a cold, starve a fever' – folk models of infection in an English suburban community, and their relation to medical treatment, *Culture, Medicine and Psychiatry*, 2, 107–37.

Helman, C.G. (1987) Heart disease and the cultural construction of time: the Type A Behaviour Pattern as a Western culture-bound syndrome, *Social Science and Medicine*, 25, 969–79.

Herzlich, C. (1973) *Health and Illness: A social psychological analysis.* trans. D. Graham. London: Academic Press.

Herzlich, C. (1985) From organic symptoms to social norm: doctors in a 'Balint Group', *History and Anthropology*, 2, 17–31.

Herzlich, C. and Pierret, J. (1985) The social construction of the patient: patients and illnesses in other ages, *Social Science and Medicine*, 20, 145–51.

Herzlich, C. and Pierret, J. (1987) *Illness and Self in Society.* trans. E. Forster. Baltimore: Johns Hopkins University Press.

Hinkle, L.E. (1973) The concept of 'stress' in the biological and social sciences, *Social Science and Medicine*, 1, 31–48.

Hinkle, L.E. (1974) 'The effect of exposure to culture change, social change, and changes in interpersonal relationships on health', in B.S. Dohrenwend and B.P. Dohrenwend (eds) *Stressful Life Events: Their nature and effects.* New York: John Wiley.

Hockey, J. and James, A. (1993) *Growing Up and Growing Old: Ageing and dependency in the life course.* London: Sage.

Holmes, R. (1993) 'Coronary heart disease: a cautionary tale', in B. Davey and J. Popay (eds) *Dilemmas in Health Care*, Ballmoor: Open University Press.

Holmes, T.S. and Masuda, M. (1974) 'Life change and illness susceptibility', in B.S. Dohrenwend and B.P. Dohrenwend (eds) *Stressful Life Events: Their nature and effects*. New York: John Wiley.

Holmes, T.S. and Rahe, R.H. (1967) The Social Readjustment Rating Scale, *Journal of Psychosomatic Research*, 11, 213–18.

Holtzman, W.H., Evans, R.I., Kennedy, S. and Iscoe, I. (1987) Psychology and health: contributions of psychology to the improvement of health and health care, *Bulletin of the World Health Organization*, 65, 913–35.

House, J.S., Landis, K.R. and Umberson, D. (1988) Social relationships and health, *Science*, 241, 540–5.

Hunt, S.J. and MacLeod, M. (1987) Health and behavioural change: some lay perspectives, *Community Medicine*, 9, 68–76.

Idler, E.L. (1979) Definitions of health and illness and medical sociology, *Social Science and Medicine*, 13A: 723–31.

Ingham, J.G. and Miller, P. McC. (1986) Self-referral to primary care: symptoms and social factors, *Journal of Psychosomatic Research*, 30, 49–56.

Jacobsen, M.M. and Eichhorn, R.L. (1964) How farm families cope with heart disease: a study of problems and resources, *Journal of Marriage and the Family*, 26, 166–73.

Janz, N.K. and Becker, M.H. (1984) The Health Belief Model: a decade later, *Health Education Quarterly*, 11, 1–47.

Jaspars, J., King, J. and Pendleton, D. (1983) 'The consultation: a social-psychological analysis', in D. Pendleton and J. Hasler (eds) *Doctor–Patient Communication*. London: Academic Press.

Jewson, N.D. (1976) The disappearance of the sick-man from medical cosmology, 1770–1870, *Sociology*, 10, 225–44.

Johnson, D.J. (1986) 'The doctor–patient relationship: an analysis of framing in general practice'. Unpublished PhD thesis, Loughborough University.

Johnston, M. (1994) Current trends, *The Psychologist*, 7, 114–18 (Special issue in health psychology).

Jones, R.A., Wiese, H.J., Moore, M.A. and Haley, J.V. (1981) On the perceived meaning of symptoms, *Medical Care*, 19, 710–17.

Kane, P. (1991) *Women's Health: from womb to tomb*. Basingstoke: Macmillan.

Kanter, R.M. (1975) Women and the structure of organizations: explorations in theory and behavior, *Sociological Inquiry*, 45, 34–74.

Kasl, S.V., Cobb, S. and Gore, S. (1972) Changes in reported illness and illness behavior related to termination of employment: a preliminary report, *International Journal of Epidemiology*, 1, 111–17.

Kaufert, P.A. and McKinlay, S.M. (1985) 'Estrogen-replacement therapy: the production of medical knowledge and the emergence of policy', in E. Lewin and V. Olesen (eds) *Women, Health and Healing: Towards a new perspective*. New York: Tavistock.

Kelly, M. (1992) Self, identity and radical surgery, *Sociology of Health and Illness*, 14, 390–415.

Kleinman, A.M. (1973) Medicine's symbolic reality: on a central problem in the philosophy of medicine, *Inquiry*, 16, 206–13.

Knowles, J.H. (1977) 'The responsibility of the individual', in J.H. Knowles (ed.) *Doing Better and Feeling Worse: Health in the United States*. New York: Norton.

Kobasa, S.C. (1979) Stressful life events, personality, and health: an inquiry into hardiness, *Journal of Personality and Social Psychology*, 37, 1–11.

Lalljee, M., Lamb, R. and Carnibella, G. (1993) Lay prototypes of illness: their content and use, *Psychology and Health*, 8, 33–49.

Lambert, H. and McPherson, K. (1993) 'Disease prevention and health promotion', in B. Davey and J. Popay (eds) *Dilemmas in Health Care*, Ballmoor: Open University Press.

Last, J.M. (1963) The iceberg: 'completing the clinical picture' in general practice, *Lancet*, 2, 28–31.

Latané, B. and Darley, J.M. (1970) *The Unresponsive Bystander: Why doesn't he help?* New York: Appleton-Century-Crofts.

Lau, R.R., Bernard, T.M. and Hartman, K.A. (1989) Further explorations of common-sense representations of common illnesses, *Health Psychology*, 8, 195–219.

Lawler, J. (1991) *Behind the Screens: Nursing, somology, and the problem of the body*. Melbourne: Churchill Livingstone.

Lazarus, R.S. (1985) 'The costs and benefits of denial', in A. Monat and R.S. Lazarus (eds) *Stress and Coping: An anthology*, 2nd edition. New York: Columbia University Press.

Lazarus, R.S. and Cohen, J.B. (1977) 'Environmental stress', in I. Altman and J. Wohlwill (eds) *Human Behavior and Environment, Volume 1*, New York: Plenum.

Lazarus, R.S. and Folkman, S. (1984) 'Coping and adaptation', in W.G. Gentry (ed.) *Handbook of Behavioural Medicine*. London: Guilford.

Leavitt, F. (1979) The Health Belief Model and utilization of ambulatory care services, *Social Science and Medicine*, 13A, 105–12.

Lehr, I., Messinger, H.B. and Rosenman, R.H. (1973) A sociobiological approach to the study of coronary heart disease, *Journal of Chronic Disease*, 26: 13–30

Leventhal, H. and Tomarken, A. (1987) 'Stress and health: perspectives from health psychology', in S.V. Kasl and C.L. Cooper (eds) *Stress and Health: Issues in research methodology*. Chichester: John Wiley.

Levine, R.M. (1992) 'Self-categorization, illness and health-related decision making: making sense of symptoms in complementary and conventional contexts'. Unpublished PhD thesis, University of Exeter.

Lewin, K. (1958) 'Group decision and social change', in E.E. Maccoby, T.M. Newcomb and E.L. Hartley (eds) *Readings in Social Psychology*, 3rd edition. New York: Holt, Rinehart and Winston.

Lewis, J. (1980) *The Politics of Motherhood: Child and maternal welfare in England, 1900–1939*. London: Croom Helm

Ley, P. (1982) Satisfaction, compliance and communication, *British Journal of Social Psychology*, 21, 241–54.

Ley, P. and Spelman, M.S. (1967) *Communicating with the Patient*. London: Staples Press.

Lopez, A.D. (1984) 'Demographic change in Europe and its health and social implications: an overview', in A.D. Lopez and R.L. Cliquet (eds) *Demographic Trends in the European Region: Health and social implications*. Copenhagen: World Health Organization.

Lorber, J. (1975) 'Women and medical sociology: invisible professionals and ubiquitous patients', in M. Millman and R.M. Kanter (eds) *Another Voice: Feminist perspectives on social life and social science*. New York: Anchor Press/Doubleday.

Lowery, B.J. and Jacobsen, B.S. (1985) Attributional analysis of chronic illness outcomes, *Nursing Research*, 34, 82–8.

McBride, A.B. and McBride, W.L. (1981) Theoretical underpinnings for women's health, *Women and Health*, 6, 37–55.

MacCormack, C. (1980) Health care problems of ethnic minority groups, *MIMS Magazine*, 15 July, 53–60.

McCrea, F.B. (1983) The politics of menopause: the 'discovery' of a deficiency disease, *Social Problems*, 31, 111–23.

MacDonald, L. (1988) 'The experience of stigma: living with rectal cancer', in R. Anderson and M. Bury (eds) *Living with Chronic Illness: The experience of patients and their families*. London: Unwin Hyman.

McGuire, W.J. (1985) 'Attitudes and attitude measurement', in G. Lindzey and E. Aronson (eds) *The Handbook of Social Psychology, Volume 2*. New York: Random House.

Macintyre, S. (1986) The patterning of health by social position in contemporary Britain: directions for sociological research, *Social Science and Medicine*, 23, 393–415.

McKeown, T. (1976) *The Modern Rise of Population*. London: Edward Arnold.

McKinlay, A. and Potter, J. (1987) Social representations: a conceptual critique, *Journal for the Theory of Social Behaviour*, 17, 471–87.

McKinlay, J.B. (1973) Social networks, lay consultation and help-seeking behavior, *Social Forces*, 51, 275–92.

MacLeod, M. (1993) 'On knowing the patient: experiences of nurses undertaking care', in A.

Radley (ed.) *Worlds of Illness: Biographical and cultural perspectives on health and disease*. London: Routledge.

Manning, P.K. and Fabrega, H. (1973) 'The experience of self and body: health and illness in the Chiapas Highlands', in G. Psathas (ed.) *Phenomenological Sociology: Issues and applications*. New York: Wiley.

Marcus, A.C. and Seeman, T.E. (1981) Sex differences in health status: a reexamination of the nurturant role hypothesis, *American Sociological Review*, 46, 119–23.

Marinker, M. (1976) The myth of family medicine, *World Medicine*, 11, 17–19.

Marmot, M. and Syme, S.L. (1976) Acculturation and coronary heart disease in Japanese-Americans, *American Journal of Epidemiology*, 104: 225–47.

Marteau, T.M. (1994) Psychology and screening: narrowing the gap between efficacy and effectiveness, *British Journal of Clinical Psychology*, 33, 1–10.

Marteau, T.M. and Johnston, M. (1986) Determinants of beliefs about illness: a study of parents of children with diabetes, asthma, epilepsy, and no chronic illness, *Journal of Psychosomatic Research*, 30, 673–83.

Marteau, T.M. and Johnston, M. (1987) Health psychology: the danger of neglecting psychological models, *Bulletin of the British Psychological Society*, 40: 82–5.

Martin, E. (1987) *The Woman in the Body: A cultural analysis of reproduction*. Milton Keynes: Open University Press.

Matarazzo, J.D. (1982) Behavioral health's challenge to academic, scientific, and professional psychology, *American Psychologist*, 37, 1–14.

Mathews, A. and Steptoe, A. (eds) (1982) Special Issue: Behavioural Medicine, *British Journal of Clinical Psychology*, 21, Whole Part 4.

Mechanic, D. (1962) The concept of illness behavior, *Journal of Chronic Disease*, 15, 189–94.

Mechanic, D. (1974) 'Discussion of research programs on relations between stressful life events and episodes of physical illness', in B.S. Dohrenwend and B.P. Dohrenwend (eds) *Stressful Life Events: Their nature and effects*. New York: John Wiley.

Mechanic, D. (1977) Illness behavior, social adaptation, and the management of illness, *Journal of Nervous and Mental Disease*, 165, 79–87.

Medawar, P. (1974) Introduction to M. Friedman, and R.H. Rosenman (eds) *Type A Behavior and Your Heart*. London: Wildwood House.

Mestrovic, S. and Glassner, B. (1983) A Durkheimian hypothesis on stress, *Social Science and Medicine*, 18, 1315–27.

Miles, A. (1991) *Women, Health and Medicine*. Ballmoor: Open University Press.

Miller, F.T., Bentz, W.K., Aponte, J.F. and Brogan, D.R. (1974) 'Perception of life event crisis events: a comparative study of rural and urban samples', in B.S. Dohrenwend and B.P. Dohrenwend (eds) *Stressful Life Events: Their nature and effects*. New York: John Wiley.

Miller, P.McC. and Ingham, J.G. (1976) Friends, confidants and symptoms, *Social Psychiatry*, 11, 51–8.

Molleman, E., Krabbendam, P.J., Annyas, A.A., Koops, H.S., Sleijfer, D. T. and Vermey, A. (1984) The significance of the doctor–patient relationship in coping with cancer, *Social Science and Medicine*, 18, 475–80.

Molleman, E., Pruyn, J. and van Knippenberg, A. (1986) Social comparison processes among cancer patients, *British Journal of Social Psychology*, 25, 1–13.

Monks, J. (1989) Experiencing symptoms in chronic illness: fatigue in multiple sclerosis, *International Disability Studies*, 11, 78–83.

Moore, J., Phipps, K. and Marcer, D. (1985) Why do people seek treatment by alternative medicine?, *British Medical Journal*, 290, 28–9.

Morgan, M., Calnan, M. and Manning, N. (1985) *Sociological Approaches to Health and Medicine*. London: Croom Helm.

Morris, J.N. (1979) Social inequalities undiminished, *Lancet*, i, 87–90.

Moscovici, S. (1984) 'The phenomenon of social representations', in R.M. Farr and S. Moscovici (eds) *Social Representations*. Cambridge: Cambridge University Press.

Moscovici, S. (1990) 'The generalized self and mass society', in H.T. Himmelweit and G. Gaskell (eds) *Societal Psychology*. Newbury Park: Sage.

Moser, K.A., Pugh, H.S. and Goldblatt, P.O. (1988) Inequalities in women's health: looking at mortality differentials using an alternative approach, *British Medical Journal*, 296, 1221–4.

Murcott, A. (1979) 'Health as ideology', in P. Atkinson, R. Dingwall and A. Murcott (eds) *Prospects for the National Health*. London: Croom Helm.

Murphy, M.A. and Fischer, C.T. (1983) Styles of living with low back injury: the continuity dimension, *Social Science and Medicine*, 17, 291–7.

Najman, J.M., Klein, D. and Munro, C. (1982) Patient characteristics negatively stereotyped by doctors, *Social Science and Medicine*, 16, 1781–9.

Natapoff, J.N. (1978) Children's views of health: a developmental study, *American Journal of Public Health*, 68, 995–1000.

Nathanson, C.A. (1975) Illness and the feminine role: a theoretical review, *Social Science and Medicine*, 9, 57–62.

Nathanson, C.A. (1980) Social roles and health status among women: the significance of employment, *Social Science and Medicine*, 14A, 463–71.

Oakley, A. (1984) *The Captured Womb: A history of the medical care of pregnant women*. Oxford: Blackwell.

Oakley, A. (1993) *Essays on Women, Medicine and Health*. Edinburgh: Edinburgh University Press.

Oborne, D.J., Gruneberg, M.M. and Eiser, J.R. (1979) *Research in Psychology and Medicine, Volume 2: Social Aspects: Attitudes, communication, care and training*. London: Academic Press.

OPCS, (1988) *General Household Survey*. London: HMSO

OPCS, (1993) *General Household Survey*. London: HMSO.

Parkes, C.M. (1971) Psycho-social transitions: a field for study, *Social Science and Medicine*, 5, 101–15.

Parkes, C.M., Benjamin, B. and Fitzgerald, R.G. (1969) Broken heart: a statistical study of increased mortality among widowers, *British Medical Journal*, 1, 740–3.

Parsons, T. (1951a) *The Social System*. Glencoe, Ill: Free Press.

Parsons, T. (1951b) Illness and the role of the physician: a sociological perspective, *American Journal of Orthopsychiatry*, 21, 452–60.

Parsons, T. (1958) 'Definitions of health and illness in the light of American values and social structure', in E. Gartley Jaco (ed.) *Patients, Physicians and Illness: A sourcebook in behavioral science and health*. New York: Free Press.

Parsons, T. and Fox, R. (1952) Illness, therapy and the modern urban American family, *Journal of Social Issues*, 8, 31–44.

Patton, C. (1985) *Sex and Germs: The politics of AIDS*. Boston: South End Press.

Payne, R. and Jones, J.G. (1987) 'Measurement and methodological issues in social support', in S.V. Kasl and C.L. Cooper (eds) *Stress and Health: Issues in research methodology*. Chichester: John Wiley.

Payne, R., Warr, P. and Hartley, J. (1984) Social class and psychological ill-health during unemployment, *Sociology of Health and Illness*, 6, 152–74.

Pearlin, L.I. (1989) The sociological study of stress, *Journal of Health and Social Behavior*, 30, 241–56.

Pearlin, L.I. and Schooler, C. (1978) The structure of coping, *Journal of Health and Social Behavior*, 19, 2–21.

Pelletier, K.R. and Lutz, R. (1991) 'Healthy people – healthy business: a critical review of stress management programs in the workplace', in A. Monat and R.S. Lazarus (eds) *Stress and Coping: An anthology*. New York: Columbia University Press.

Pendleton, D. and Hasler, J. (1983) 'Introduction' to D. Pendleton and J. Hasler (eds) *Doctor–Patient Communication*. London: Academic Press.

Petch, M.C. (1983) Coronary bypasses, *British Medical Journal*, 287, 514–16.

Pfeffer, N. (1985) 'The hidden pathology of the male reproductive system', in H. Homans (ed.) *The Sexual Politics of Reproduction*. Aldershot: Gower.

Phillimore, P., Beattie, A. and Townsend, P. (1994) Widening inequality of health in northern England, 1981–1991, *British Medical Journal*, 308, 1125–8.

Phillips, D.L. and Segal, B.E. (1969) Sexual status and psychiatric symptoms, *American Sociological Review*, 34, 58–72.

Pierret, J. (1992) 'Coping with AIDS in everyday life', in M. Pollack (ed.) *AIDS: A problem for sociological research*. London: Sage.

Pierret, J. (1993) 'Constructing discourses about health and their social determinants', in A. Radley (ed.) *Worlds of Illness: Biographical and cultural perspectives on health and disease*. London: Routledge.

Pilisuk, M. and Froland, C. (1978) Kinship, social networks, social support and health, *Social Science and Medicine*, 12B, 273–80.

Pill, R. and Stott, N.C.H. (1982) Concepts of illness causation and responsibility: some preliminary data from a sample of working-class mothers, *Social Science and Medicine*, 16, 43–52.

Pill, R. and Stott, N.C.H. (1985) Preventive procedures and practices among working class women: new data and fresh insights, *Social Science and Medicine*, 21, 975–83.

Pill, R., Jones-Elwyn, G. and Stott, N.C.H. (1989) Opportunistic health promotion: quantity or quality?, *Journal of the Royal College of General Practitioners*, 39, 196–200.

Pinder, R. (1990) *The Management of Chronic Illness: Patient and doctor perspectives on Parkinson's disease*. Basingstoke: Macmillan.

Pollock, K. (1988) On the nature of social stress: production of a modern mythology, *Social Science and Medicine*, 26, 381–92.

Pollock, K. (1993) 'Attitude of mind as a means of resisting illness', in A. Radley (ed.) *Worlds of Illness: Biographical and cultural perspectives on health and disease*. London: Routledge.

Porter, R. and Porter, D. (1988) *In Sickness and in Health: The British experience 1650–1850*. London: Fourth Estate.

Potter, J. and Litton, I. (1985) Some problems underlying the theory of social representations, *British Journal of Social Psychology*, 24, 81–90.

Potter, J. and Wetherell, M. (1987) *Discourse and Social Psychology: Beyond attitudes and behaviour*. London: Sage.

Pratt, L. (1972) Conjugal organization and health, *Journal of Marriage and the Family*, 34, 85–95.

Pratt, L. (1973) Child rearing methods and children's health behavior, *Journal of Health and Social Behavior*, 14, 61–9.

Price, L. (1984) Art, science, faith and medicine: the implications of the placebo effect, *Sociology of Health and Illness*, 6, 61–73.

Radley, A. (1982) Theory and data in the study of 'coronary proneness' (Type A Behaviour Pattern), *Social Science and Medicine*, 16, 107–14.

Radley, A. (1984) The embodiment of social relations in coronary heart disease, *Social Science and Medicine*, 19, 1227–34.

Radley, A. (1988) *Prospects of Heart Surgery: Psychological adjustment to coronary bypass grafting*. New York: Springer-Verlag.

Radley, A. (1989) Style, discourse and constraint in adjustment to chronic illness, *Sociology of Health and Illness*, 11, 230–52.

Radley, A. (1991) *The Body and Social Psychology*. New York: Springer-Verlag.

Radley, A. (1993) 'The role of metaphor in adjustment to chronic illness', in A. Radley (ed.) *Worlds of Illness: Biographical and cultural perspectives on health and disease*. London: Routledge.

Radley, A. and Green, R. (1985) Styles of adjustment to coronary graft surgery, *Social Science and Medicine*, 20, 461–72.

Radley, A. and Green, R. (1987) Illness as adjustment: a methodology and conceptual framework, *Sociology of Health and Illness*, 9, 179–207.

Radley, A. and Kennedy, M. (1992) Reflections upon charitable giving: a comparison of individuals from business, 'manual' and professional backgrounds, *Journal of Community and Applied Psychology*, 2, 113–29.

Rahe, R.H. (1972) Review Article: Subjects' recent life changes and their near-future illness reports, *Annals of Clinical Research*, 4, 250–65.

Reid, J., Ewan, C. and Lowy, E. (1991) Pilgrimage of pain: the illness experiences of women with repetition strain injury and the search for credibility, *Social Science and Medicine*, 32, 601–12.

Reisine, S.T., Goodenow, C. and Grady, K.E. (1987) The impact of rheumatoid arthritis on the homemaker, *Social Science and Medicine*, 25, 89–95.

Repetti, R.L., Matthews, K.A. and Waldron, I. (1989) Employment and women's health: effects of paid employment on women's mental and physical health, *American Psychologist*, 44, 1394–401.

Robinson, D. (1971) *The Process of Becoming Ill*. London: Routledge and Kegan Paul.

Robinson, D. (1980) 'Self-help health groups', in P.B. Smith (ed.) *Small Groups and Personal Change*. London: Methuen.

Rodin, J. and Ickovics, J.R. (1990) Women's health: review and research agenda as we approach the 21st century, *American Psychologist*, 45, 1018–34.

Rodin, M. (1992) The social construction of premenstrual syndrome, *Social Science and Medicine*, 35, 49–56.

Romanyshyn, R.D. (1982) *Psychological Life: From science to metaphor*. Milton Keynes: Open University Press.

Rook, K.S. (1984) The negative side of social interaction: impact on psychological well-being, *Journal of Personality and Social Psychology*, 46, 1097–108.

Rook, K.S. (1987) Social support versus companionship: effects on life stress, loneliness, and evaluation by others, *Journal of Personality and Social Psychology*, 52, 1132–47.

Rosenblatt, D. and Suchman, E.A. (1964) 'Blue-collar attitudes and information toward health and illness', in A.B. Shostak and W. Gomberg (eds), *Blue-Collar World: Studies of the American worker*. Englewood Cliffs, N.J: Prentice-Hall.

Rosenstock, I.M. (1974) The Health Belief Model and preventive health behavior, *Health Education Monographs*, 2, 354–86.

Roter, D., Lipkin, M. and Korsgaard, A. (1991) Sex differences in patients' and physicians' communication during primary care visits, *Medical Care*, 29, 1083–93.

Ruberman, W., Weinblatt, A.B., Goldberg, J.D. and Chaudhary, B.S. (1984) Psychosocial influences on mortality after myocardial infarction, *New England Journal of Medicine*, 311, 552–9.

Rutter, D. (1989) Models of belief-behaviour relationships in health, *Health Psychology Update*, 4, 3–10.

Ruzek, S.B. (1978) *The Women's Health Movement: Feminist alternatives to medical control*. New York: Praeger.

Ryan, W. (1976) *Blaming the Victim*. New York: Vintage Books.

Sabatier, R. (1988) *Blaming Others: Prejudice, race and worldwide AIDS*. London: Panos Publications.

Sacks, H. (1992) *Lectures on Conversation* (2 vols). Oxford: Blackwell.

Salloway, J.C. and Dillon, P.B. (1973) A comparison of family networks and friend networks in health care utilization, *Journal of Comparative and Family Studies*, 4, 131–42.

Sampson, E.E. (1977) Psychology and the American ideal, *Personality and Social Psychology*, 35, 767–82.

Sanders, G.S. (1982) 'Social comparison and perceptions of health and illness', in G.S. Sanders and J. Suls (eds) *Social Psychology of Health and Illness*. Hillsdale, N.J: Lawrence Erlbaum.

Saward, E. and Sorensen, A. (1978) The current emphasis on preventive medicine, *Science*, 200, 889–94.

Scambler, A., Scambler, G. and Craig, D. (1981) Kinship and friendship networks and women's demand for primary care, *Journal of the Royal College of General Practitioners*, 26, 746–50.

Schacter, S. and Singer, J. (1962) Cognitive, social and physiological determinants of emotion, *Psychological Review*, 69, 379–99.

Scheper-Hughes, N. and Lock, M.M. (1987) The mindful body: a prolegomenon to future work in medical anthropology, *Medical Anthropology Quarterly*, 1, 6–41.

Schneider, J.W. and Conrad, P. (1980) In the closet with illness: epilepsy, stigma potential and information control, *Social Problems*, 28, 32–44.

Segall, A. (1976) The sick role concept: understanding illness behavior, *Journal of Health and Social Behavior*, 17, 163–70.

Selye, H. (1956) What is stress? *Metabolism*, 5, 525–30.

Sharma, U. (1992) *Complementary Medicine Today*. London: Tavistock/Routledge.

Sharp, K., Ross, C.E. and Cockerham, W.C. (1983) Symptoms, beliefs, and the use of physician services among the disadvantaged, *Journal of Health and Social Behavior*, 24, 255–63.

Sharrock, W. (1979) 'Portraying the professional relationship', in D.C. Anderson (ed.) *Health Education in Practice*, London: Croom Helm.

Shillitoe, R.W. and Christie, M.J. (1989) Determinants of self-care: the Health Belief Model, *Holistic Medicine*, 4, 3–17.

Silverman, D. (1987) *Communication and Medical Practice: Social relations in the clinic*. London: Sage.

Skelton, J.A. and Pennebaker, J. (1982) 'The psychology of physical symptoms and sensation', in G.S. Sanders and J. Suls (eds) *Social Psychology of Health and Illness*. Hillsdale, NJ: Lawrence Erlbaum.

Skevington, S. (1981) Intergroup relations and nursing, *European Journal of Social Psychology*, 11, 43–59.

Smith, D.E. (1974) Women's perspective as a radical critique of sociology, *Sociological Inquiry*, 44, 7–13.

Smith-Rosenberg, C. (1972) The hysterical woman: sex roles and role conflict in 19th-century America, *Social Research*, 39, 652–78.

Sontag, S. (1991) *Illness as Metaphor – Aids and its Metaphors*. Harmondsworth: Penguin.

Stacey, M. (1988) *The Sociology of Health and Healing*. London: Unwin Hyman.

Stainton Rogers, W. (1991) *Explaining Health and Illness: An exploration of diversity*. Hemel Hempstead: Harvester Wheatsheaf.

Starrin, B. and Larsson, G. (1987) Coping with unemployment – a contribution to the understanding of women's unemployment, *Social Science and Medicine*, 25, 163–71.

Stewart, D.C. and Sullivan, T.J. (1982) Illness behavior and the sick role in chronic disease, *Social Science and Medicine*, 16, 1397–404.

Stewart, I.M.G. (1950) Coronary disease and modern stress, *Lancet*, i, 867–70.

Stimson, G. (1974) Obeying doctor's orders: a view from the other side, *Social Science and Medicine*, 8, 97–104.

Stimson, G. and Webb, B. (1975) *Going to See the Doctor: The consultation process in general practice*. London: Routledge and Kegan Paul.

Stone, G.C. (1979) Patient compliance and the role of the expert, *Journal of Social Issues*, 35, 34–59.

Stott, N.C.H. and Pill, R.M. (1990) 'Advise yes, dictate no': patients' views on health promotion in the consultation, *Family Practice*, 7, 125–31.

Strauss, A.L. (1975) *Chronic Illness and the Quality of Life*. St Louis: The C.V. Mosby Company.

Stroebe, M.S. and Stroebe, W. (1983) Who suffers more? Sex differences in health risks of the widowed, *Psychological Bulletin*, 93, 279–301.

Strong, P.M. (1977) 'Medical errands: a discussion of routine patient work', in A. Davis and G. Horobin (eds) *Medical Encounters: The experience of illness and treatment*. London. Croom Helm.

Strong, P.M. (1979a) *The Ceremonial Order of the Clinic: Patients, doctors and medical bureaucracies*. London: Routledge and Kegan Paul.

Strong, P.M. (1979b) Sociological imperialism and the profession of medicine: a critical examination of the thesis of medical imperialism, *Social Science and Medicine*, 13A, 199–215.

Suchman, E.A. (1965) Stages of illness and medical care, *Journal of Health and Human Behavior*, 6, 114–28.

Susman, J. (1994) Disability, stigma and deviance, *Social Science and Medicine*, 38, 15–22.

Syme, S.L. and Berkman, L.F. (1976) Social class, susceptibility and sickness, *American Journal of Epidemiology*, 104, 1–8.

Szasz, T.S., Knoff, W.F. and Hollender, M.H. (1958) The doctor–patient relationship and its historical context, *American Journal of Psychiatry*, 115, 522–8.

Tagliacozzo, D.L. and Mauksch, H.O. (1972) 'The patient's view of the patient's role', in E. Gartley Jaco (ed.) *Patients, Physicians and Illness: A sourcebook in behavioral science and health*, 2nd edition. New York: Free Press.

Taussig, M.T. (1980) Reification and the consciousness of the patient, *Social Science and Medicine*, 14B, 3–13.

Taylor, S.E. (1979) Hospital patient behavior: reactance, helplessness, or control?, *Journal of Social Issues*, 35, 156–84.

Taylor, S.E. (1983) Adjustment to threatening events: a theory of cognitive adaptation, *American Psychologist*, 38, 1161–73.

Taylor, S.E. (1990) Health psychology: the science and the field, *American Psychologist*, 45, 40–50.

Taylor, S.E., Lichtman, R. and Wood, J.V. (1984) Attributions, beliefs about control, and adjustment to breast cancer, *Journal of Personality and Social Psychology*, 46, 489–502.

Telles, J.L. and Pollack, M.H. (1981) Feeling sick: the experience and legitimation of illness, *Social Science and Medicine*, 15A, 243–51.

Temoshok, L. (1990) 'Applying the biophysical model to research on HIV/AIDS', in P. Bennett, J. Weinman and P. Spurgeon (eds) *Current Developments in Health Psychology*. Chur: Harwood.

Thoits, P.A. (1982) Conceptual, methodological, and theoretical problems in studying social support as a buffer against life stress, *Journal of Health and Social Behavior*, 23, 145–59.

Thomas, K.B. (1978) The consultation and the therapeutic illusion, *British Medical Journal*, 1, 1327–8.

Thomas, K.J., Carr, J., Westlake, L. and Williams, B.T. (1991) Use of non-orthodox and conventional health care in Great Britain, *British Medical Journal*, 302, 207–10.

Totman, R. (1979) What makes 'life events' stressful? A retrospective study of patients who have suffered a first myocardial infarction, *Journal of Psychosomatic Research*, 23, 193–201.

Totman, R. (1987) *Social Causes of Illness*, 2nd edition. London: Souvenir Press.

Townsend, P. and Davidson, N. (1982) *Inequalities in Health*. Harmondsworth: Penguin.

Turner, J.C. (1987) *Rediscovering the Social Group*. Oxford: Blackwell.

Twaddle, A.C. (1969) Health decisions and sick role variations: an exploration, *Journal of Health and Social Behavior*, 10, 105–15.

Tyroler, H.A. and Cassel, J. (1964) Health consequences of culture change – II: the effect of urbanization on coronary heart mortality in rural residents, *Journal of Chronic Disease*, 17, 167–77.

Umberson, D. (1992) Gender, marital status and the social control of health behavior, *Social Science and Medicine*, 34, 907–17.

Ussher, J.M. (1989) *The Psychology of the Female Body*. London: Routledge.

Verbrugge, L.M. (1980a) Sex differences in complaints and diagnoses, *Journal of Behavioral Medicine*, 3, 327–55.

Verbrugge, L.M. (1980b) Comment on Walter R. Gove and Michael Hughes, 'Possible causes of the apparent sex differences in physical health', *American Sociological Review*, 45, 507–12.

Verbrugge, L.M. (1983) Multiple roles and physical health of women and men, *Journal of Health and Social Behavior*, 24, 16–29.

Verbrugge, L.M. (1989) The twain meet: empirical explanations of sex differences in health and mortality, *Journal of Health and Social Behavior*, 30, 282–304.

Vincent, J. (1992) 'Self-help groups and health care in contemporary Britain', in M. Saks (ed.) *Alternative Medicine in Britain*, Oxford: Oxford University Press.

Viney, L.L. and Westbrook, M.T. (1982) Coping with chronic illness: the mediating role of biographic and illness-related factors, *Journal of Psychosomatic Research*, 26, 595–605.

Voysey, M. (1972) Official agents and the legitimation of suffering, *Sociological Review*, 20, 533–51.

Voysey, M. (1975) *A Constant Burden: The reconstitution of family life*. London: Routledge and Kegan Paul.

Waldron, I. (1983) Sex differences in illness incidence, prognosis and mortality: issues and evidence, *Social Science and Medicine*, 17, 1107–23.

Wallen, J., Waitzkin, H. and Stoeckle, J.D. (1979) Physician stereotypes about female health and illness: a study of patient's sex and the informative process during medical interviews, *Women and Health*, 4, 135–46.

Wang, C. (1992) Culture, meaning and disability: injury prevention campaigns and the production of stigma, *Social Science and Medicine*, 9, 1093–102.

Warr, P. and Parry, G. (1982) Paid employment and women's psychological well-being, *Psychological Bulletin*, 91, 498–516.

Weinman, J. (1990) 'Health psychology: progress, perspective and prospects', in P. Bennett, J. Weinman and P. Spurgeon (eds) *Current Developments in Health Psychology*. Chur: Harwood.

Weisman, C.S. and Teitelbaum, M.A. (1985) Physician gender and the physician-patient relationship: recent evidence and relevant questions, *Social Science and Medicine*, 20, 1119–27.

Westbrook, M.T. and Viney, L.L. (1982) Psychological reactions to the onset of chronic illness, *Social Science and Medicine*, 16, 899–905.

Wiener, C.L. (1975) The burden of rheumatoid arthritis: tolerating the uncertainty, *Social Science and Medicine*, 9, 97–104.

Wilkinson, R.G. (1992) Income distribution and life expectancy, *British Medical Journal*, 304, 165–8.

Wilkinson, S. and Kitzinger, C. (1993) Whose breast is it anyway?: a feminist consideration of advice and 'treatment' for breast cancer, *Women's Studies International Forum*, 16, 229–38.

Williams, G.H. (1984) The genesis of chronic illness: narrative reconstruction, *Sociology of Health and Illness*, 6, 174–200.

Williams, G.H. (1989) Hope for the humblest? The role of self-help in chronic illness: the case of ankylosing spondylitis, *Sociology of Health and Illness*, 11, 135–59.

Williams, G.H. (1993) 'Chronic illness and the pursuit of virtue in everyday life', in A. Radley (ed.) *Worlds of Illness: Biographical and cultural perspectives on health and disease*. London: Routledge.

Williams, G.H. and Wood, P.H.N. (1986) Common-sense beliefs about illness: a mediating role for the doctor, *Lancet*, ii, 1435–7.

Williams, R. (1983) Concepts of health: an analysis of lay logic, *Sociology*, 17, 185–204.

Williams, R. (1990) *A Protestant Legacy: Attitudes to death and illness among older Aberdonians*. Oxford: Clarendon Press.

Willis, P. (1977) *Learning to Labour: How working-class kids get working-class jobs*. Farnborough: Saxon House.

Wills, T.A. (1991) 'Social support and interpersonal relationships', in M.S. Clark (ed.) *Prosocial Behavior*. Newbury Park: Sage.

Wood, P.H.N. (1980) *The International Classification of Impairments, Disabilities and Handicaps*. Geneva: World Health Organization.

World Health Organization (1987) *Evaluation of the Strategy for Health for all by the Year 2000. Seventh report on the world health situation*. Geneva: WHO.

Wright, J. and Weber, E. (1987) *Homelessness and Health*. Washington, DC: McGraw-Hill.

Wright, P. and Treacher, A. (1982) 'Introduction' to P. Wright and A. Treacher (eds) *The Problem of Medical Knowledge: Examining the social construction of medicine*. Edinburgh: Edinburgh University Press.

Young, A. (1976) Internalizing and externalizing medical belief systems: an Ethiopian example, *Social Science and Medicine*, 10, 147–56.

Young, A. (1980) The discourse on stress and the reproduction of conventional knowledge, *Social Science and Medicine*, 14B, 133–46.

Young, A. (1981) When rational men fall sick: an inquiry into some assumptions made by medical anthropologists, *Culture, Medicine and Psychiatry*, 5, 317–35.

Young, A. (1982) The anthropologies of illness and sickness, *Annual Review of Anthropology*, 11, 257–85.

Young, K. (1989) 'Narrative embodiments: enclaves of the self in the realm of medicine', in J. Shotter and K. Gergen (eds) *Texts of Identity*. London: Sage.

Zborowski, M. (1952) Cultural components in responses to pain, *Journal of Social Issues*, 8, 16–30.

Zelditch, M. (1956) 'Role differentiation in the nuclear family', in T. Parsons and R.F. Bales (eds) *Family Socialization and Interaction Process*. London: Routledge and Kegan Paul.

Zola, I.K. (1966) Culture and symptoms – an analysis of patients' presenting complaints, *American Sociological Review*, 31, 615–30.

Zola, I.K. (1972) Medicine as an institution of social control, *Sociological Review*, 20, 487–504.

Zola, I.K. (1973) Pathways to the doctor – from person to patient, *Social Science and Medicine*, 7, 677–89.

Zola, I.K. (1991) Bringing our bodies and ourselves back in: reflections on a past, present, and future 'medical sociology', *Journal of Health and Social Behavior*, 32, 1–16.

Author Index

Subject Index